JAPANESE COOKING WITH MANGA

EASY RECIPES YOUR FRIENDS WILL LOVE!

T0161139

BY THE GOURMAND GOHAN TEAM

Alexis Aldeguer, Maiko-san & Ilaria Mauro

TUTTLE Publishing

Tokyo | Rutland, Vermont | Singapore

Contents

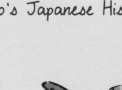

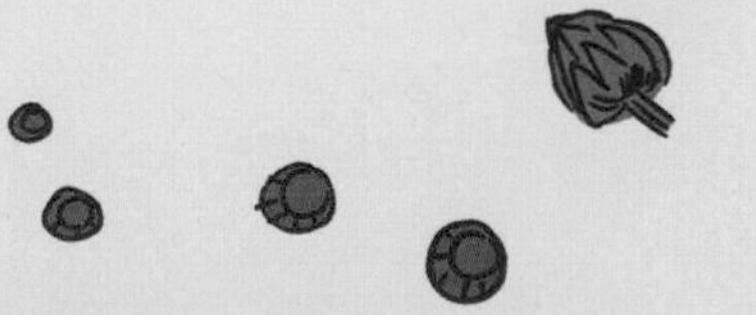

CHAPTER 5

Meat & Chicken

CHAPTER 6

Fish & Seafood

CHAPTER 7

Noodles & Rice

CHAPTER 8

Desserts & Drinks

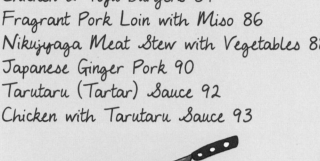

How the Gourmand Gohan team started...

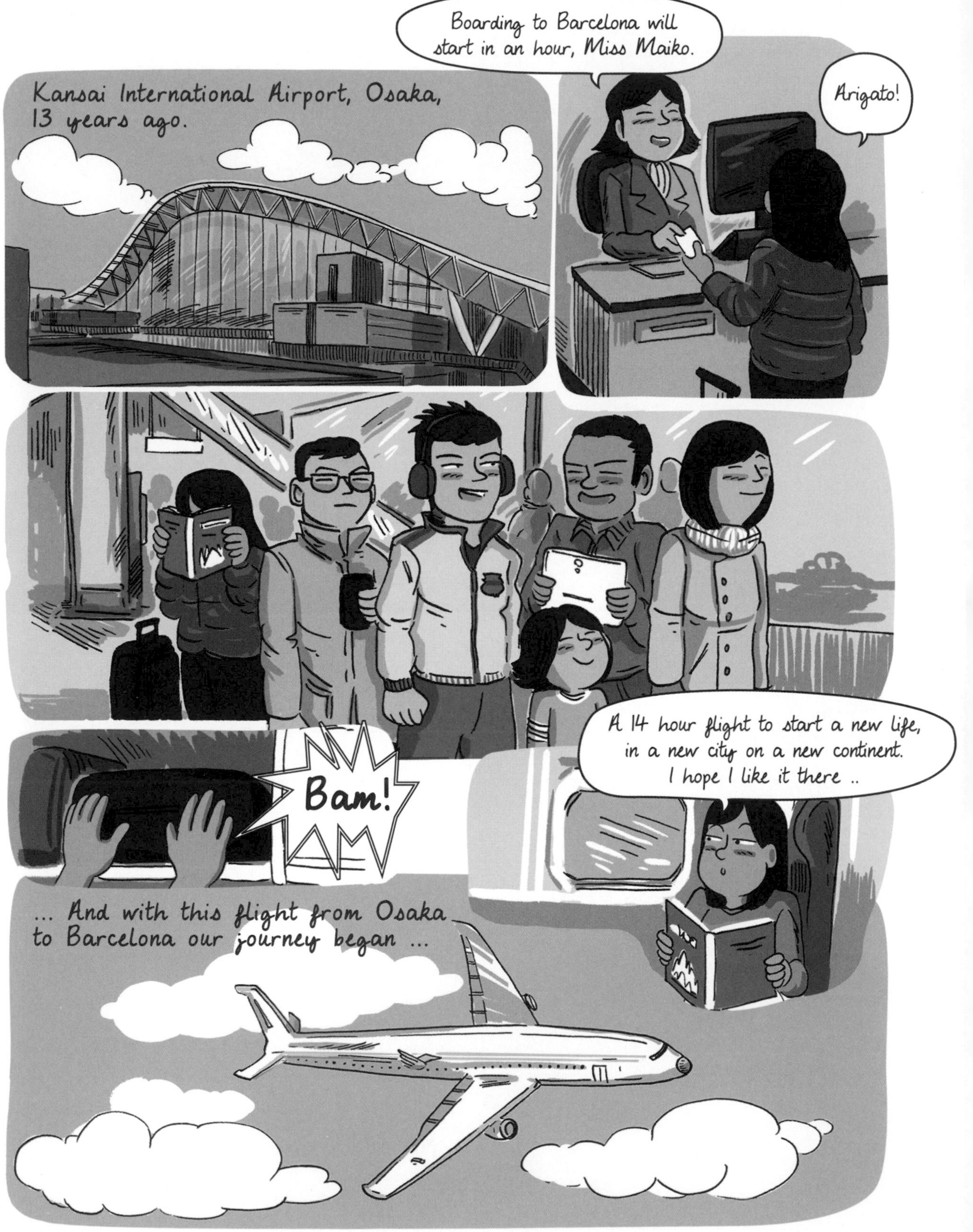
Kansai International Airport, Osaka, 13 years ago.
Boarding to Barcelona will start in an hour, Miss Maiko.
Arigato!
Bam!
A 14 hour flight to start a new life, in a new city on a new continent. I hope I like it there ..
... And with this flight from Osaka to Barcelona our journey began ...

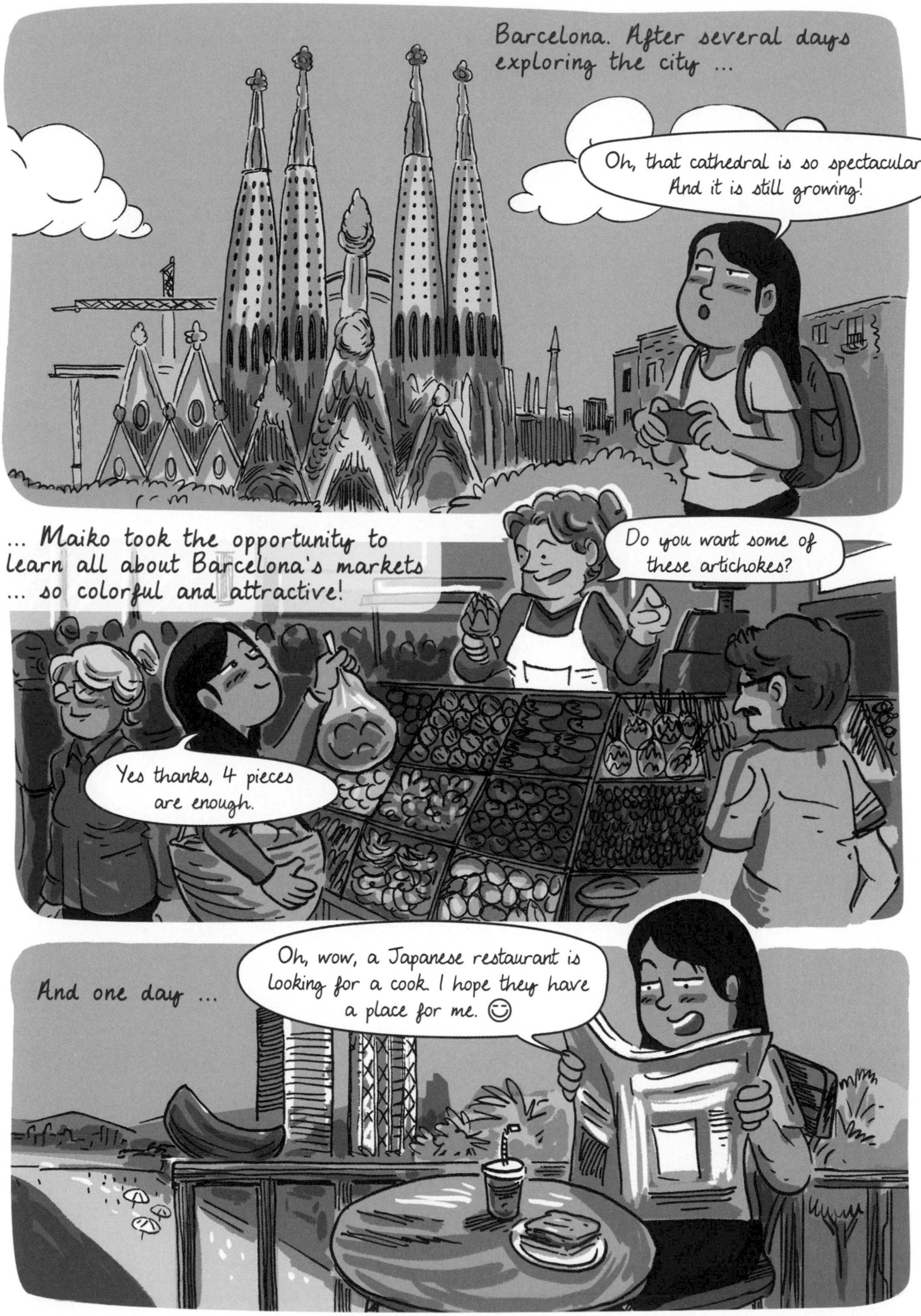
Barcelona. After several days exploring the city ...
Oh, that cathedral is so spectacular! And it is still growing!
... Maiko took the opportunity to learn all about Barcelona's markets ... so colorful and attractive!
Do you want some of these artichokes?
Yes thanks, 4 pieces are enough.
And one day ...
Oh, wow, a Japanese restaurant is looking for a cook. I hope they have a place for me. ☺

A few months later ...

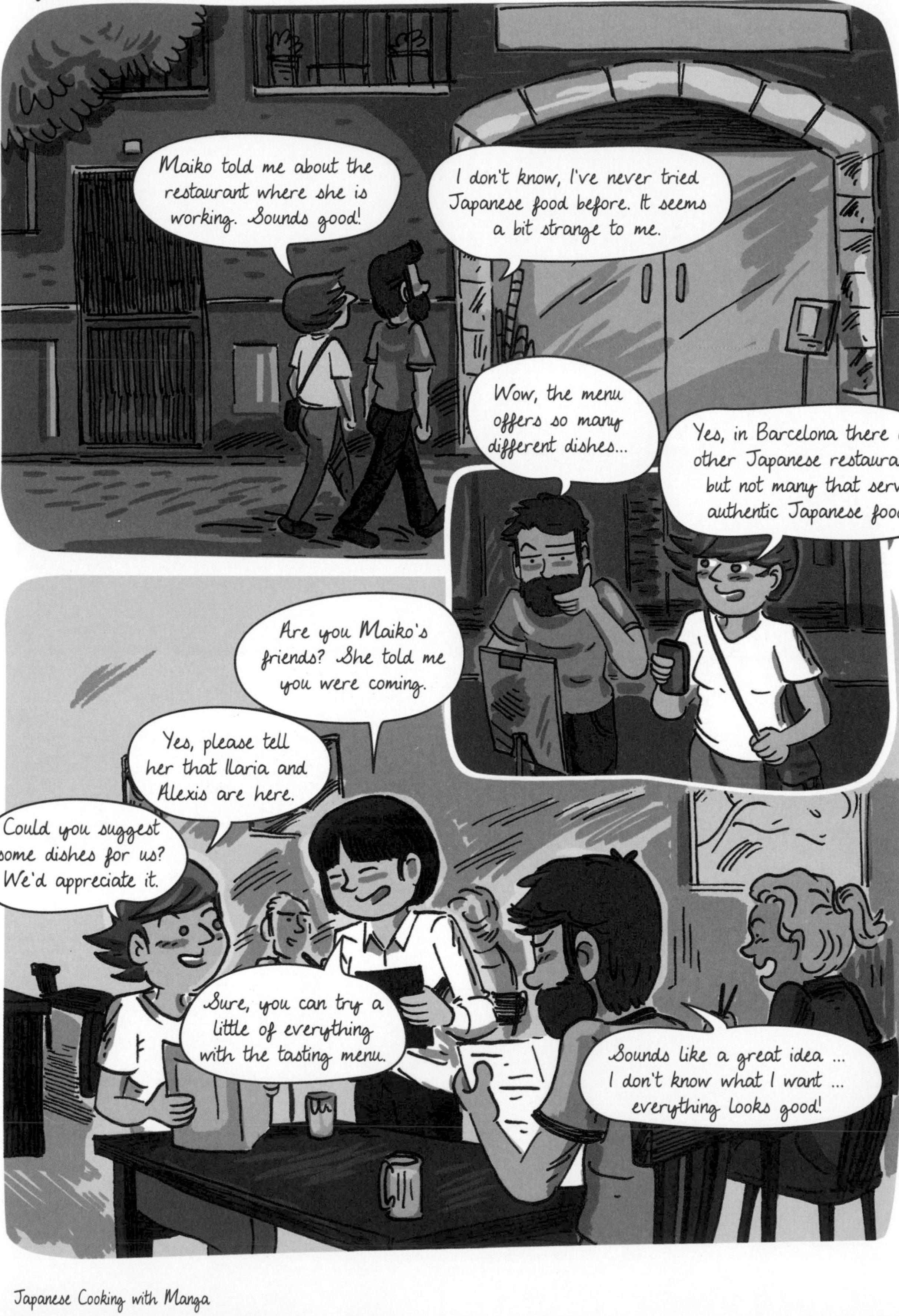

Maiko told me about the restaurant where she is working. Sounds good!
I don't know, I've never tried Japanese food before. It seems a bit strange to me.
Wow, the menu offers so many different dishes...
Yes, in Barcelona there are other Japanese restaurants, but not many that serve authentic Japanese food.
Are you Maiko's friends? She told me you were coming.
Yes, please tell her that Ilaria and Alexis are here.
Could you suggest some dishes for us? We'd appreciate it.
Sure, you can try a little of everything with the tasting menu.
Sounds like a great idea ... I don't know what I want ... everything looks good!

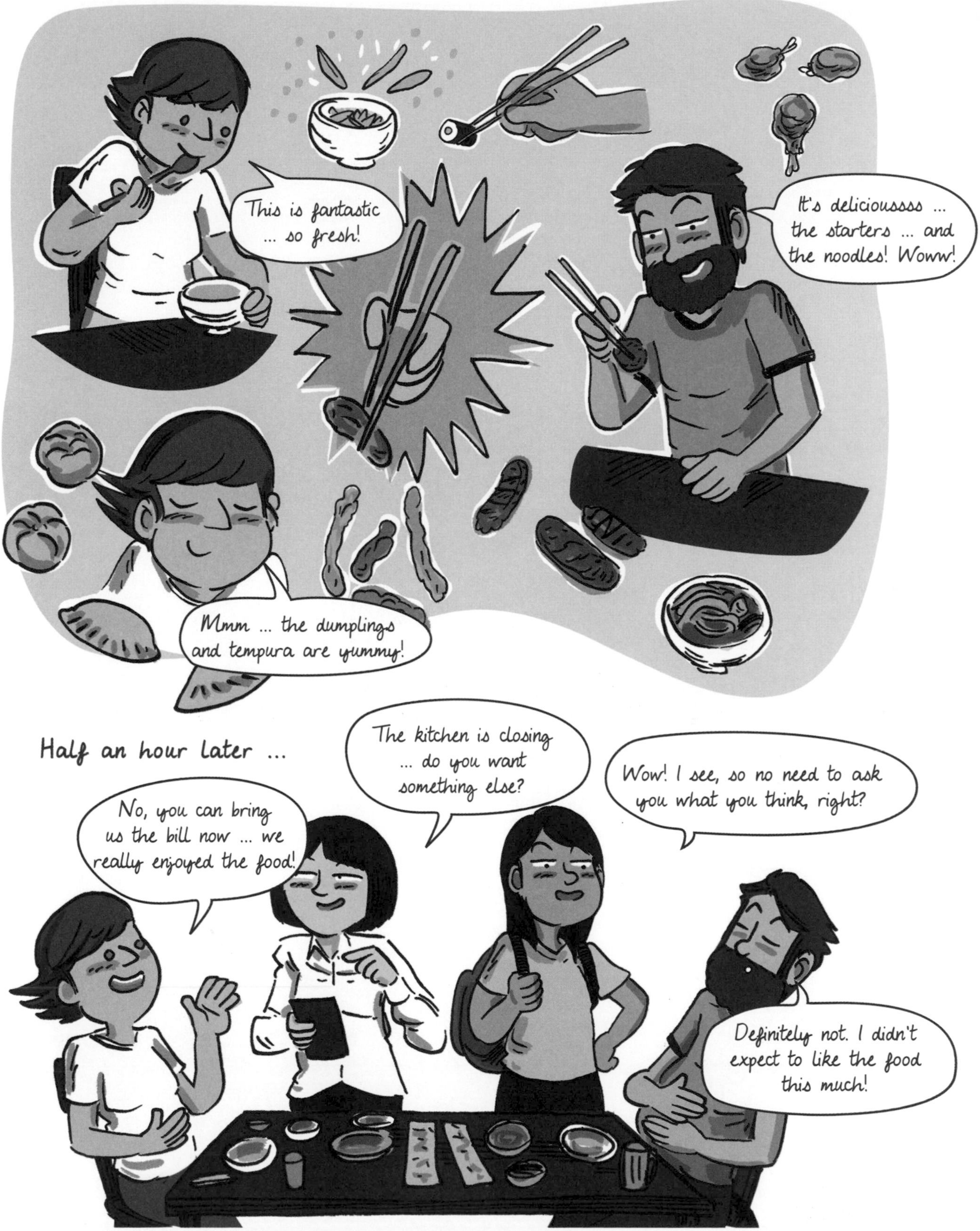
This is fantastic ... so fresh!
It's deliciousssss ... the starters ... and the noodles! Woww!
Mmm ... the dumplings and tempura are yummy!
Half an hour later ...
No, you can bring us the bill now ... we really enjoyed the food!
The kitchen is closing ... do you want something else?
Wow! I see, so no need to ask you what you think, right?
Definitely not. I didn't expect to like the food this much!

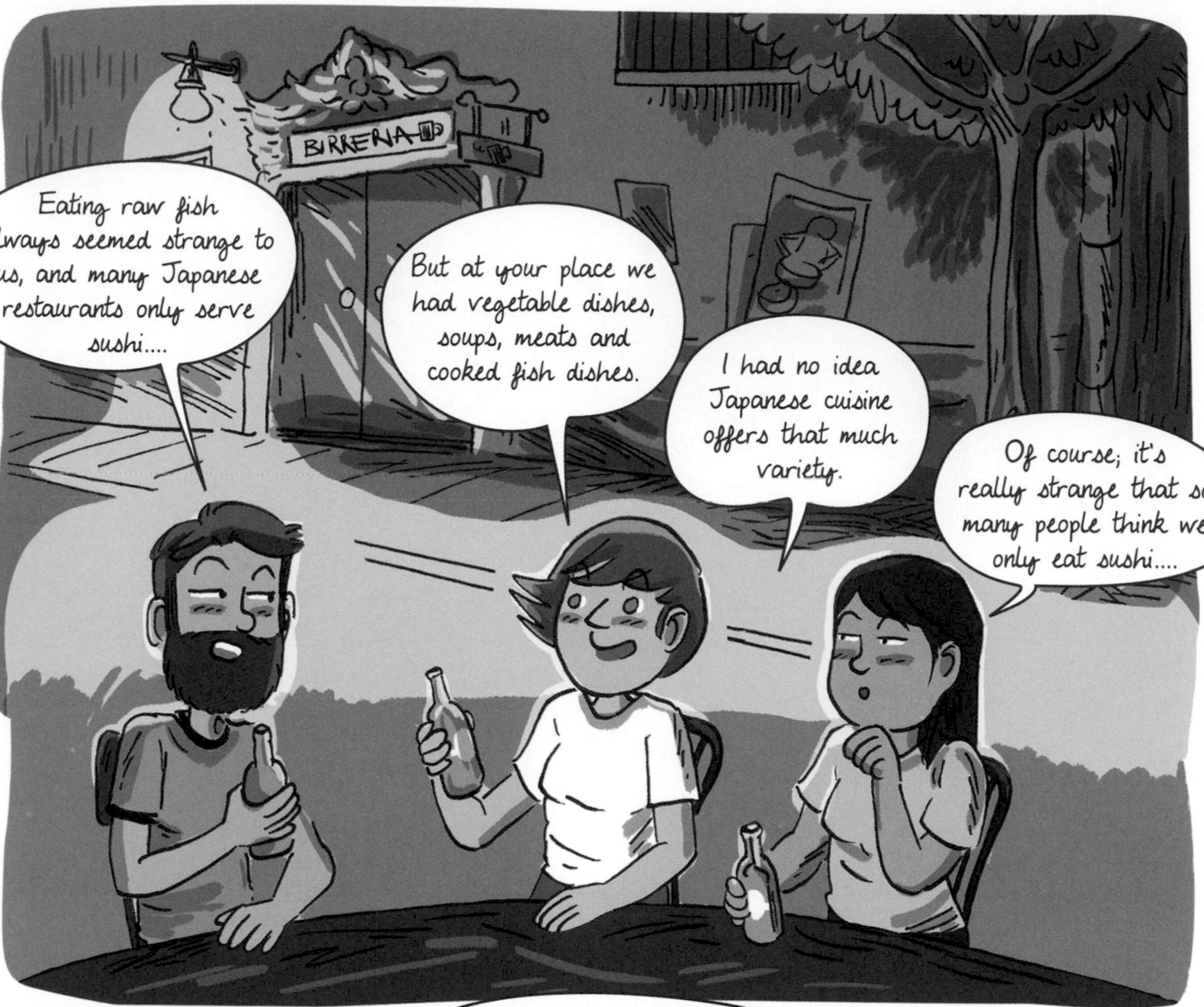
BIRRERIA
Eating raw fish always seemed strange to us, and many Japanese restaurants only serve sushi....
But at your place we had vegetable dishes, soups, meats and cooked fish dishes.
I had no idea Japanese cuisine offers that much variety.
Of course; it's really strange that so many people think we only eat sushi....

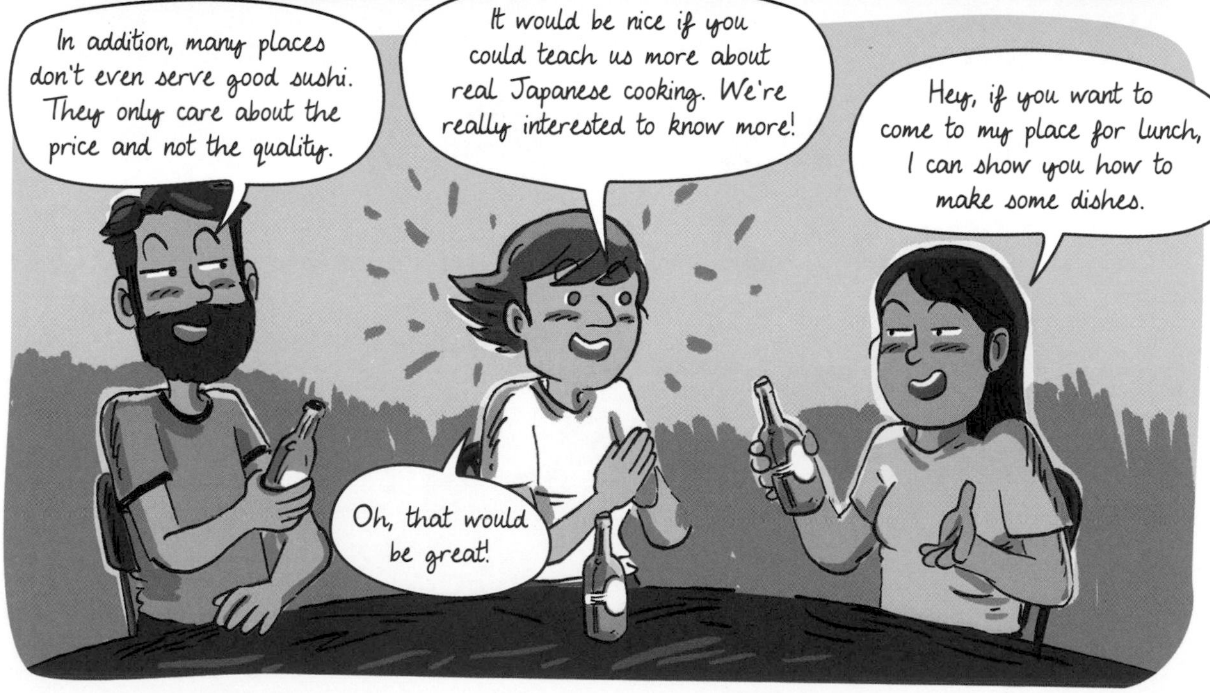
In addition, many places don't even serve good sushi. They only care about the price and not the quality.
It would be nice if you could teach us more about real Japanese cooking. We're really interested to know more!
Oh, that would be great!
Hey, if you want to come to my place for lunch, I can show you how to make some dishes.

First of all, before you start cooking, wash your hands with soap and water.

Okay, now I have a page to tell you my secrets ... First of all, paying attention to simple things is the way to prepare delicious food and learn something from each recipe.

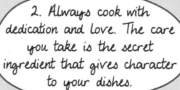

Our hands are our most important tools and you have to take care of them. And always treat every product with maximum care and respect.

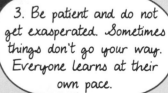

1. Keep your kitchen clean and tidy. That will bring you calm and clarity of mind.

2. Always cook with dedication and love. The care you take is the secret ingredient that gives character to your dishes.

3. Be patient and do not get exasperated. Sometimes things don't go your way. Everyone learns at their own pace.

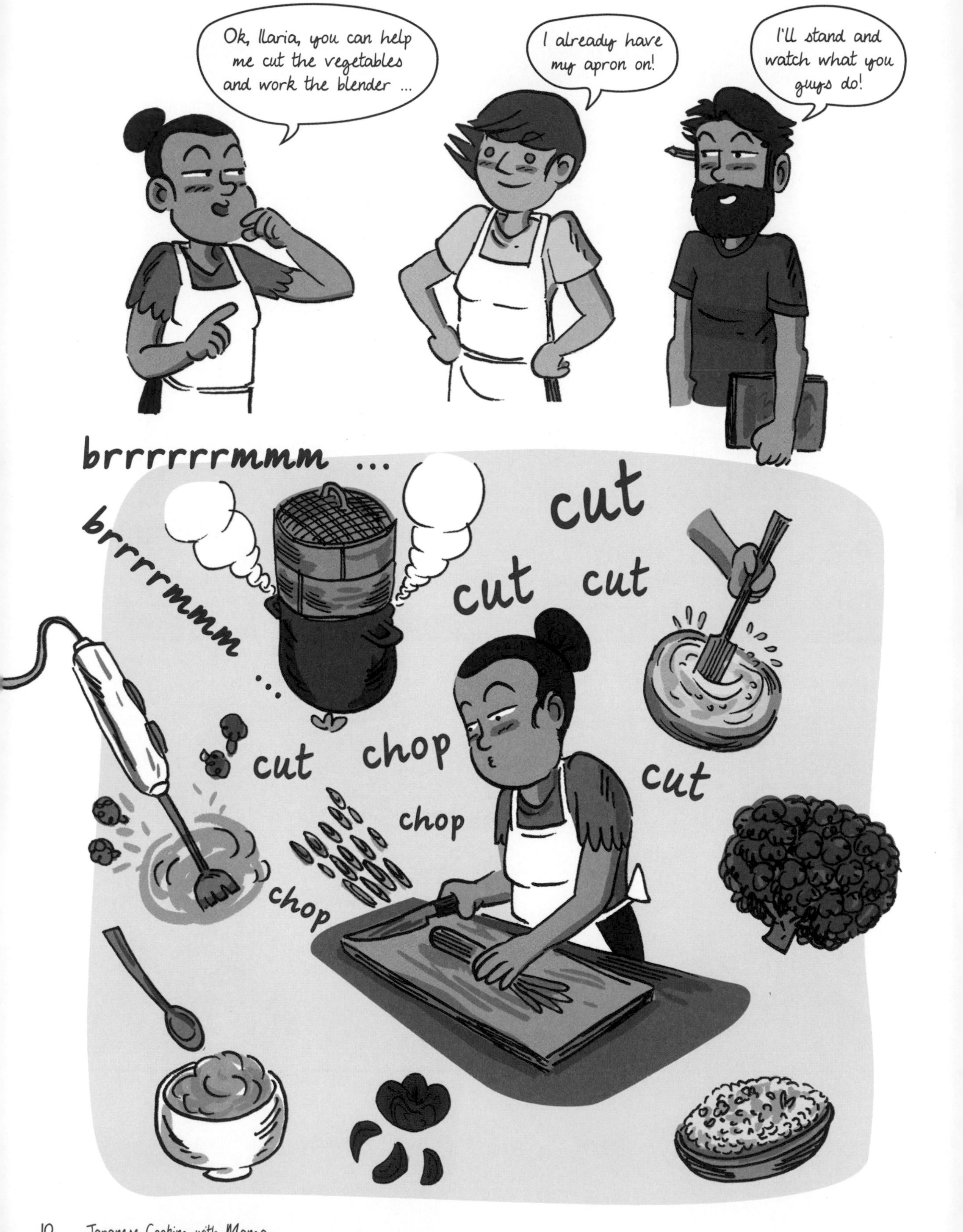

Ok, Ilaria, you can help me cut the vegetables and work the blender ...
I already have my apron on!
I'll stand and watch what you guys do!
brrrrrrmmm ...
brrrrrmmm ...
cut
cut
cut
cut
chop
chop
cut
chop

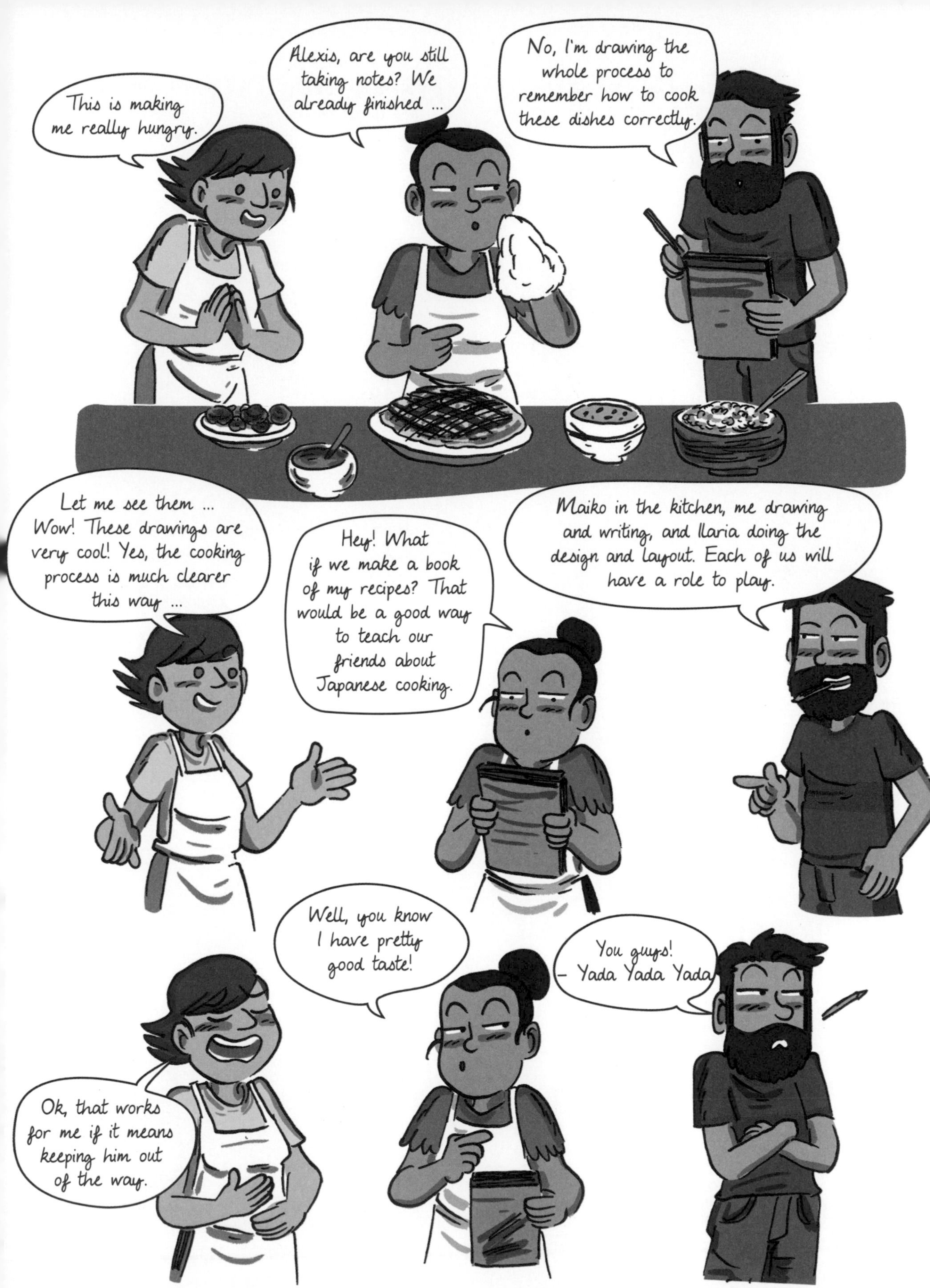
This is making me really hungry.
Alexis, are you still taking notes? We already finished ...
No, I'm drawing the whole process to remember how to cook these dishes correctly.
Let me see them ... Wow! These drawings are very cool! Yes, the cooking process is much clearer this way ...
Hey! What if we make a book of my recipes? That would be a good way to teach our friends about Japanese cooking.
Maiko in the kitchen, me drawing and writing, and Ilaria doing the design and layout. Each of us will have a role to play.
Well, you know I have pretty good taste!
You guys! - Yada Yada Yada
Ok, that works for me if it means keeping him out of the way.

Essential Japanese Ingredients

Many Japanese ingredients are now available at supermarkets everywhere. The international section has short-grain rice, soy sauce and rice vinegar. You will also find gyoza wrappers, fresh tofu and even miso in the refrigerated section.

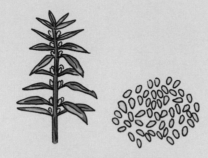

Dashi Powder is the ubiquitous Japanese fish stock powder used in many Japanese dishes. Dashi soup stock can be made fresh from dried bonito flakes but it is also available in an instant powdered version that you just dissolve in water. Instant dashi stock powder comes in small packets or bottles and is useful when a small amount of dashi stock is required.

Sesame Seeds White sesame seeds are more commonly used than black ones, which have a stronger flavor. You can buy them toasted or dry toast them yourself in a pan over medium heat, moving them around until they turn golden brown—but do not burn them! Black sesame seeds are used as a garnish and are sometimes used as a decoration for sushi.

Rice Vinegar is available in Asian food stores and many supermarkets. Make sure the rice vinegar you purchase has only rice and water as the ingredients. Store it in a cool, dry place. The flavor of rice vinegar is more delicate than other vinegars. If you cannot find it, use diluted wine or cider vinegar.

Dried Bonito Flakes are dried shavings of bonito fish sold in small plastic packets. The shavings come in varying sizes—the larger ones are used to make dashi soup stock whereas the finer ones are used as a garnish. They are available in Japanese stores and many supermarkets.

Seaweed comes in many varieties, normally dried. **Wakame** is from the seas around Japan and Korea and has an intense color, sweet flavor and delicate texture. It is great in salads. **Nori** is a small and rugged seaweed. After being crushed and pressed, it is sold in packets as dried sheets, ready to make sushi! **Kombu** is a dark green seaweed, rich in minerals. Once reconstituted it's used in salads and soups, and to flavor rice when cooking. Kombu is usually discarded after the dish or rice is cooked.

Nori Seaweed

Wakame Seaweed

Kombu Seaweed

Miso is a fermented soybean paste similar to Chinese black bean paste. It is available in the refrigerated section of Asian supermarkets and some health food stores. White, red or special blends are the commonly available miso varieties. Typically, the lighter the color of the miso, the sweeter and lighter the flavor.

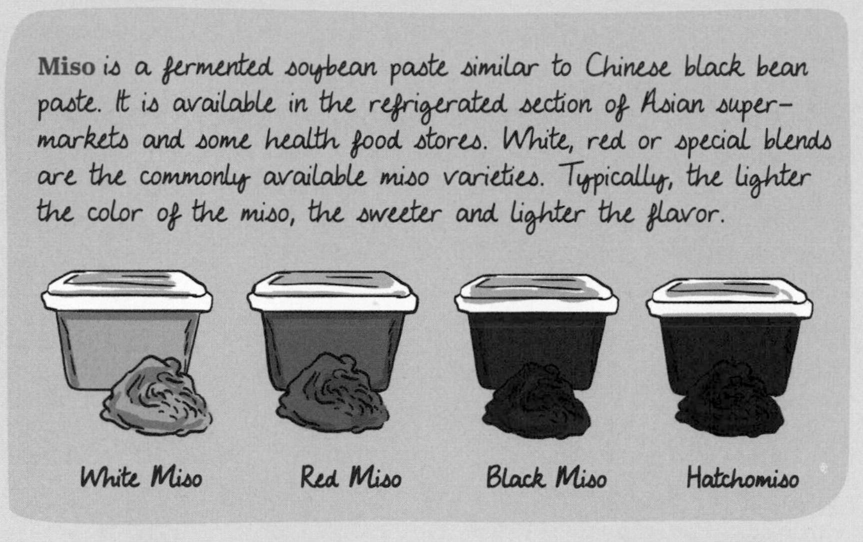

White Miso | Red Miso | Black Miso | Hatchomiso

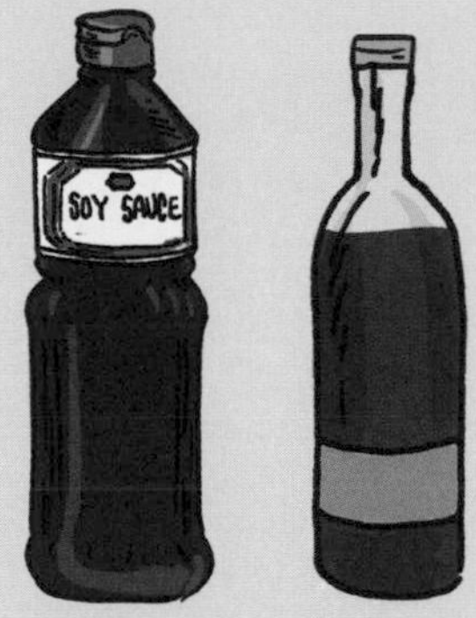
SOY SAUCE

Soy Sauce is an essential ingredient in Japanese dishes. It is made of soybeans, wheat and salt. Generally, at the table, **light soy sauce** is used whereas in cooking, **dark soy sauce** is used.

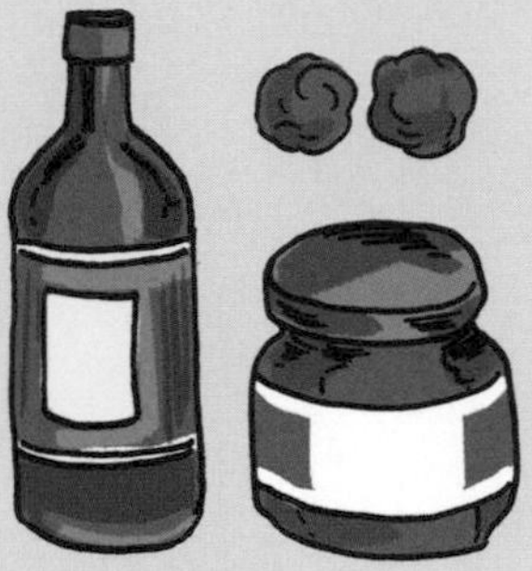

Umeboshi is a preserved Japanese sour plum. You can buy them whole, or as jars of umeboshi paste or in the form of umeboshi vinegar. Umeboshi has a sour and salty flavor and is used for salads, vegetables and over rice.

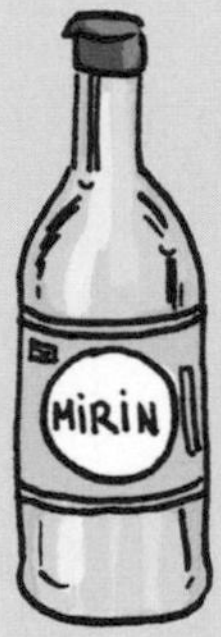
MIRIN

Mirin is a sweet, amber-colored rice wine used as a flavoring in soups and sauces. It has low alcohol content and a high sugar content. Readily available in Japanese food stores and many supermarkets. If mirin is unavailable, cooking sherry may be substituted.

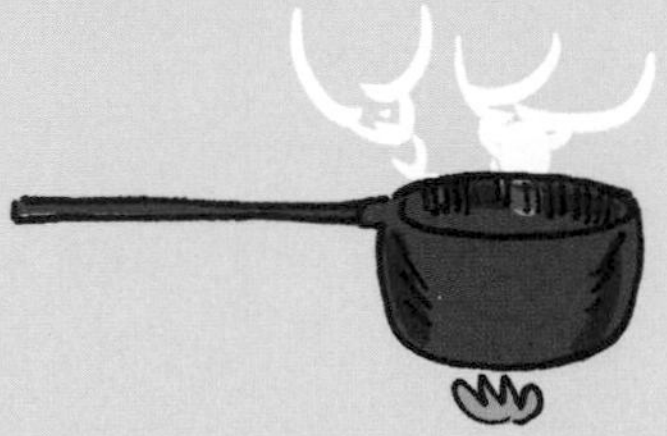

You can make your own **sushi soy sauce** by heating 7 parts of light soy sauce + 3 parts of mirin in a saucepan until it comes to a boil. Allow it to cool, then pour into a bottle and refrigerate.

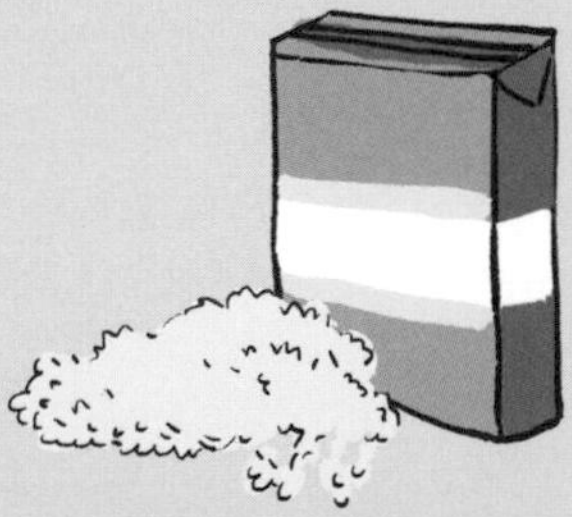

Panko Breadcrumbs are dried white breadcrumbs that come in fine and coarse varieties. Used to coat deep-fried foods, they are crunchier than Western varieties. Substitute regular breadcrumbs if you cannot find them.

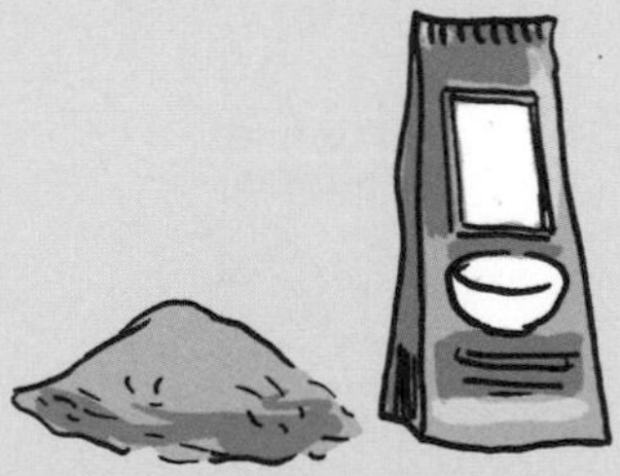

Matcha Powder is a green tea powder with a light, sweet flavor. Green tea is associated with the traditional Japanese tea ceremony and is also used to make desserts like ice cream or cake.

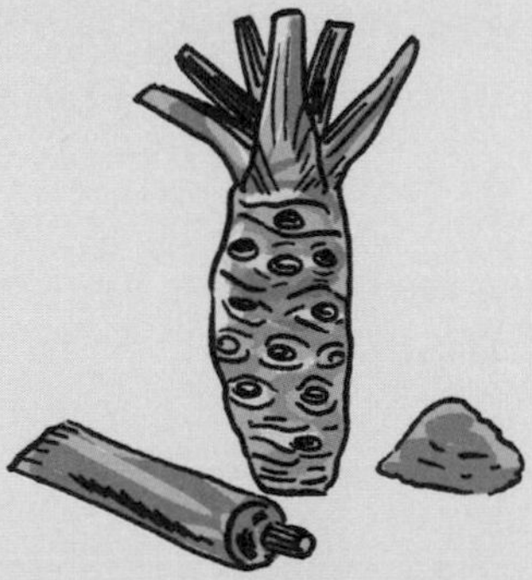

Wasabi is a spicy Japanese horseradish that is sold in powdered form or as a paste in a tube. It is normally eaten with sushi or sashimi.

Tofu is a white curd made from soybean milk. Both silken and firm tofu are used in recipes throughout the book. Opt for varieties that are packed in water in your grocer's refrigerated section. Once opened, tofu must be kept refrigerated, covered in water. Change the water daily. Stored this way, tofu can last for several days.

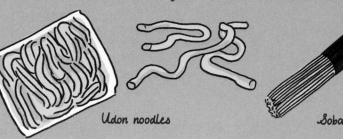

Noodles There are many different kinds of Japanese noodles. **Udon** are thick noodles made from wheat flour, and are available round or flat, fresh or dried. They have a soft and smooth texture and can be used in stir-fries, but are particularly good served in a hot dashi broth. **Soba** are thin noodles made with buckwheat flour, and have a soft texture. Substitute Chinese ramen or whole wheat spaghetti if you cannot find them.

Udon noodles

Soba noodles

SUSHI RICE

Rice Sushi is usually made with special Japanese short-grain rice, commonly called sushi rice. It is a high quality rice that is sticky and slightly sweet (not to be mistaken for glutinous rice). Its high starch content creates the stickiness needed to make your favorite types of sushi.

Sake is a clear rice wine made by brewing short grain rice in porcelain or wooden casks. It is for cooking or drinking. White wine, Chinese rice wine or dry sherry may be substituted.

Shiitake Mushrooms are sometimes called black mushrooms or Chinese mushrooms. They are available fresh or dried. Dried ones must be reconstituted by soaking them in warm water for a few minutes and are more intensely flavored than fresh shiitake. Porcini mushrooms or Chinese mushrooms may be substituted.

SESAME OIL

Sesame Oil should be used sparingly as a seasoning and never for deep-frying. Japanese sesame oil is milder than the Chinese or Korean varieties.

MAYONAISE

Mayonnaise Japanese mayannoaise is lighter and creamier than regular mayonnaise. Store it in the refrigerator after opening. If you are unable to find it, add a little sugar and rice vineagr to regular mayonnaise.

How to Make a Japanese Omelette

Kinshi tamago is a shredded omelette that is used to garnish sushi bowls and also in other recipes and types of sushi. Here we show you how to make a very thin Japanese-style omelette that can be sliced into shreds.

Makes about 1 cup of shredded omelette
Time: 15 minutes

2 eggs
Pinch of salt, to taste
Oil, for frying

1. Break the eggs into a bowl and beat them with a whisk. Add a pinch of salt.

2. Pass the mixture through a fine sieve to give it a finer texture.

3. Heat a skillet over medium heat and add a little oil. Add a tablespoon of the egg batter and spread it around the pan ... so it looks like a thin pancake.

4. Flip it over to cook on the other side. After each omelette is done, place it on a paper towel to absorb the oil.

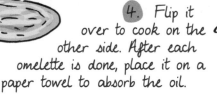

5. When the omelettes have cooled, cut them first in half and then into strips.

And the kinshi tamago is ready!

This is a a very simple preparation that can be used to accompany lots of dishes.

The Importance of Seasonal Produce

We want to emphasize to you the importance of cooking with seasonal ingredients. This is a very important point if you want to eat healthy, sustainable and tasty meals. In Japanese cooking, every detail counts. (Although this is true also for any other type of cooking.)

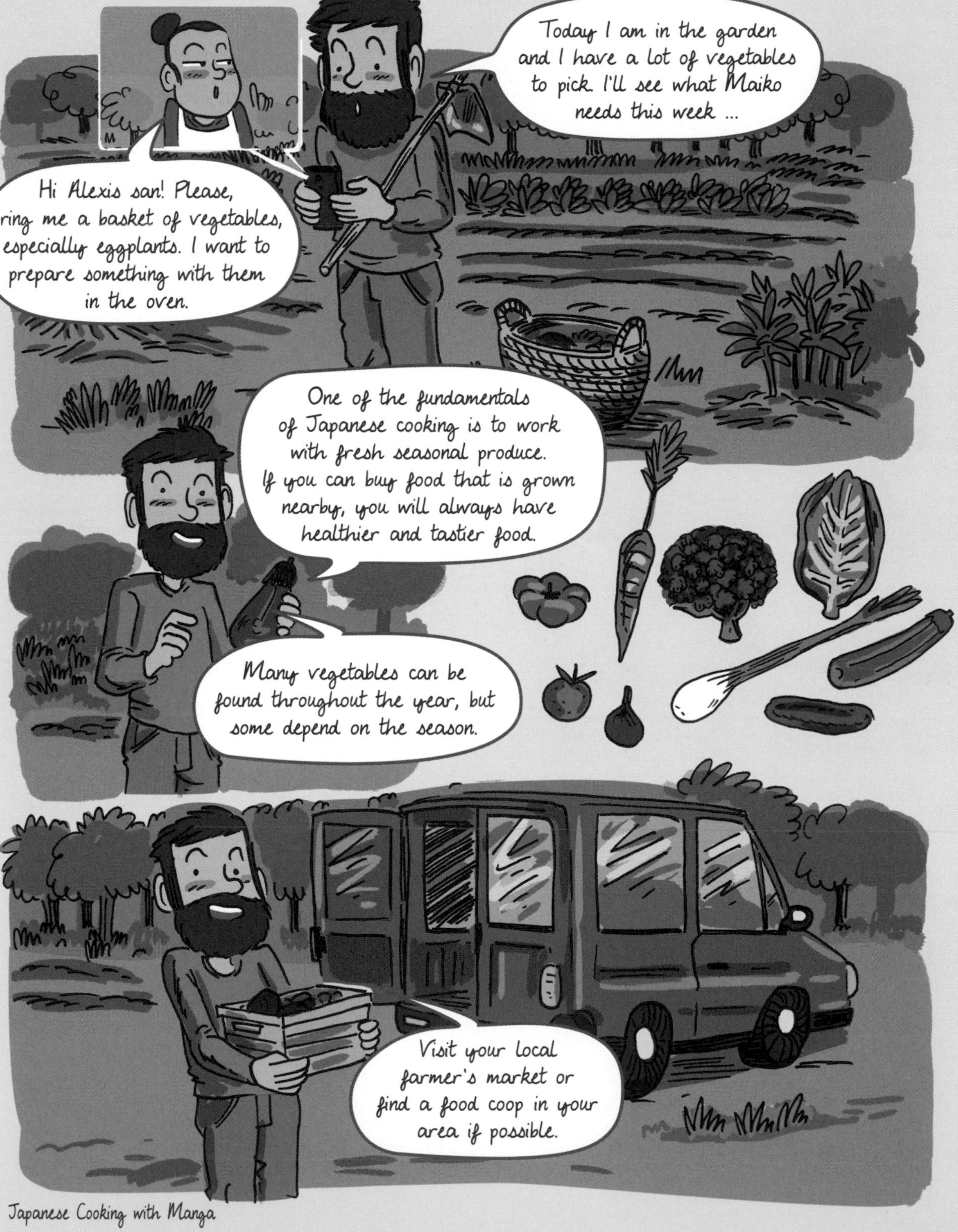
Today I am in the garden and I have a lot of vegetables to pick. I'll see what Maiko needs this week ...
Hi Alexis san! Please, bring me a basket of vegetables, especially eggplants. I want to prepare something with them in the oven.
One of the fundamentals of Japanese cooking is to work with fresh seasonal produce. If you can buy food that is grown nearby, you will always have healthier and tastier food.
Many vegetables can be found throughout the year, but some depend on the season.
Visit your local farmer's market or find a food coop in your area if possible.

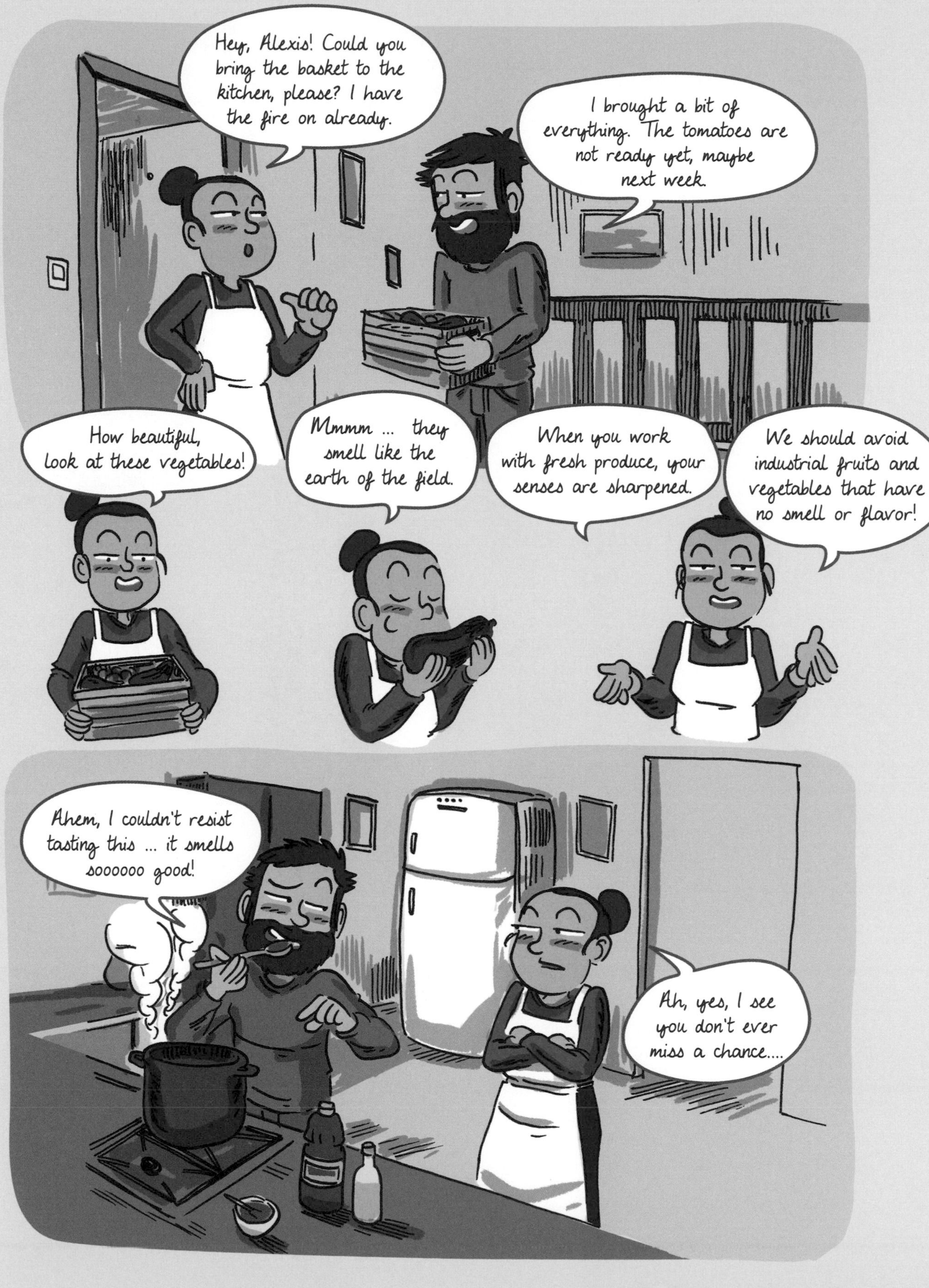
Hey, Alexis! Could you bring the basket to the kitchen, please? I have the fire on already.
I brought a bit of everything. The tomatoes are not ready yet, maybe next week.
How beautiful, look at these vegetables!
Mmmm ... they smell like the earth of the field.
When you work with fresh produce, your senses are sharpened.
We should avoid industrial fruits and vegetables that have no smell or flavor!
Ahem, I couldn't resist tasting this ... it smells soooooo good!
Ah, yes, I see you don't ever miss a chance....

Chapter 1

STARTERS & SNACKS

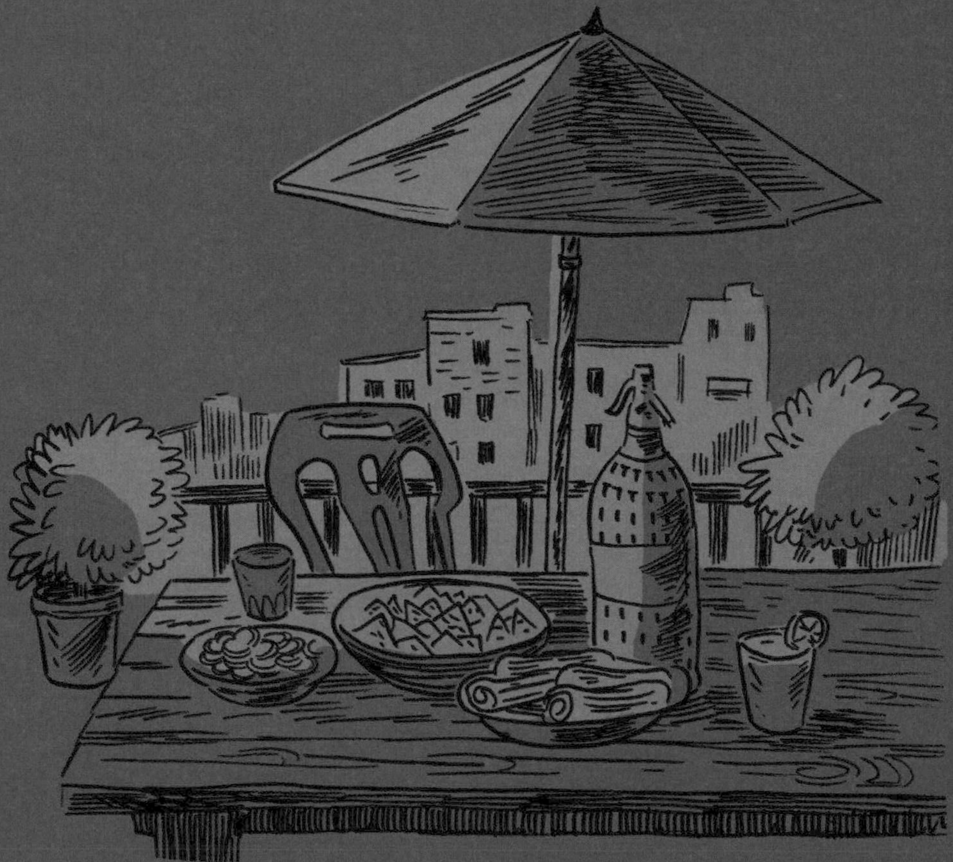

Hey guys, now that you know our story and a bit more about Japanese ingredients and our philosophy of cooking, it's time to get to work! Let's start the adventure; ready to go? To get you started, we'll make some easy things that are fun to share with friends ... party snacks, light meals and appetizers. Your food will definitely be the hit of the party!! Here we go!

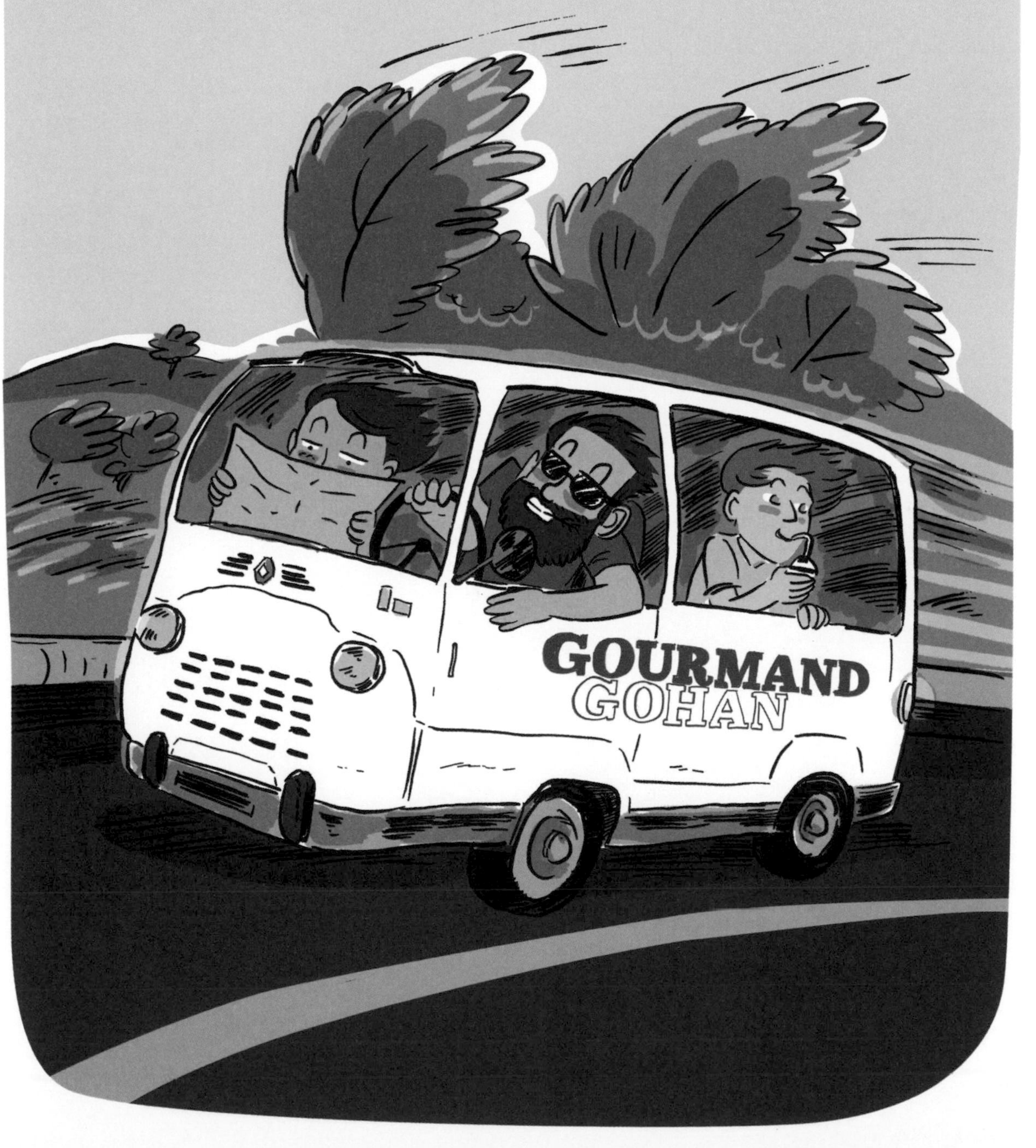
GOURMAND
GOHAN

Japanese Pizza Okonomiyaki

Okonomiyaki is a popular snack in Japan, sold by street vendors at temple festivals. It's like a stuffed pancake or a pizza—you can put anything you want on it! The name actually means "whatever you like"! Our version uses scallions, cabbage and tuna but you can also use chopped ham, bacon, calamari, onions, chicken, cheese or anything else you have on hand. The sauce is what makes it special—you can buy bottled Okonomiyaki Sauce in Asian food stores, or make your own using the simple recipe on the opposite page!

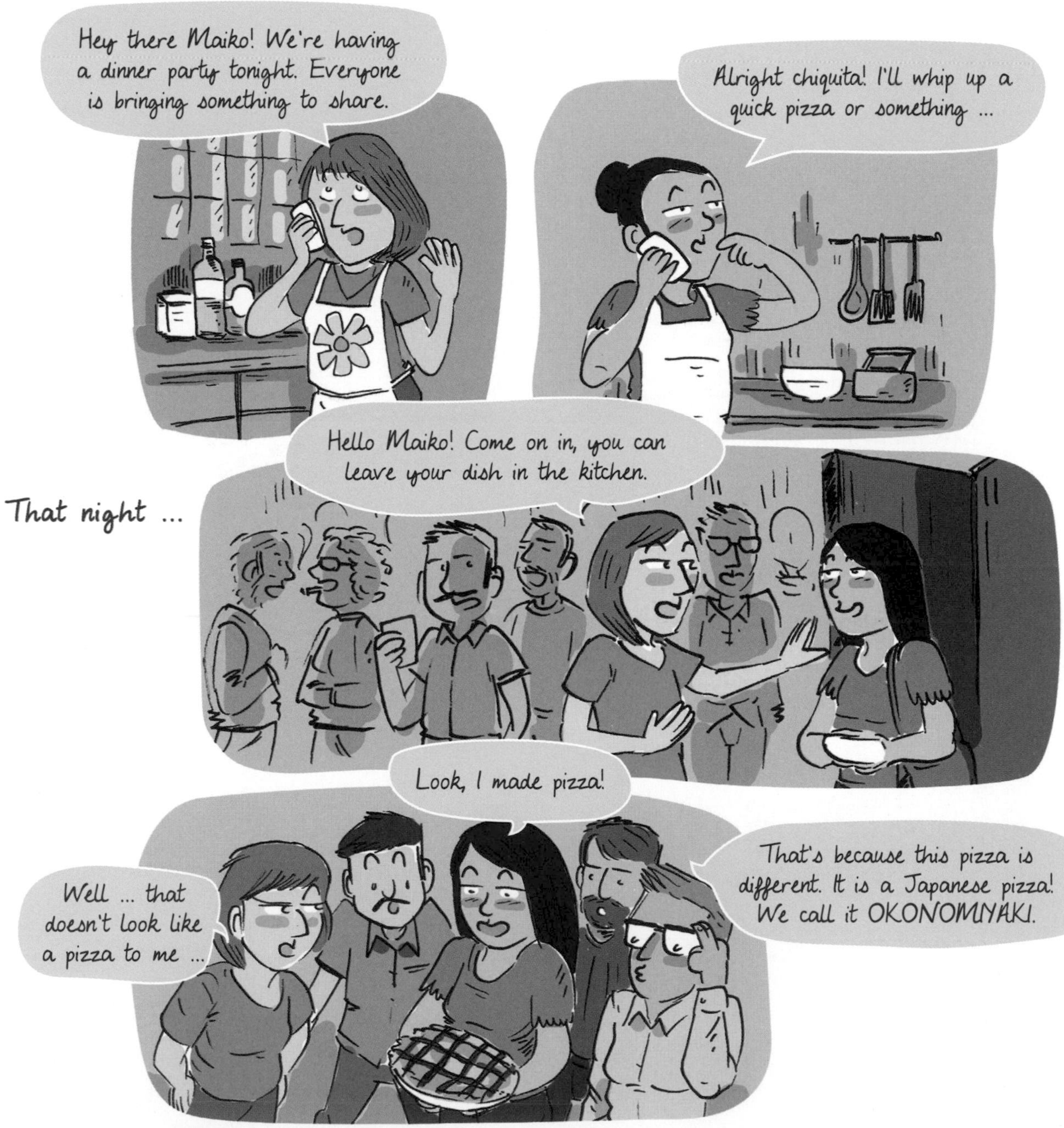
Hey there Maiko! We're having a dinner party tonight. Everyone is bringing something to share.
Alright chiquita! I'll whip up a quick pizza or something ...
That night ...
Hello Maiko! Come on in, you can leave your dish in the kitchen.
Look, I made pizza!
Well ... that doesn't look like a pizza to me ...
That's because this pizza is different. It is a Japanese pizza! We call it OKONOMIYAKI.

Serves 4
(as a light snack)
Time: 20 minutes

- 1 scallion (spring onion), washed and chopped (both green and white parts)
- 1½ cups (150 g) shredded cabbage (2–3 large leaves of cabbage, washed and sliced very thinly into threads)
- ½ cup (125 ml) water
- 3 tablespoons flour
- 3 eggs
- Salt and pepper, to taste
- 1 can (6 oz /160 g) tuna in water or brine, drained and flaked
- 3 tablespoons olive oil, for frying
- Dried bonito flakes, to garnish (optional)

Okonomiyaki Sauce

- 8 tablespoons mayonnaise
- 4 tablespoons tomato ketchup
- 2 tablespoons soy sauce

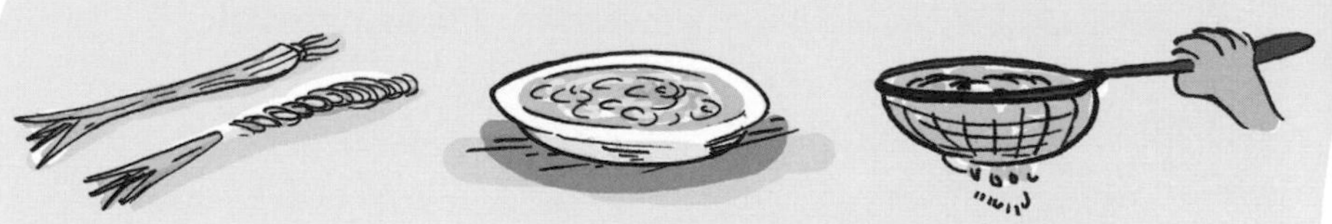

1. Finely chop the white and green parts of the scallion... soak it in water... and drain.

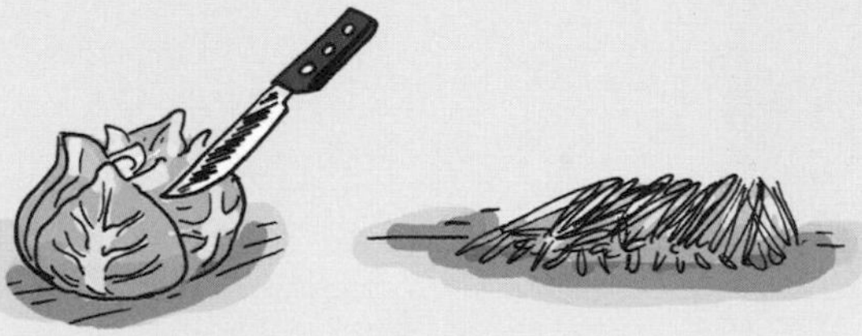

2. Wash the cabbage leaves, drain and fold them, then slice very finely into thread-like strips.

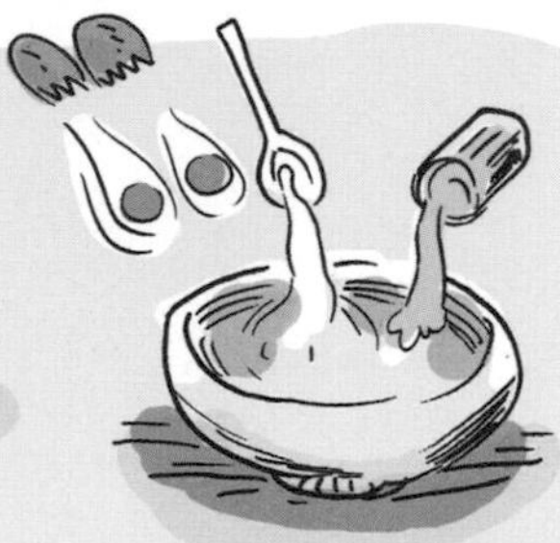

3. In a mixing bowl, combine the water, flour, eggs, salt and pepper and beat with a fork to make a batter.

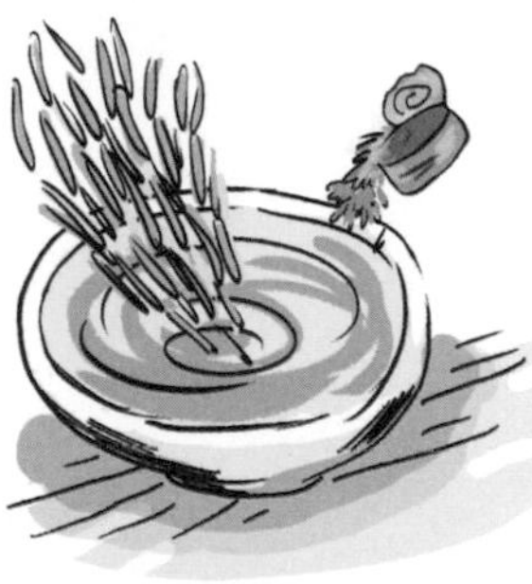

4. Flake the tuna with a fork, then add it to the batter. Also add the sliced cabbage and scallion and stir everything together.

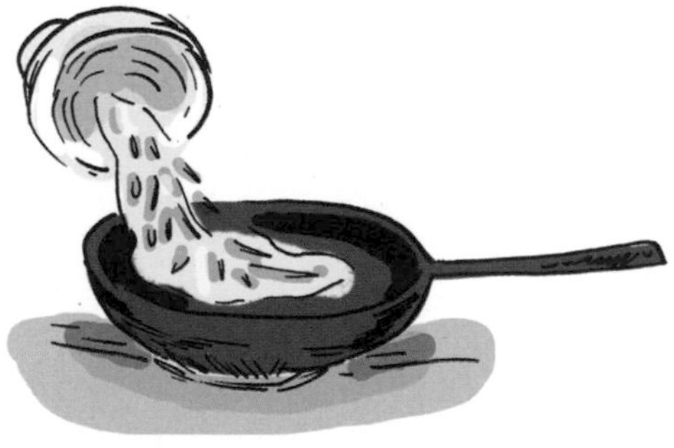

5. Add the oil to a large skillet over medium heat. Once the oil is very hot and begins to smoke, pour in the mixture. When the pancake sets on one side, after about 3 minutes, turn it over and cook it on the other side.

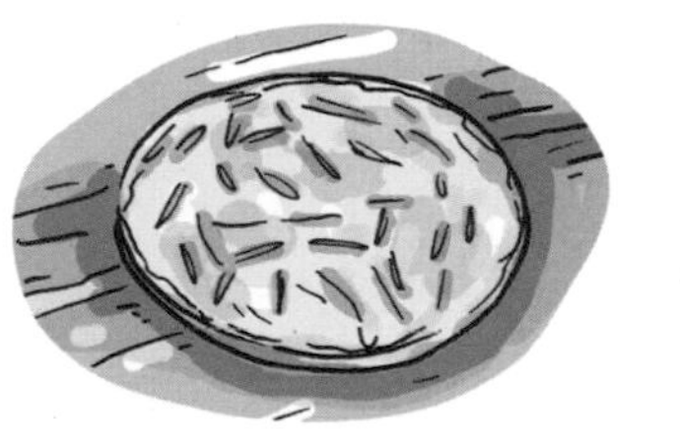

6. Serve on a plate or board like an omelette.

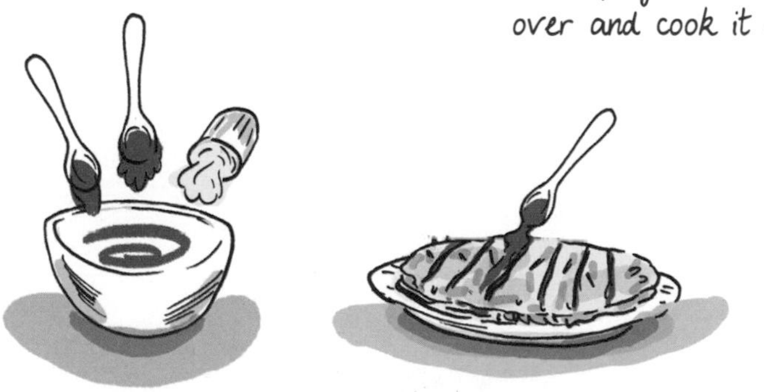

7. Mix the Okonomiyaki Sauce ingredients in a small bowl and spread it on top of the pancake with a spoon. Serve the extra sauce on the side.

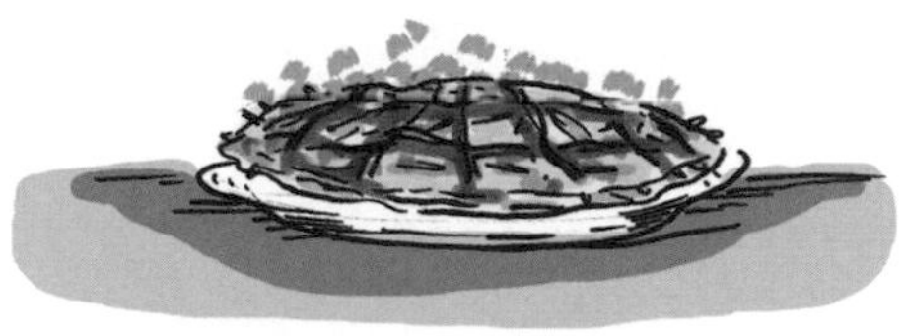

8. (Optional) Sprinkle dried bonito flakes on top for that extra flavor!

Baked Cheese Crackers Cheese Senbei

Senbei means "crackers" in Japanese and these baked crackers are absolutely delicious and very easy to make! They go great with beer and are a perfect party snack!

1. Preheat oven to 400°F (200°C).

2. Place half the gyoza wrappers on a greased baking tray (or use baking parchment).

Makes 18 crackers
Time: 20 minutes

1 packet (1 lb/450 g) pot sticker (gyoza) wrappers (around 36 wrappers)**
1 tablespoon water
1 tablespoon cornstarch or potato starch
¾ cup (80 g) grated cheese (any kind of cheese—a mixture of cheddar and parmesan works great!)
2 tablespoons soy sauce
2 tablespoons sesame oil
2 teaspoons freshly ground pepper
4 teaspoons white sesame seeds
4 teaspoons fresh rosemary leaves

**You can buy gyoza or pot sticker wrappers in the refrigerated section of your supermarket. They normally come in 1 lb (450 g) packets.

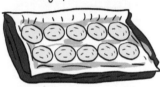

3. Combine the water and cornstarch in a small bowl, mix well, and moisten the edges of each wrapper with the mixture using a small basting brush (or your finger). Add another wrapper on top of each one to create a double layer.

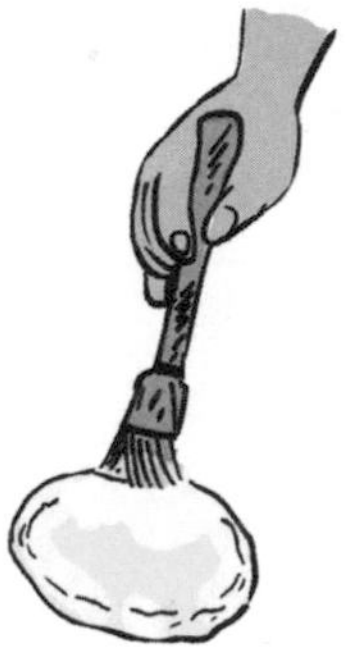

4. Combine the grated cheese, soy sauce and sesame oil in another bowl.

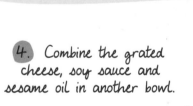

5. Coat each wrapper with the cheese mixture.

6. Sprinkle the pepper, sesame seeds and rosemary leaves on each cracker.

7. Bake until golden brown, about 10-15 minutes, and they're ready!

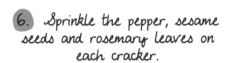

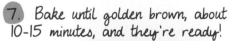

Ham & Cheese Potstickers Gyoza

These gyozas are filled with goat cheese and slices of Parma ham (or Iberico ham). They are quick and easy to make and perfect for parties. You can also use other ingredients like salami or prosciutto.

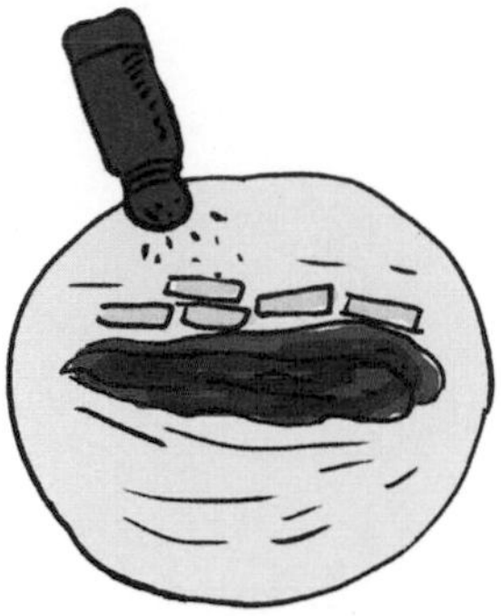

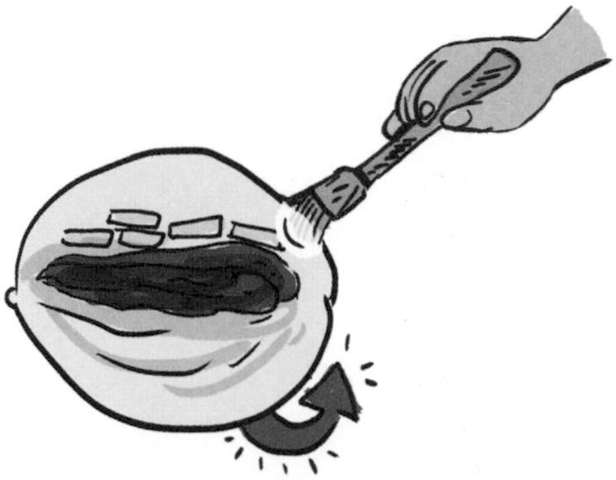

Makes 24 small gyoza
Time: 30 minutes

- 1 packet (1 lb/450 g) pot sticker or gyoza wrappers (around 36 wrappers)—see note on facing page
- ½ lb (250 g) Parma or Iberico ham (or dried salami or prosciutto), sliced into strips
- ½ lb (250 g) goat cheese, sliced or crumbled
- Ground pepper, to taste
- 1 tablespoon water
- 1 tablespoon cornstarch or potato starch
- Oil, for frying

1. Spread a gyoza wrapper on a work surface and place a few slices of ham and some cheese in the middle. Sprinkle a little ground pepper to taste.

2. Combine the water and cornstarch in a small bowl, mix well, and moisten the edges of the gyoza with this mixture, using a brush or your finger.

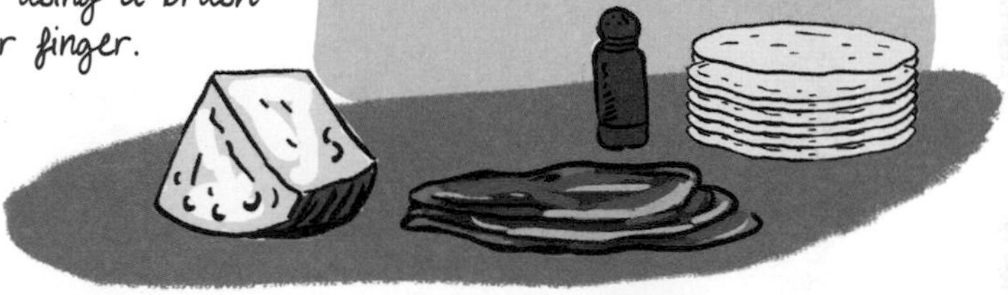

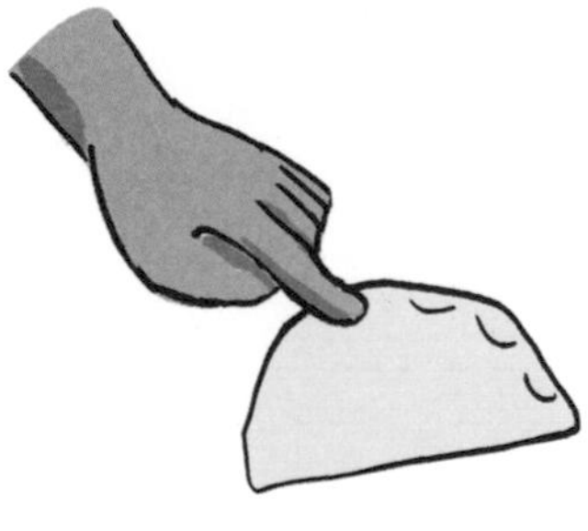

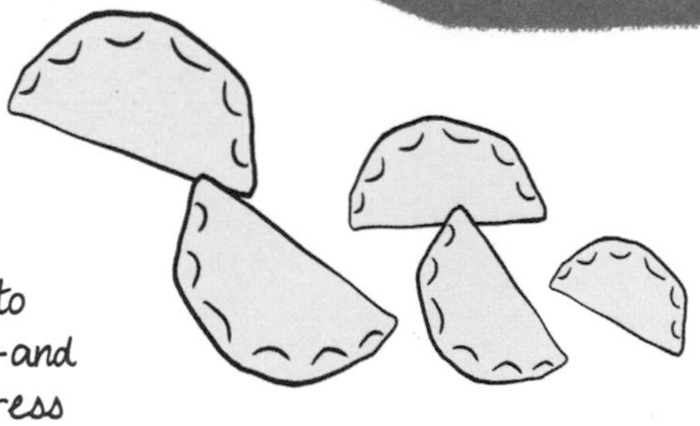

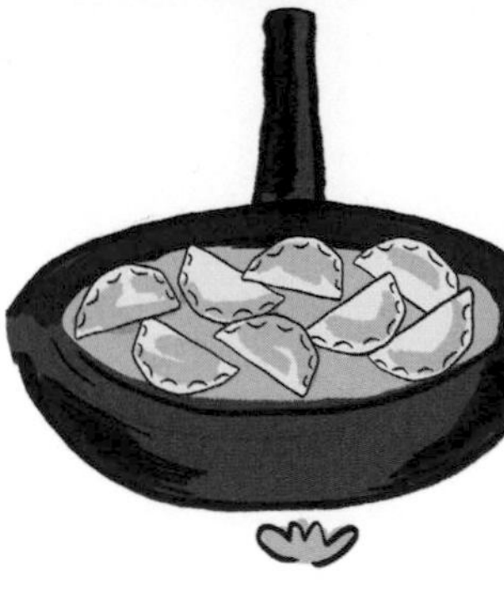

3. Fold the wrapper up to enclose the filling as shown—and form it into a half circle. Press the edges to seal well. Do the same with all the other wrappers.

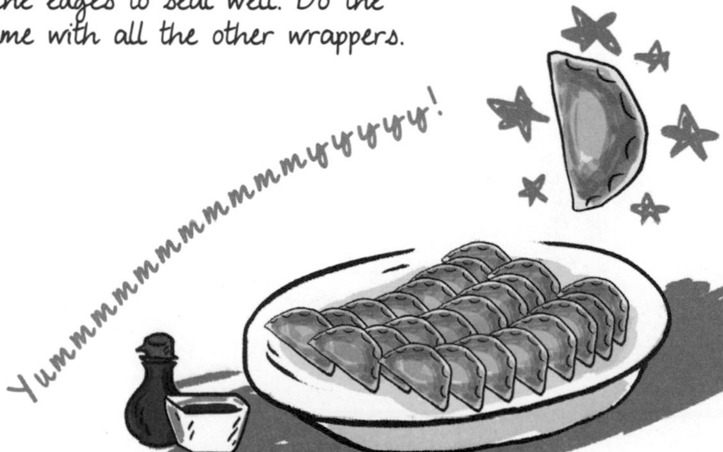
Yummmmmmmmmmmmmyyyyy!

4. Add a little oil to a skillet over medium heat and fry a dozen of the gyoza at a time until golden brown on both sides, about 6 minutes.

Japanese Omelette Rolls Dashi-Maki Tamago

Japanese omelettes are really different! They have bonito stock, sweet rice wine (mirin) and soy sauce added, which gives them lots of flavor! And the "rolling" method of cooking them is different too. You can eat them as a main dish, with rice, or slice and serve them as an appetizer.

Makes 1 large omelette
(for 2-3 people)
Time: 20 minutes

5 eggs
1 tablespoon dashi stock
   powder
3 tablespoons warm water
1 tablespoon mirin or cooking
   sherry
1 tablespoon soy sauce
1 tablespoon cornstarch or
   potato starch
Pinch of salt
Oil, for frying

1. Beat the eggs with a whisk or fork in a large bowl.

2. Strain the mixture through a fine sieve to obtain a softer texture.

3. Mix the dashi powder and water together in a bowl or glass to form dashi stock. Then add it to the eggs along with the mirin or sherry, soy sauce and cornstarch ... and a pinch of salt. Blend well.

4. Heat a skillet with some oil over medium-high heat until smoking hot.

5. Scoop about one-sixth of the mixture into the skillet and swirl it around to cover the skillet with a thin layer of egg.

6. Cook for about 1 minute or until set. Then roll the omelette up using two spatulas.

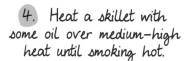

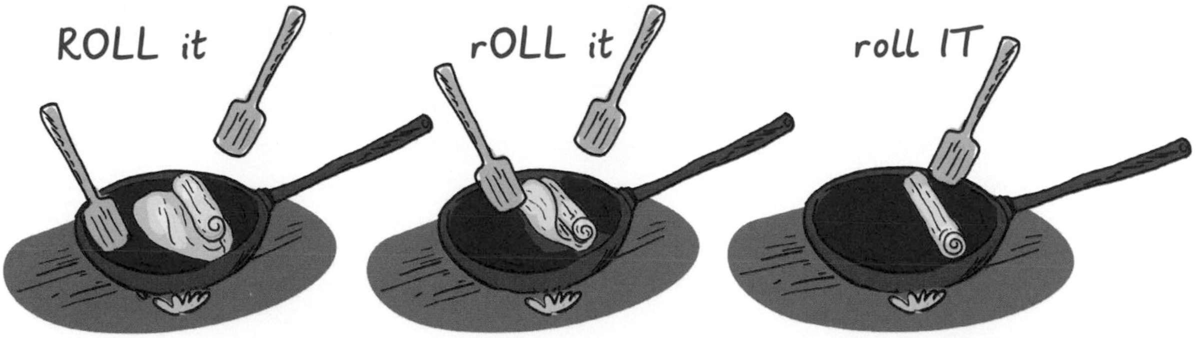
ROLL it
rOLL it
roll IT

7. Push the cooked omelette to one side of the skillet, add a little more oil and pour another scoop of the egg mixture into the skillet to form a thin layer. Once it sets, roll the new layer around the previous one to form a bigger roll.

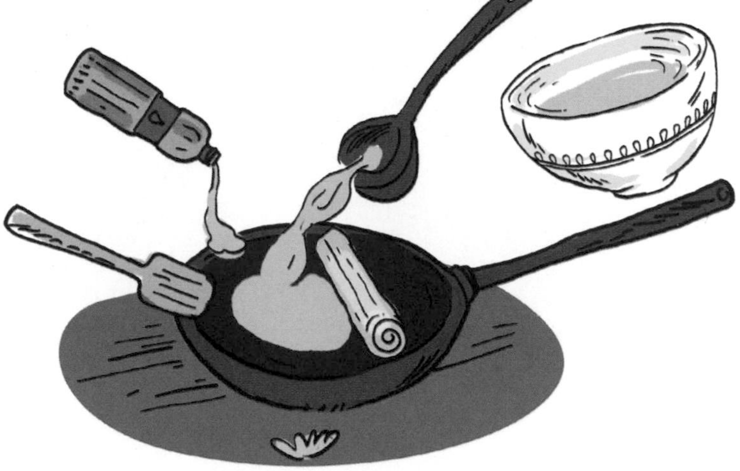

8. Repeat four more times or until the egg mixture is all used up, each time rolling the new layer around the old ones. You'll get ... an XXL omelette! And voilá! You can serve it with rice and soy sauce, or a salad.

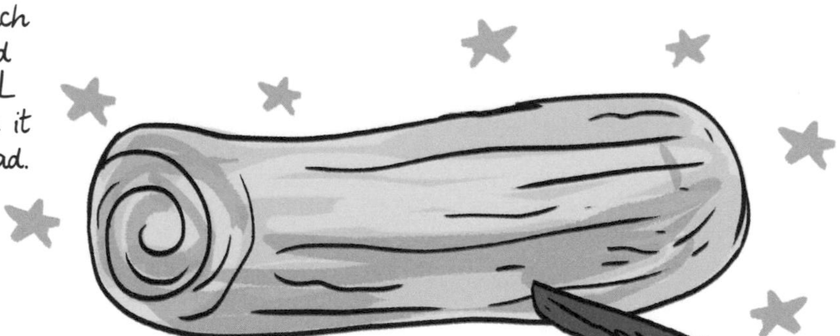

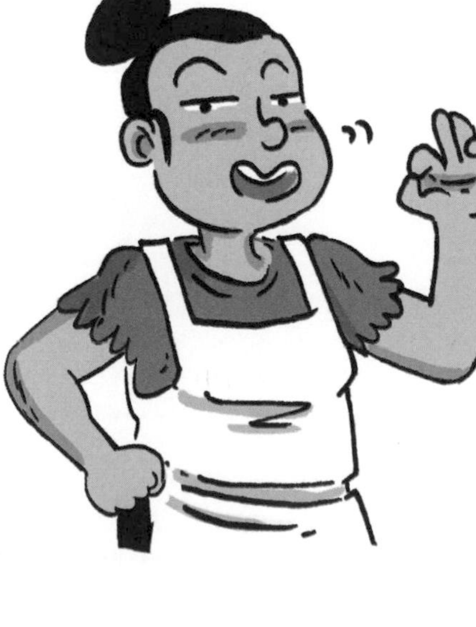

9. Alternatively, slice the omelette and serve the slices as an appetizer!

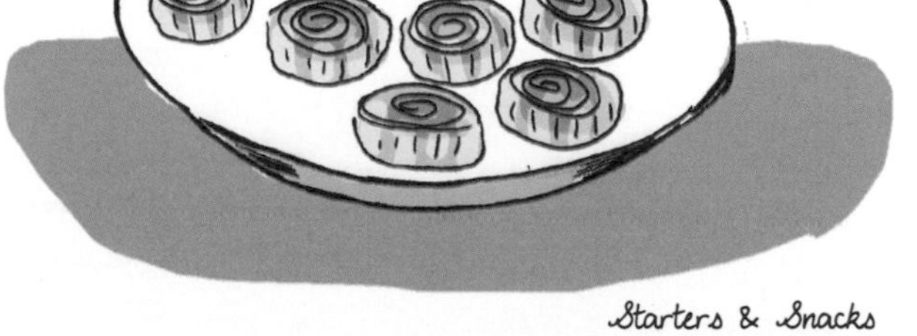

Italian Summer Rolls

The ingredients in this dish reflect Italy's national colors—green, white and red. They also reflect the classic flavors of Italy but with a Japanese twist! When you are looking for something fresh and light, this recipe is perfect! The rolls are not cooked—you just need to put in all the ingredients and roll them up.

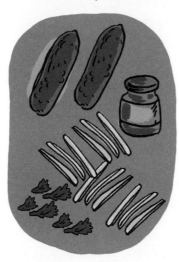

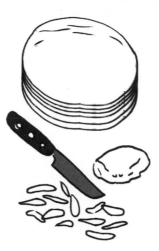

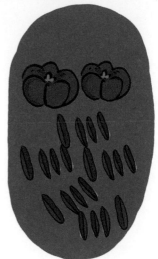

Makes 16 rolls
Time: 20 minutes

1 packet dry Vietamese rice paper wrappers
½ cup (150 g) bottled pesto sauce
2 Japanese cucumbers (or baby cucumbers), sliced into small sticks
1 bunch of arugula (rocket) or baby spinach leaves
1 lb (450 g) fresh mozzarella, cut into long strips
2–3 large tomatoes, blanched, skins and watery pulp removed, flesh diced

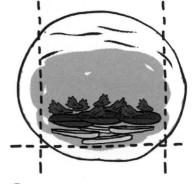

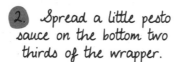

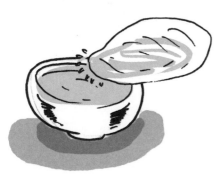

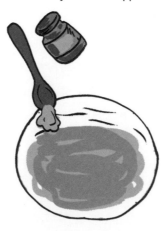

1. Moisten one rice paper wrapper with water until it is soft. Remove the excess water.

2. Spread a little pesto sauce on the bottom two thirds of the wrapper.

3. Add the cucumber, arugula, mozzarella and tomato on top to form green, white and red layers.

4. It is important to only place ingredients on the bottom part of the wrapper and leave 2 in (5 cm) at the top and sides around the fillings so the wrapper can be folded up to hold them. The broken lines show how the wrapper is to be folded.

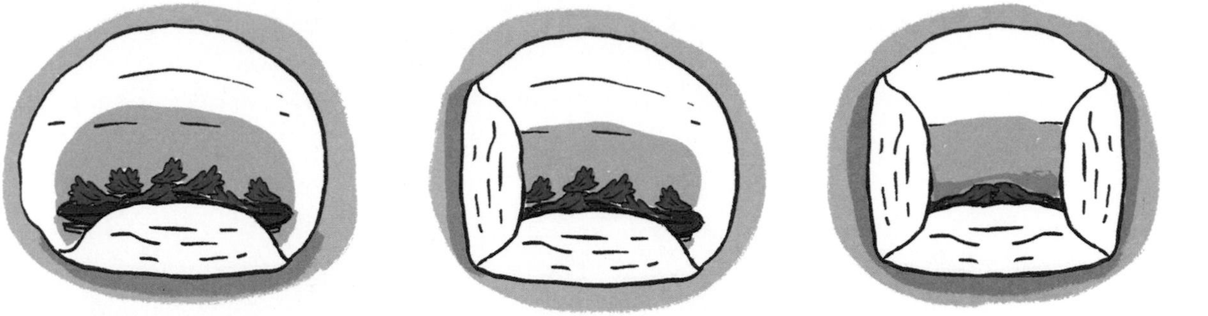

5. Fold the bottom edge up first, followed by the left and right sides. Hold the wrapper and pinch the edges together with your fingers so the filling does not leak out. (This may take some practice!)

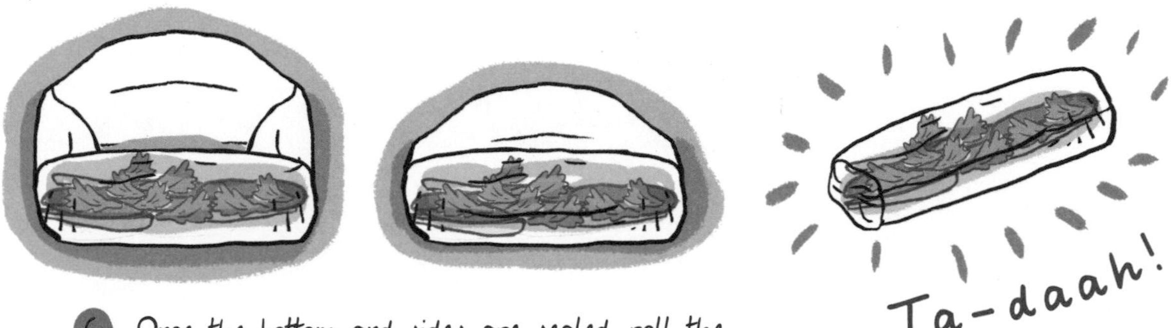
Ta-daah!

6. Once the bottom and sides are sealed, roll the wrapper up over the filling to create a cylinder. Press the edge down lightly to seal it.

There'll always be someone who makes a mess but don't let them get discouraged ...

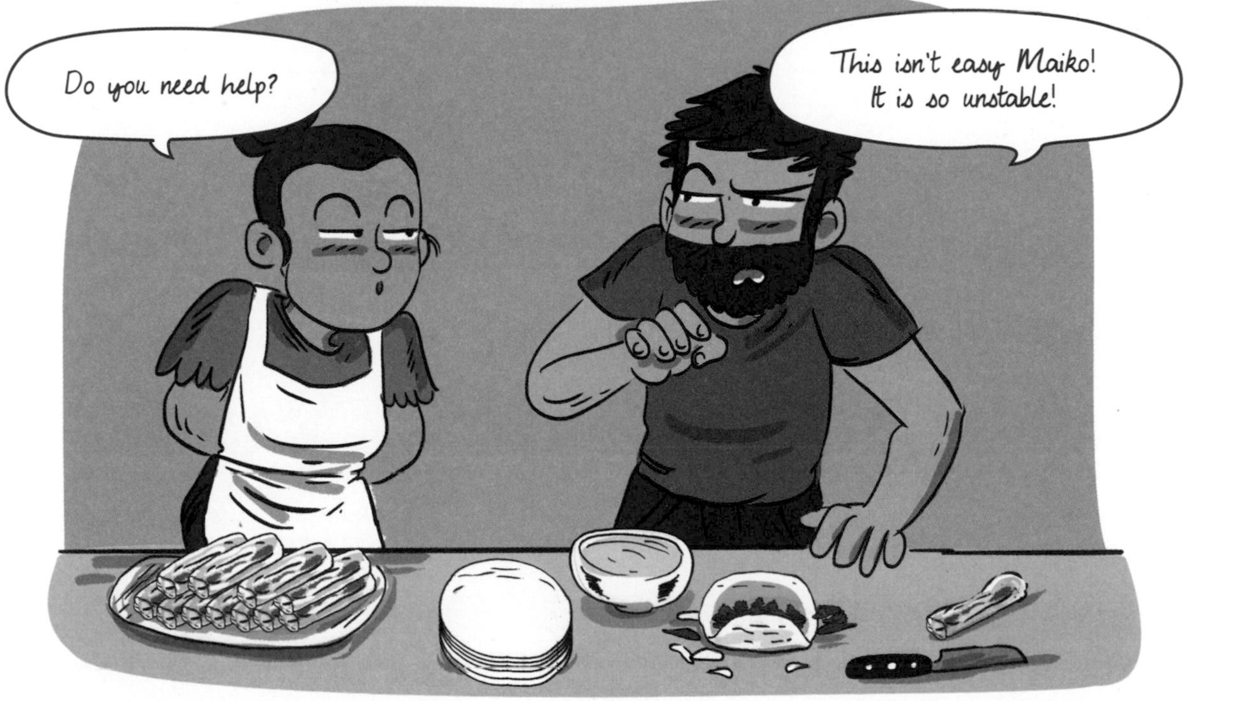
Do you need help?
This isn't easy Maiko! It is so unstable!

Japanese Shrimp & Egg Custard Chawan Mushi

This is a classic Japanese dish served in many Japanese restaurants, and it is very simple to make at home. It is normally cooked and served in small individual teacups (hence the Japanese name, chawan mushi, which means "teacup custard"). You can use small soup bowls or mugs instead. The delicate taste and soft texture of this dish is truly heavenly!

Makes 4 bowls
Time: 30 minutes

Few drops of sake or sherry
8 small fresh prawns, shelled and deveined
4 eggs
4 thin stalks of young asparagus, tough stems removed
2 or 3 shiitake mushrooms, stems removed, tops thinly sliced (if using dried mushrooms, soak them in warm water for 20 minutes drain them before slicing)
2 cups (500 ml) water
2 tablespoons dashi stock (made with 2 teaspoons dashi powder + 4 teaspoons hot water)
2 tablespoons mirin or cooking sherry
2 tablespoons soy sauce

1. Pour a few drops of sake over the prawns to remove any fishy smell.

2. After 10 minutes, peel the prawns and discard the shells, heads and tails.

3. Whisk the eggs in a bowl and strain the mixture through a fine sieve to obtain a softer texture.

4. Slice the asparagus and shiitake mushrooms.

5. Blanch the mushrooms, asparagus and prawns in a saucepan with a little boiling water for 3-4 minutes until barely cooked. Remove and drain.

6. Divide the pieces of cooked asparagus, prawn and mushrooms into 4 bowls.

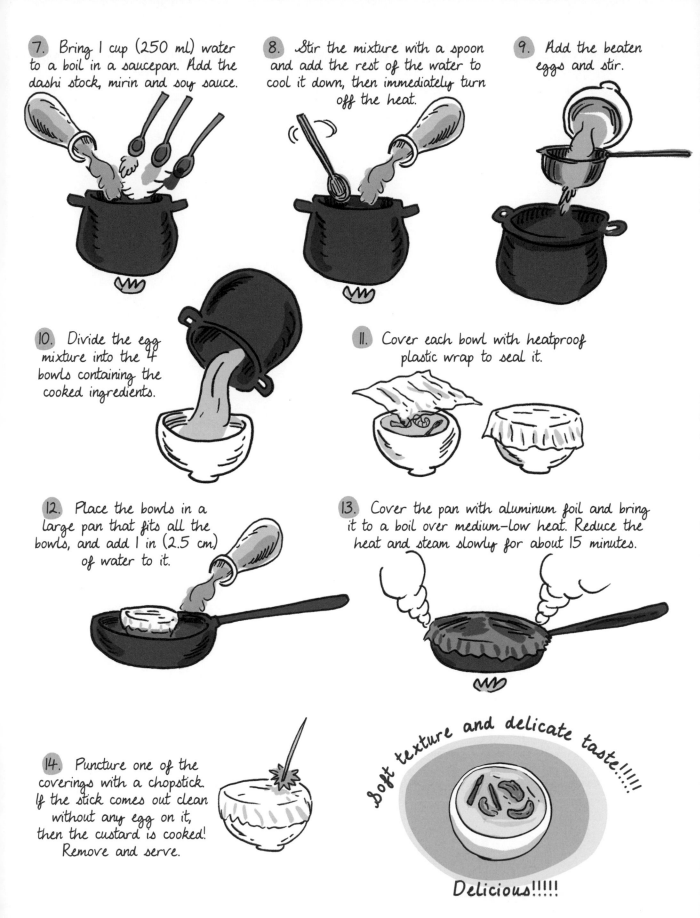

7. Bring 1 cup (250 ml) water to a boil in a saucepan. Add the dashi stock, mirin and soy sauce.

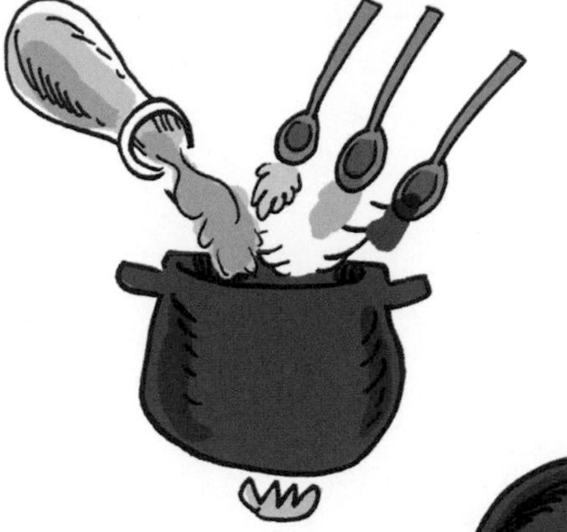

8. Stir the mixture with a spoon and add the rest of the water to cool it down, then immediately turn off the heat.

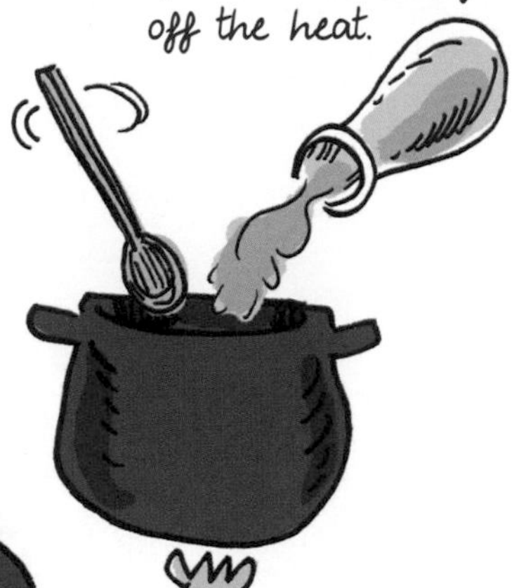

9. Add the beaten eggs and stir.

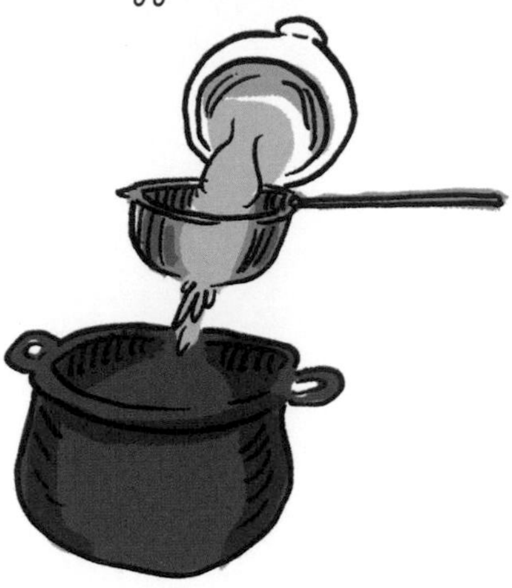

10. Divide the egg mixture into the 4 bowls containing the cooked ingredients.

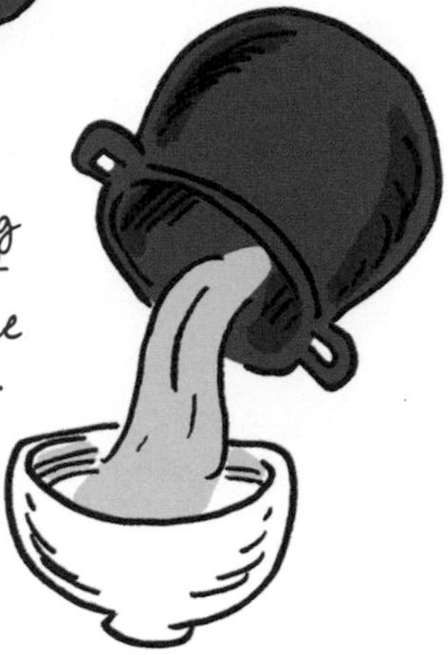

11. Cover each bowl with heatproof plastic wrap to seal it.

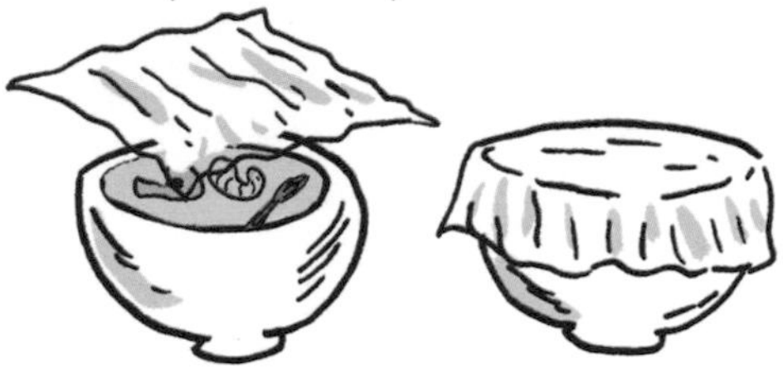

12. Place the bowls in a large pan that fits all the bowls, and add 1 in (2.5 cm) of water to it.

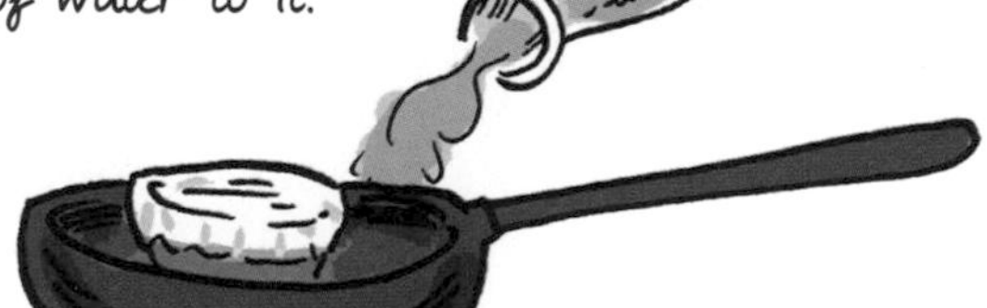

13. Cover the pan with aluminum foil and bring it to a boil over medium-low heat. Reduce the heat and steam slowly for about 15 minutes.

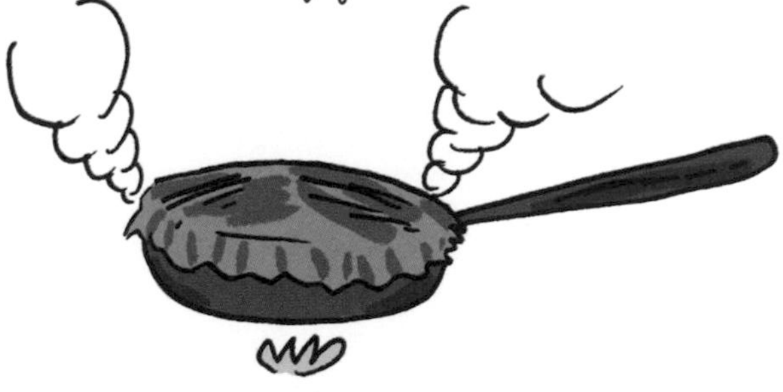

14. Puncture one of the coverings with a chopstick. If the stick comes out clean without any egg on it, then the custard is cooked! Remove and serve.

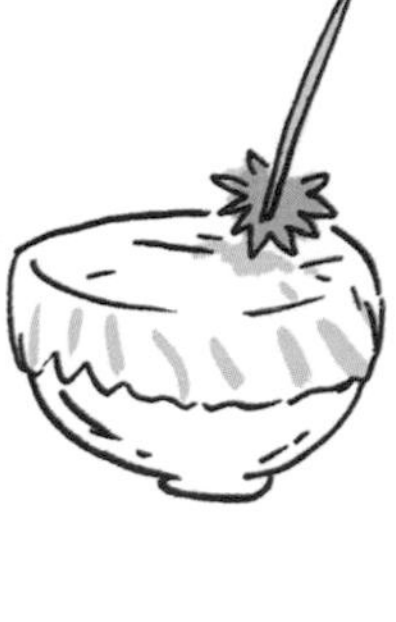

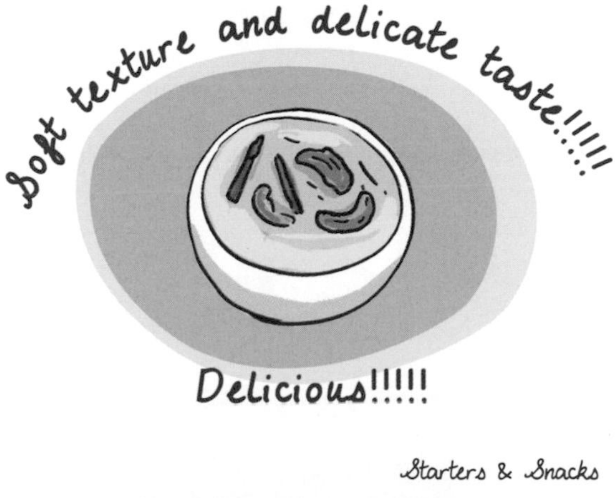
Soft texture and delicate taste!!!!!
Delicious!!!!!

Miso Marinated Mozzarella

This is a simple recipe that can be served in different ways! Mozzarella has a mellow flavor and when miso, mirin and soy sauce are added, it creates something special!!! You can eat it on its own as an appetizer or serve them in a salad or meat dishes.

Makes 4 servings
Time: 10 minutes

1 lb (450 g) fresh mozzarella (big or small balls)
2 tablespoons soy sauce
2 tablespoons mirin or cooking sherry
2 tablespoons miso paste

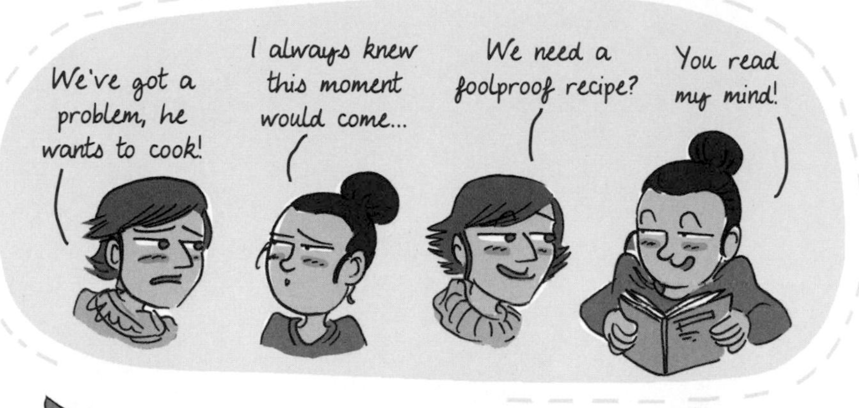
We've got a problem, he wants to cook!
I always knew this moment would come...
We need a foolproof recipe?
You read my mind!

1. Drain the water off the mozzarella (place them on an inclined cutting board in the sink). If the mozzarella is big, cut into 2-3 pieces.

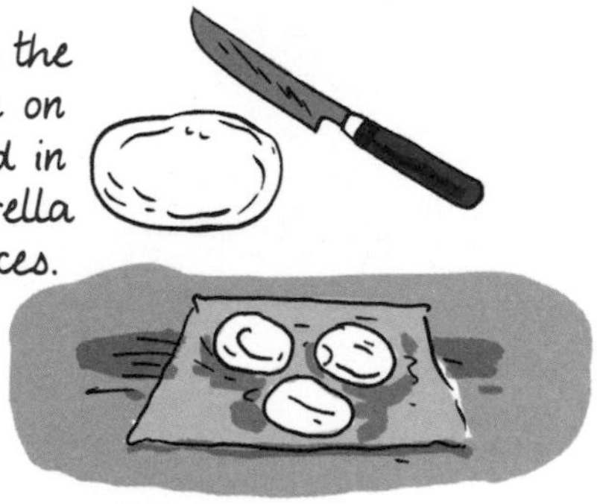

2. Place the mozzarella in a bowl and add the soy sauce, mirin or sherry, and miso.

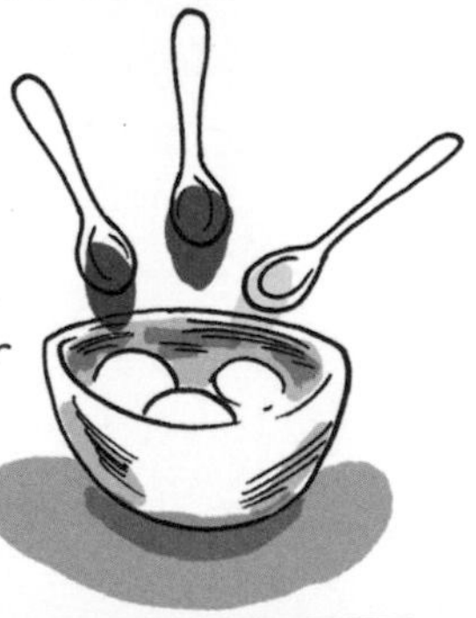

3. Here's where it gets tricky. Gently mix the ingredients and coat the mozzarella, try not to break it up as you do this!

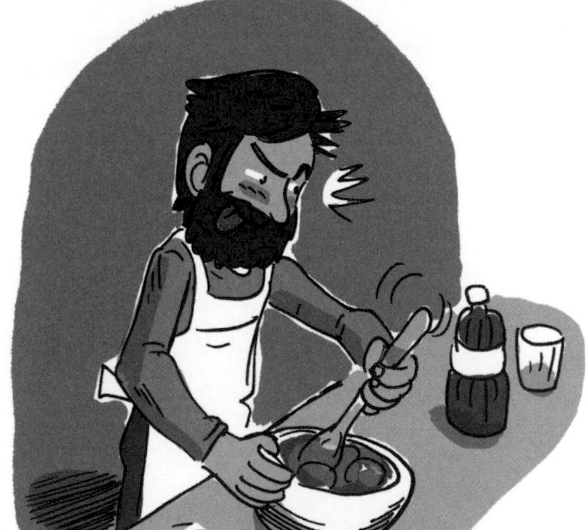

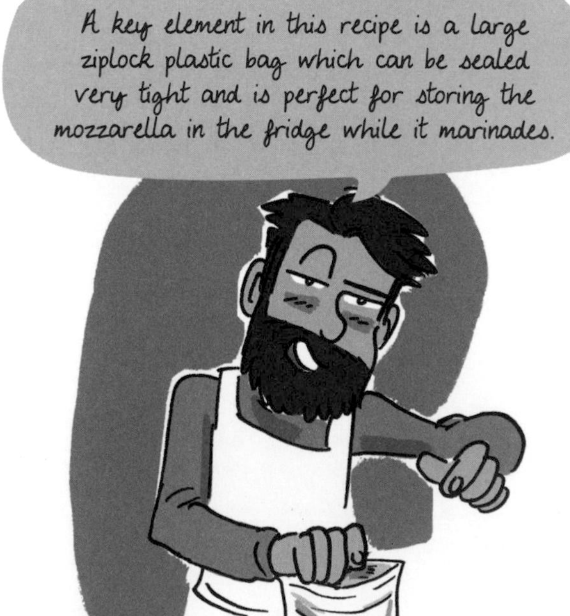
A key element in this recipe is a large ziplock plastic bag which can be sealed very tight and is perfect for storing the mozzarella in the fridge while it marinades.

4. Transfer everything to a large ziplock bag.

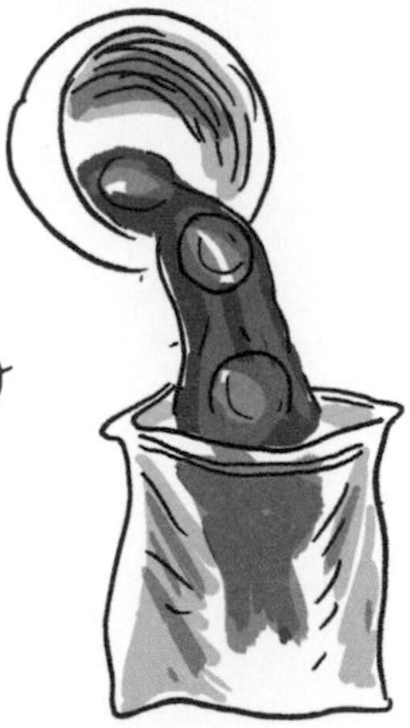

5. Seal the bag tightly making sure no air is trapped inside.

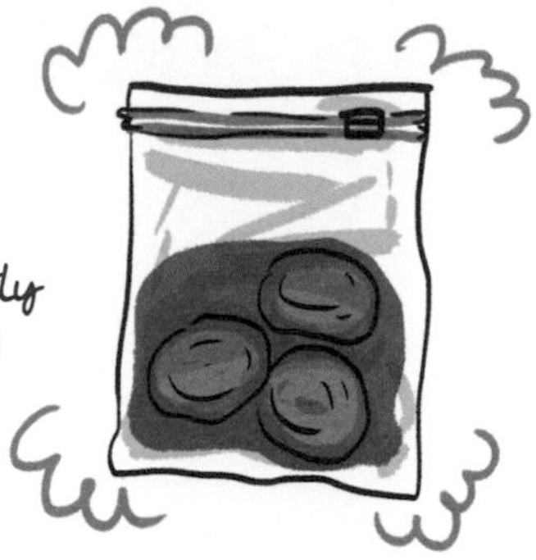

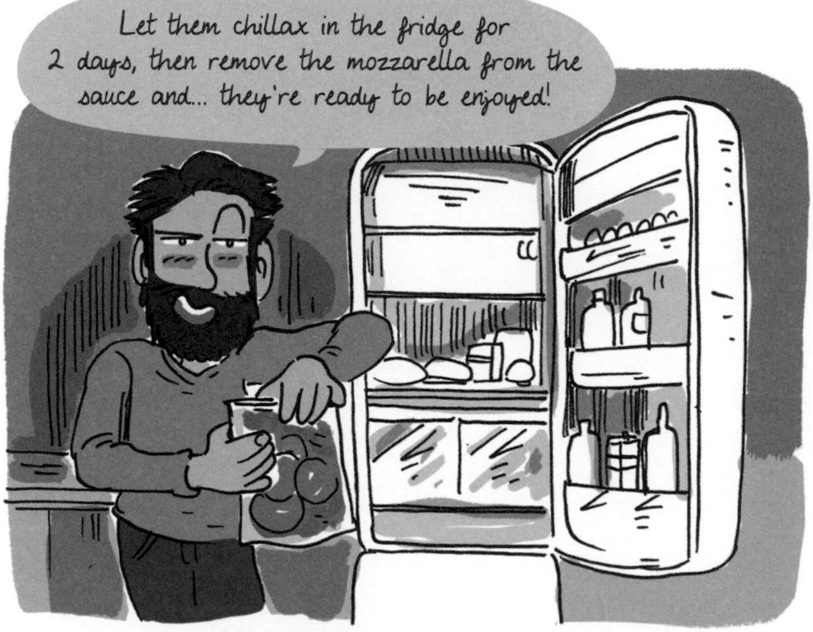
Let them chillax in the fridge for 2 days, then remove the mozzarella from the sauce and... they're ready to be enjoyed!

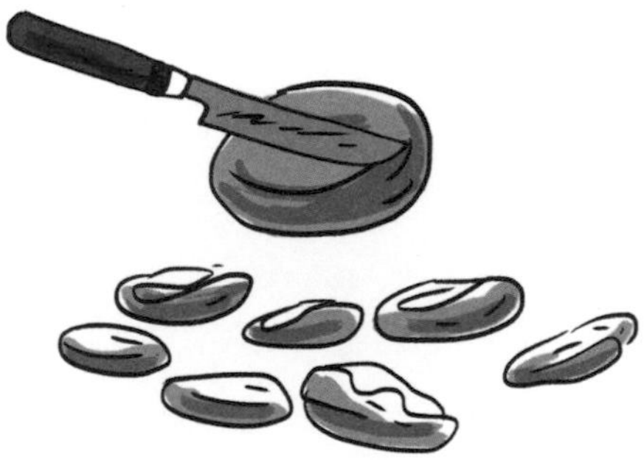

6. When ready to serve, slice the mozzarella and serve it in a salad or as a sidedish with your favorite fish or meat dishes.

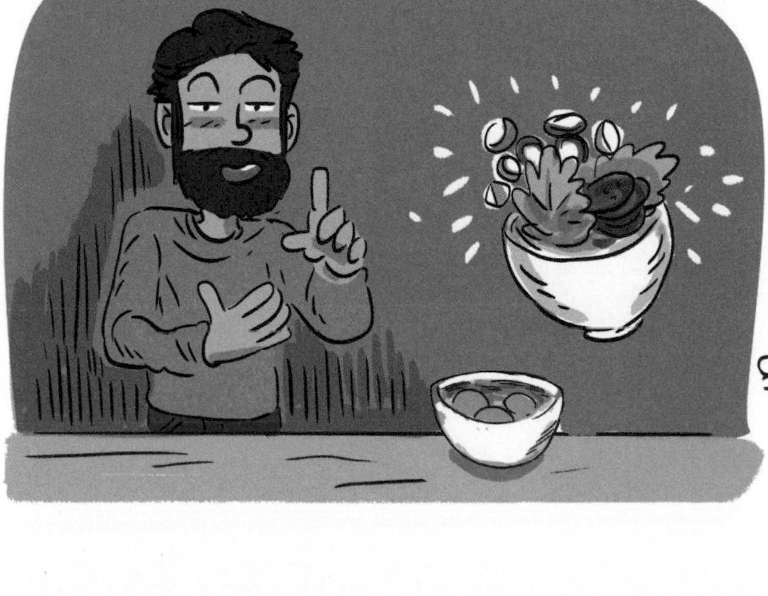

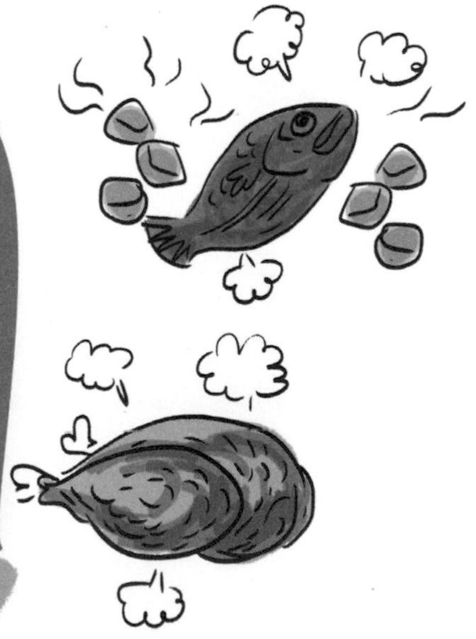

Chapter 2

SOUPS & SALADS

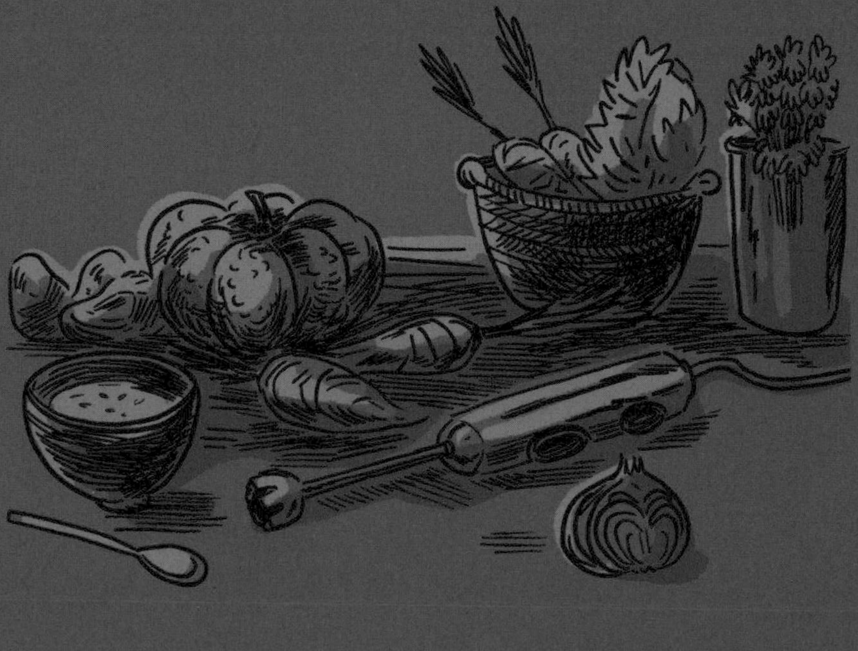

We have selected a few healthy soup and salad recipes that you can serve on their own or combined with other Japanese dishes in various ways. Soups and salads are a great way to complete a dinner menu, and some are ideal to take with you in a lunchbox. Also they are very easy to prepare, so you don't need to be an experienced cook to enjoy these!

Miso Soup with Pork & Vegetables

On a cold day, what can be better than a nice warm soup? This version of miso soup is enriched with vegetables and pork. This is a traditional recipe, perfect for cold and bleak winter days. If you cook it very slowly for a longer time, it tastes even better!!!!!!!!!!..........

Serves 4
Time: 1h 15 minutes

1 lb (450 g) boneless pork loin
2 carrots, peeled
1 turnip, peeled
1 scallion (spring onion, white part only)
1 parsnip, peeled
1 stalk celery
5 cups (1.25 l) water
2 heaping tablespoons miso paste
1 stock cube
1 teaspoon salt
1 teaspoon freshly grated ginger

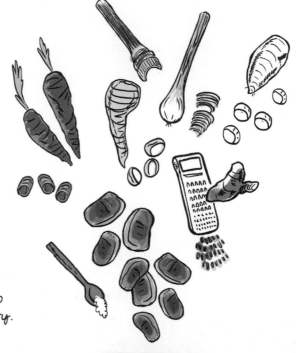

1. Cut the pork into bite-sized pieces. Also the carrots, turnip, scallion, parsnip and celery.

2. Put all the ingredients into a pot with a bit of oil and stir-fry them for 3 minutes over medium-high heat.

3. Pour in the water and add the miso, stock cube, salt and grated ginger.

4. Simmer over low heat for about 1 hour.

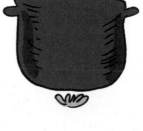

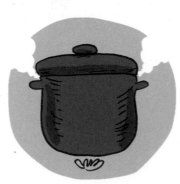

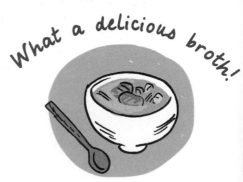

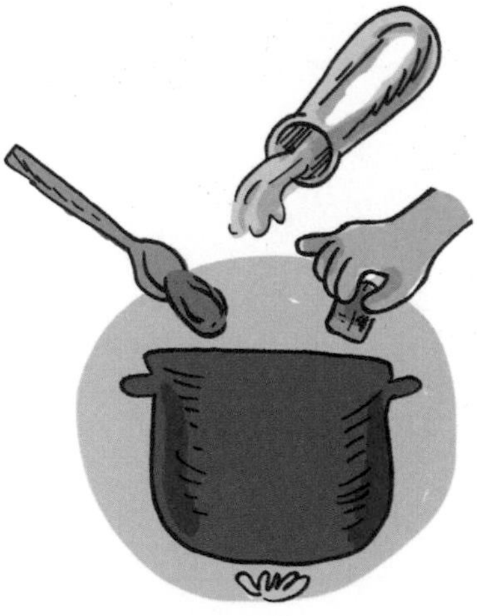

What a delicious broth!

5. You'll have a delicious Japanese-style soup, capable of satisfying demanding appetites and defeating low temperatures.

Broccoli Miso Soup

Broccoli is very healthy and can be cooked in many different ways. When enriched with miso in a soup, it becomes a super powerful and healthy dish!

Serves 2
Time: 30 minutes

2 cloves garlic, peeled
2 scallions (spring onions)
1 tablespoon oil
1 small head broccoli
2 cups (500 ml) water
1 tablespoon miso paste
Pumpkins seeds, to garnish

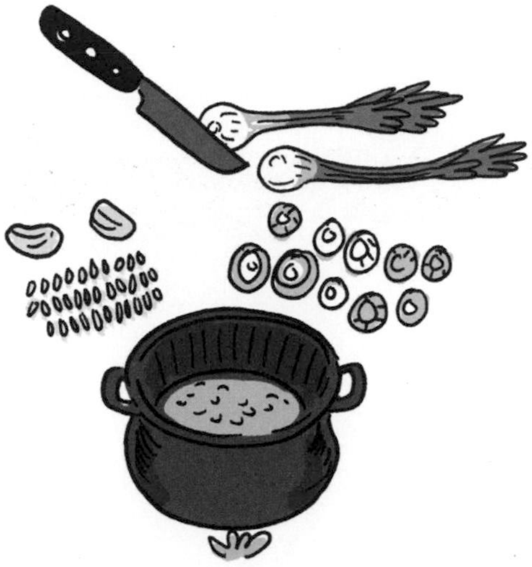

1. Slice the garlic cloves and scallions, then stir-fry them in a large pot with a little bit of oil.

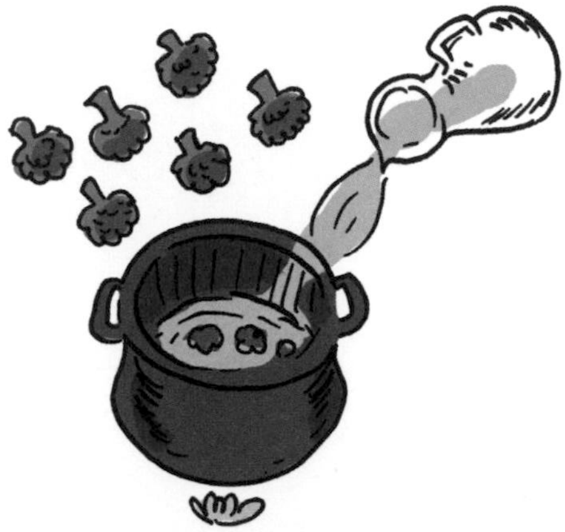

2. Cut the broccoli into bite-sized pieces and add them to the pot with the water. Let them simmer for 20 minutes over low heat.

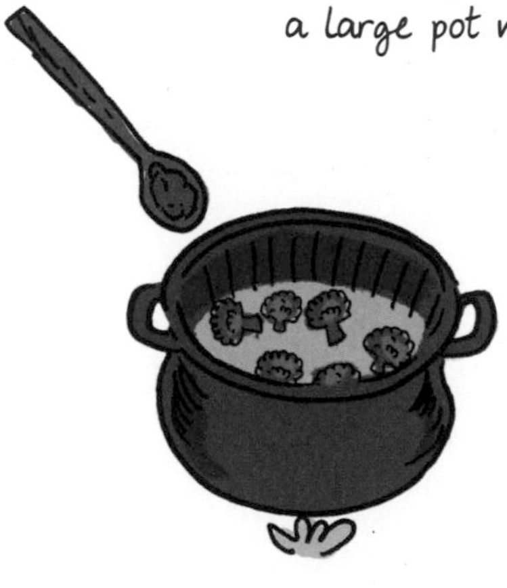

3. Now add the miso...

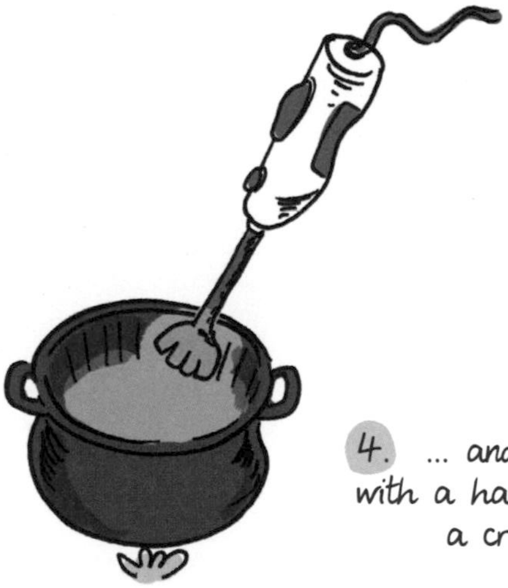

4. ... and whisk the mixture with a hand blender to obtain a creamy texture.

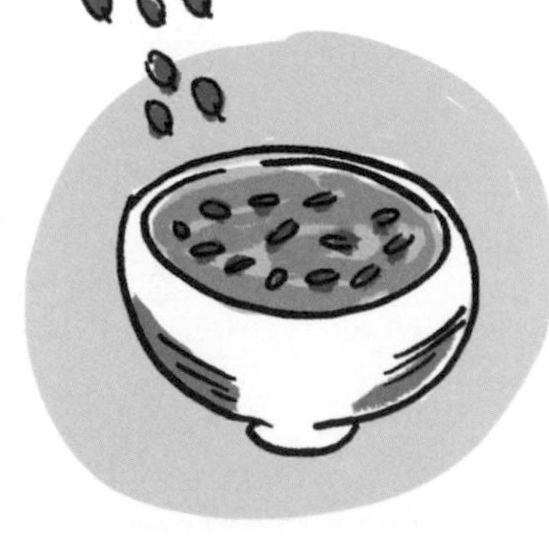

5. To serve, top with a few pumpkin seeds (it also looks great with a dash of fresh cream).

Clear Clam Soup Osuimono

Osuimono is a very simple soup that is perfect to accompany your seafood dishes—a clear and light broth with a characteristic clam aroma. Just be sure to buy good fresh clams and don't overcook them! You can serve this as a starter and it goes particularly well with sushi.

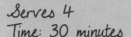

Serves 4
Time: 30 minutes

2¼ lbs (1 kg) fresh clams in their shells
2 tablespoons salt
4 cups (1 l) water
2 tablespoons dashi stock powder
1 bunch chives

1. Place the clams in a large bowl and cover them with water. Add 2 tablespoons of salt.

2. Let the bowl sit in the refrigerator for at least two hours.

3. Remove the bowl from the refrigerator, drain the clams and wash them well with water.

4. Place the clams in a pot and add about 4 cups (1 liter) of water.

5. Add 2 tablespoons of dashi stock powder, cover and bring to a boil over medium heat.

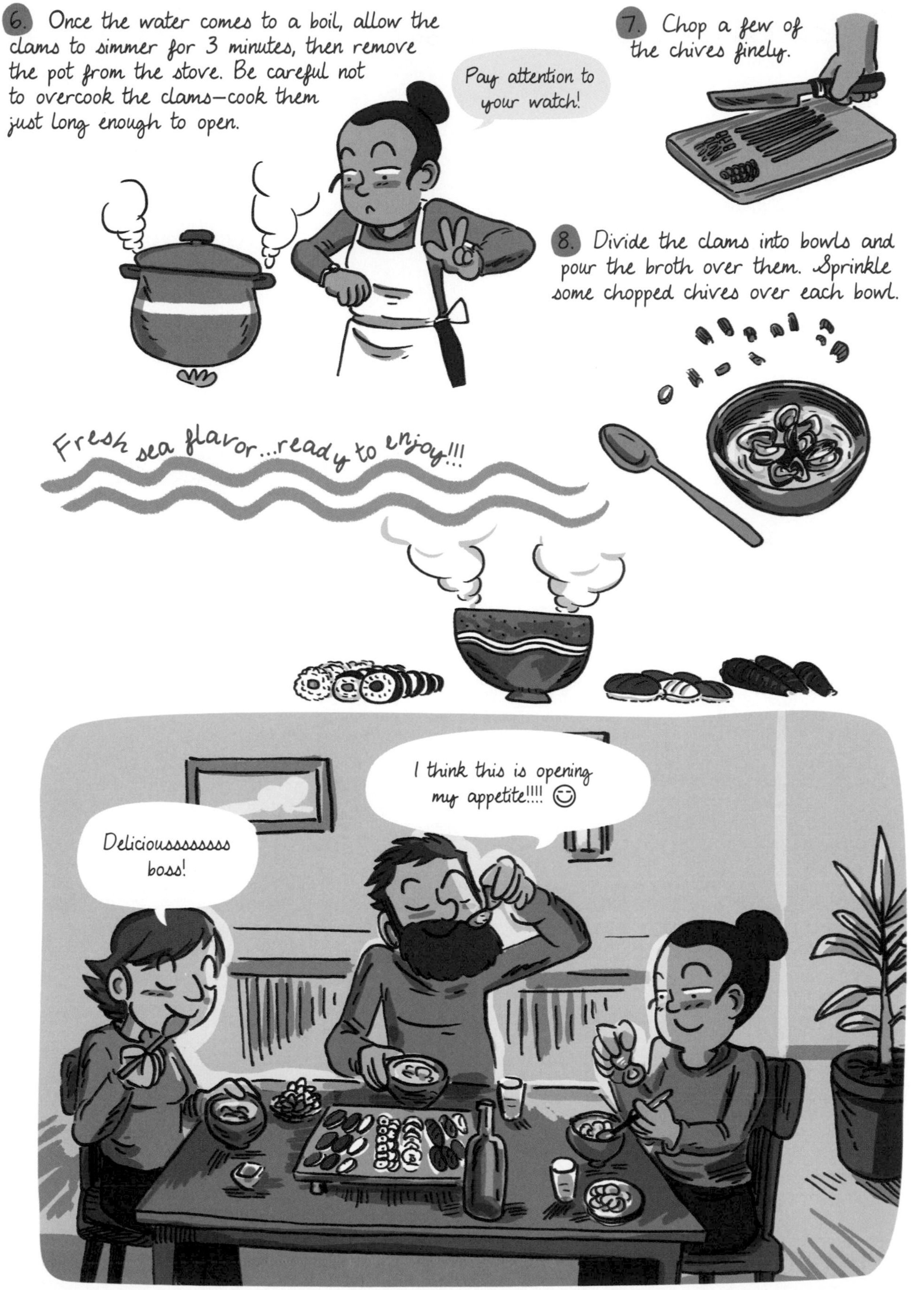
6. Once the water comes to a boil, allow the clams to simmer for 3 minutes, then remove the pot from the stove. Be careful not to overcook the clams—cook them just long enough to open.
Pay attention to your watch!
7. Chop a few of the chives finely.
8. Divide the clams into bowls and pour the broth over them. Sprinkle some chopped chives over each bowl.
Fresh sea flavor...ready to enjoy!!!
Deliciousssssss boss!
I think this is opening my appetite!!!! ☺

Radish Pickles Asazuke

Pickles are a basic condiment in Japanese cooking, served with most meals. In fact, there are hundreds of varieties. They can be prepared with radishes, cucumbers, ginger, ume (sour plums) or eggplant preserved in a vinegar mixture. They have a very fresh flavor, slightly salty and sour.

Serves 4
Time: 10 minutes

1 bunch radishes
1 tablespoon soy sauce
1 tablespoon sugar
1 tablespoon umeboshi (sour plum) vinegar
1 teaspoon sesame oil
1 tablespoon dashi stock powder

**Umeboshi vinegar is a vinegar made with umeboshi, that is a kind of salted plums. It can be substituted with apple cider vinegar.

1. Trim the tops off the radishes and wash them.

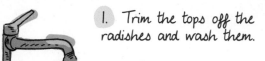

2. Cut them into even slices.

3. Put the sliced radishes into a large ziplock bag.

4. Add the other ingredients

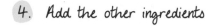

1 tablespoon soy sauce
1 tablespoon sugar
1 tablespoon umeboshi vinegar or apple cider vinegar
1 tablespoon dashi stock powder
1 teaspoon sesame oil

5. Zip close the bag and shake it up!

Shake shake shake.
Shake shake shake.

6. Let it cool in the fridge for at least an hour and it's ready to eat!!!

Hearty Vegetable Soup

Vegetable soup is an easy and nutritious dish and adds perfect balance to your diet. You can use whatever vegetables you have on hand. Carrots and fresh artichokes work great! You can always add your own special touches, take a look!

Serves 4
Time: 45 minutes

- 3 carrots
- 4 fresh artichoke hearts
- 1 onion, peeled
- Beef or chicken drippings (the juice remaining after cooking up a roast) or 1 stock cube
- 4 cups (1 l) water
- 1 teaspoon salt
- 2 tablespoons dashi stock powder

We are going to show you a magic trick. When you prepare a roast (roast beef or chicken for example), reserve the leftover bits and the juices in the pan. This will become the secret ingredient in your next soup!

1. Slice the carrots, artichoke hearts and the onion. Put them in a pot with the drippings.

2. Add the water, salt and dashi stock powder.

3. Bring to a boil over high heat then lower the heat and simmer for about 45 minutes.

The secret of a great soup is in the drippings and leftovers you add to the pot!

After a long day at work ... a veggie soup to fight the cold. Take that John Snow!

Mashed Potato Salad

This is a very popular recipe in Japanese homes. It is a classic dish that kids take in their bento boxes to school and also a great option to take with you to the office. It is similar to a Russian or German potato salad, because the main ingredients are potatoes and mayonnaisse, but a Japanese potato salad also has a spicy touch!

Serves 2
Time: 30 minutes

3 large potatoes (1 lb/450 g)
2 tablespoons butter
1 Japanese or baby cucumber, peeled
4 slices (7 oz /200 g) ham
3 tablespoons mayonnaise
1 teaspoon mustard seeds
Ground black pepper and salt, to taste

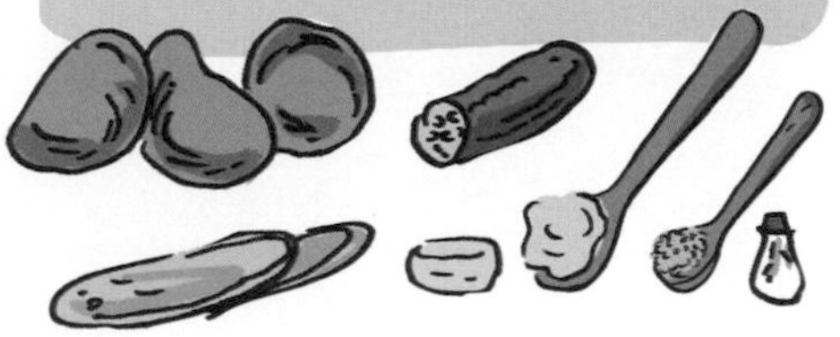

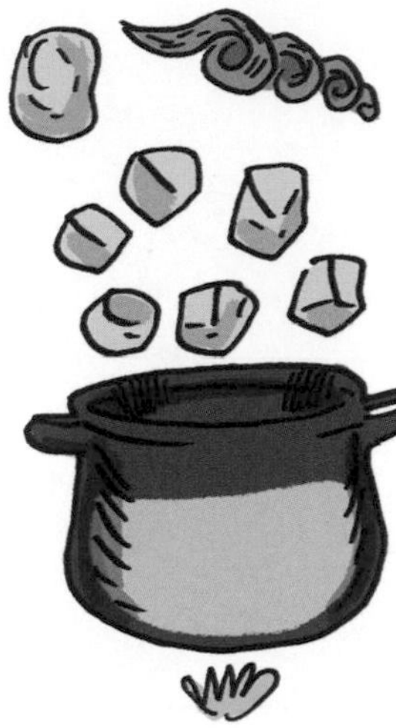

1. Peel the potatoes, put them in a pot with water and boil for 20 minutes or until done.

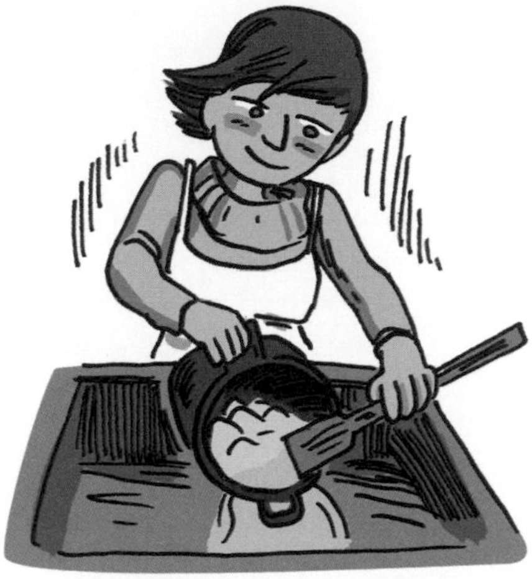

2. When the potatoes are cooked, drain them well to remove all the water.

3. Now add the butter.

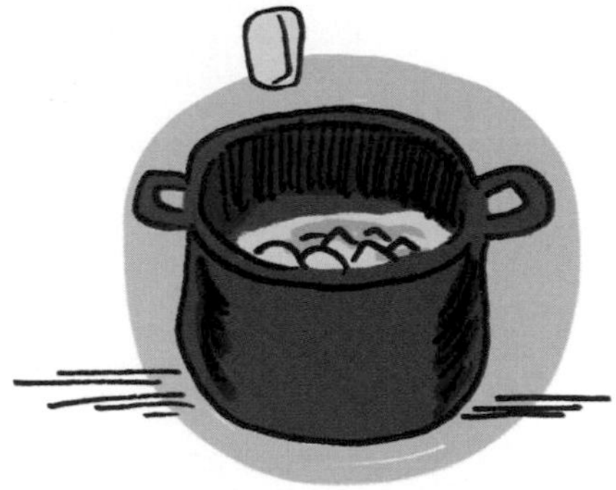

4. Using a wooden spoon or spatula, mash the potatoes and mix well to melt the butter.

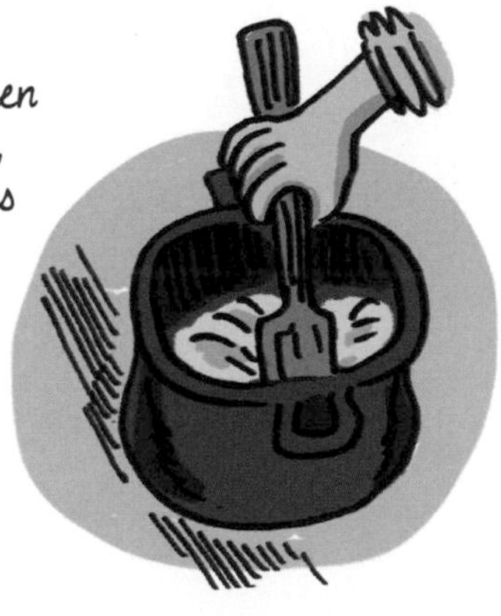

5. Peel and cut the cucumber into thin slices. Sprinkle some salt over the slices to dehydrate them.

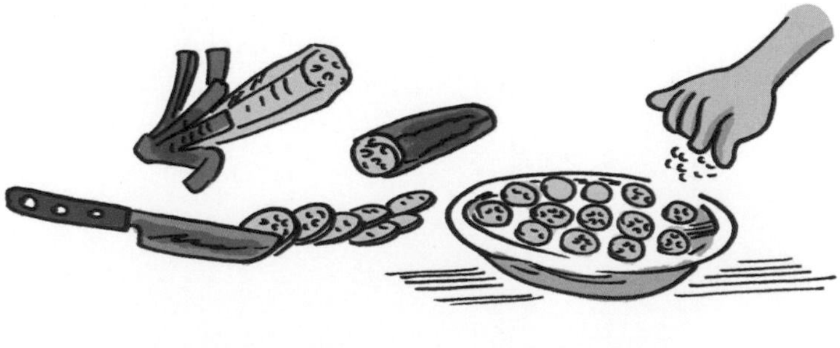

6. Now cut the ham into thin strips.

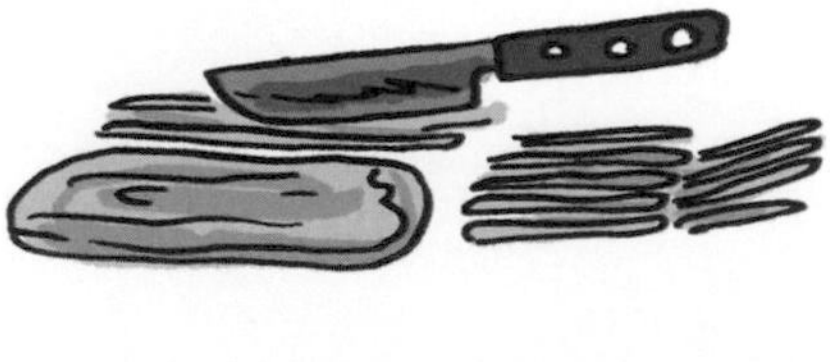

7. Drain off the water from the cucumber slices.

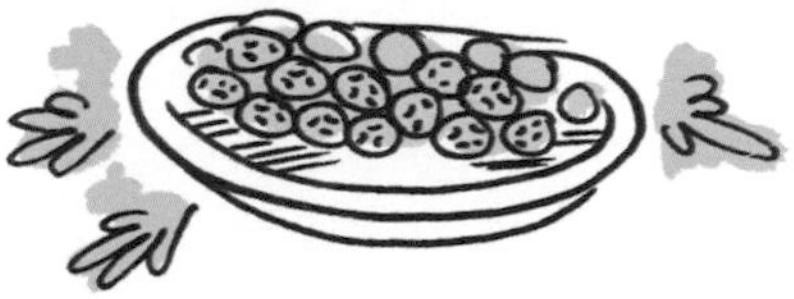

8. Once the potatoes have cooled, add the cucumber slices, strips of ham, mayonnaise, mustard seeds and black pepper.

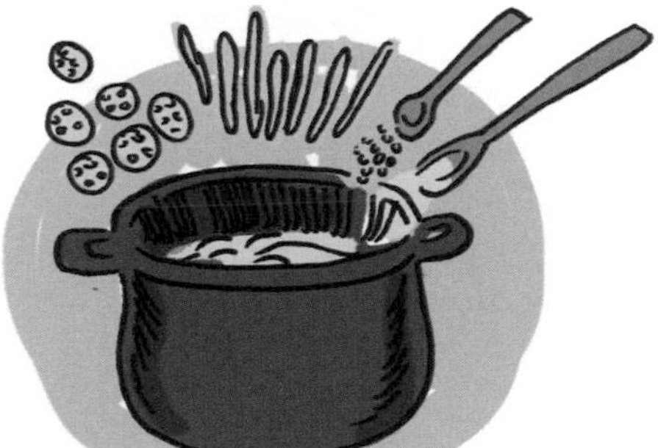

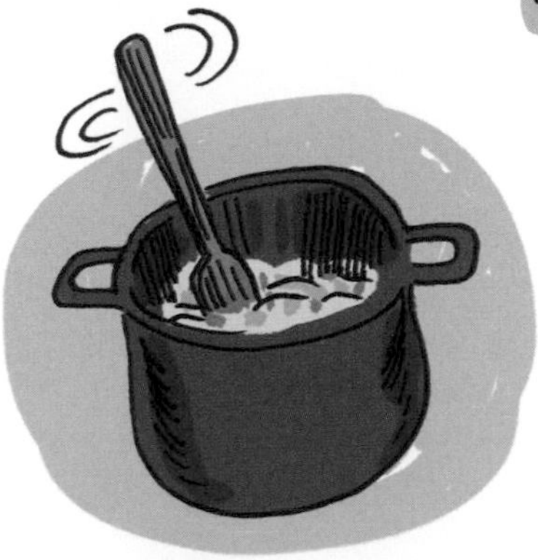

9. Mix all the ingredients well with a wooden spoon and add a bit of salt, tasting to make sure you have the right amount.

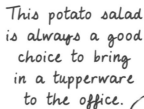

Extra Bonus:
Add more ingredients if you want! Peas, sliced cheese, hard boiled egg, sweet corn ...

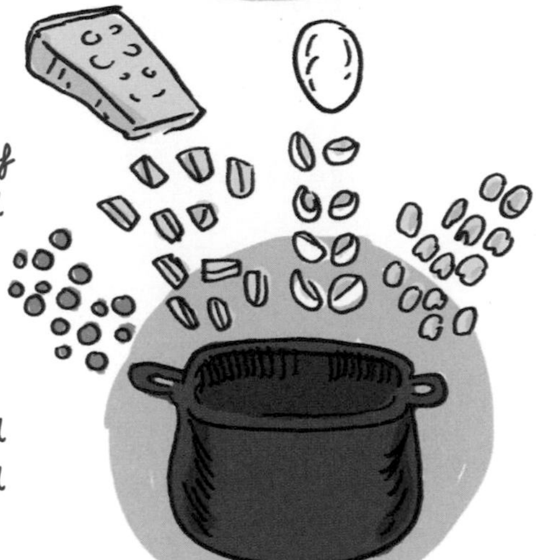

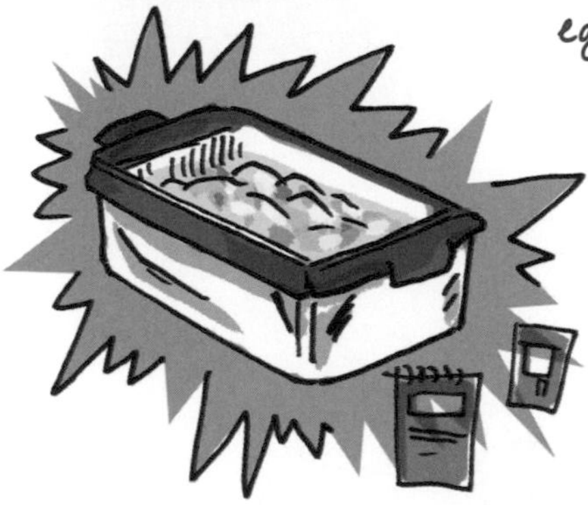

This potato salad is always a good choice to bring in a tupperware to the office.

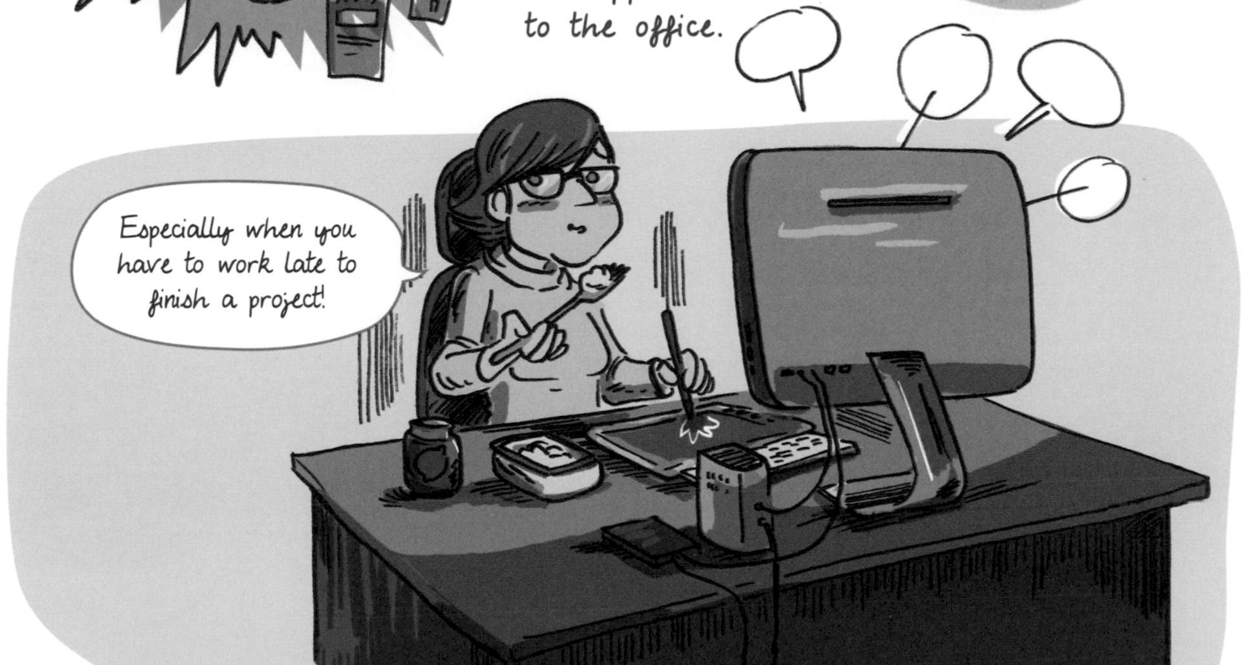
Especially when you have to work late to finish a project!

Sunomono Summer Salad

Sunomono is a classic Japanese salad which literally means "something with vinegar". Most kinds of sunomono contain seaweed and cucumber with a vinegar dressing. Here we use wakame seaweed with lemon juice. It's very simple to prepare and is particularly refreshing on a hot summer day. This recipe will surprise you for sure!

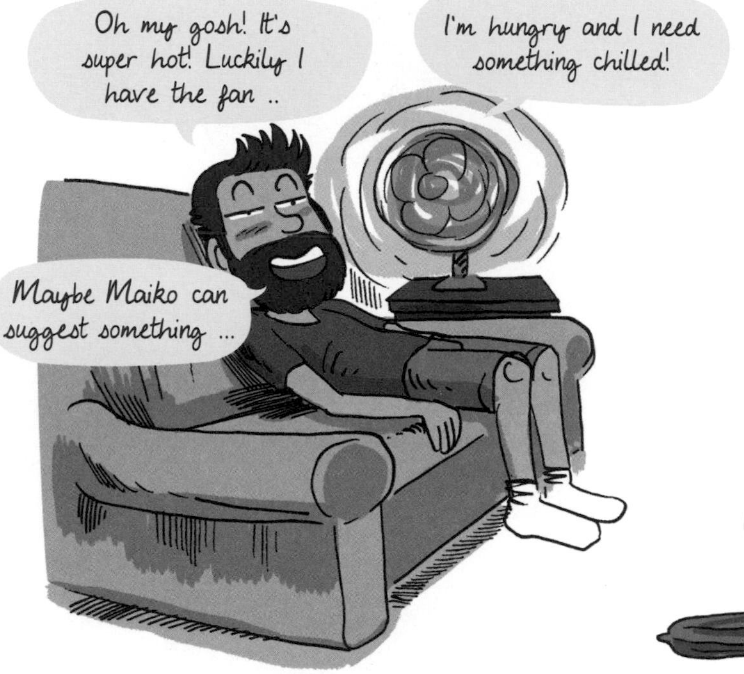

Oh my gosh! It's super hot! Luckily I have the fan ..
I'm hungry and I need something chilled!
Maybe Maiko can suggest something ...

Serves 2
Time: 20 minutes

2 Japanese cucumbers or baby cucumbers
2 tablespoons dried wakame seaweed
3 radishes
3 teaspoons lemon juice
1 teaspoon sesame oil
1 teaspoon soy sauce
1 teaspoon brown sugar
1 teaspoon toasted sesame seeds*
Salt, to taste

*Dry roast sesame seeds in a skillet for a few minutes over medium heat until they are lightly browned, stirring them with a wooden spatula. Be careful not to burn them!

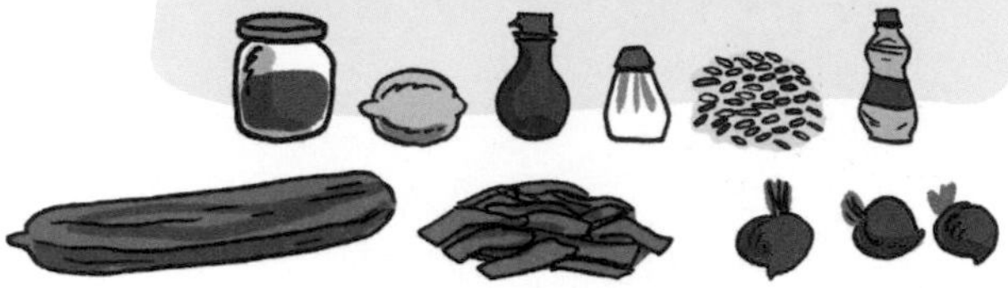

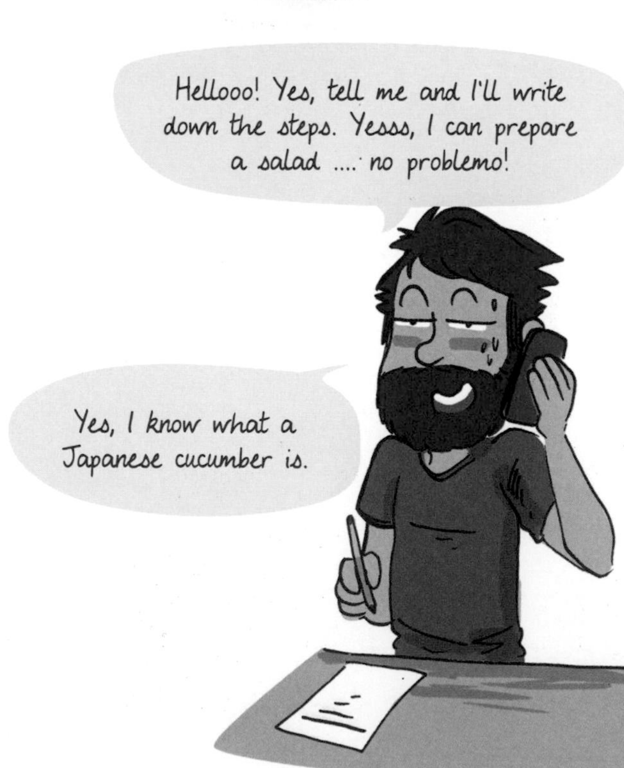

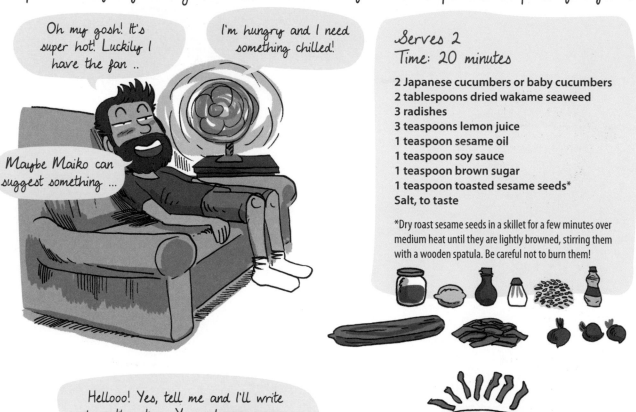

Hellooo! Yes, tell me and I'll write down the steps. Yesss, I can prepare a salad .... no problemo!
Yes, I know what a Japanese cucumber is.

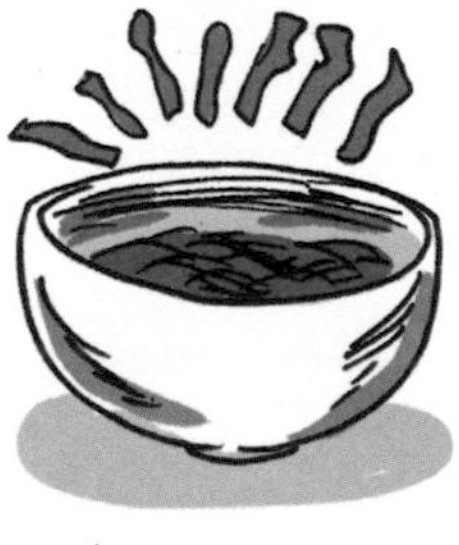

1. Put the wakame seaweed in a bowl of room temperature water to reconstitute it.

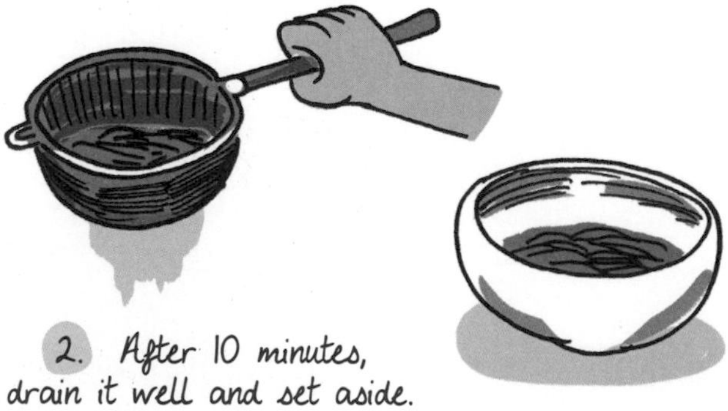

2. After 10 minutes, drain it well and set aside.

3. Cut the cucumbers and radishes into thin slices.

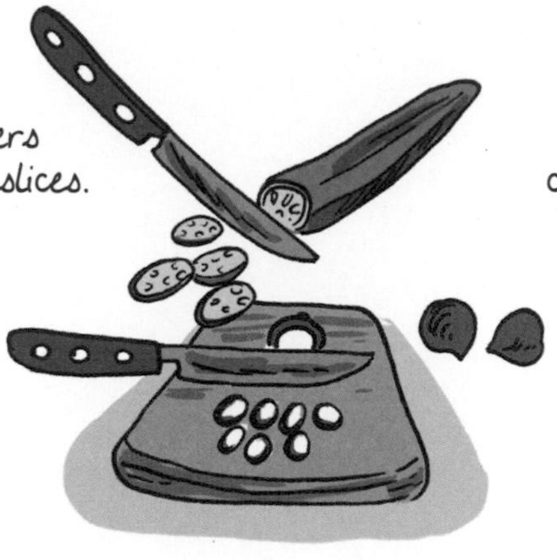

4. Put the seaweed, cucumber and radish into a serving bowl.

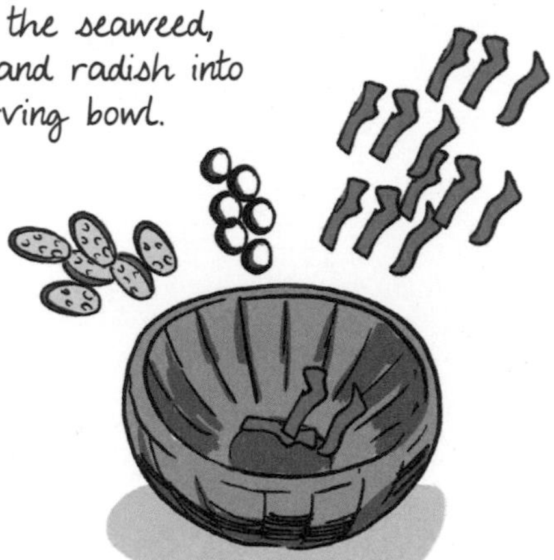

5. In another small bowl, prepare the dressing for the salad by adding the lemon juice, sesame oil, soy sauce, sesame seeds, brown sugar and salt.

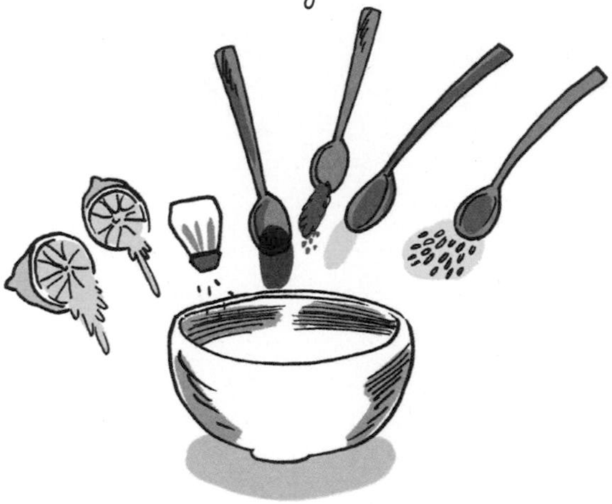

6. Stir the mixture well until the sugar has dissolved and the consistency is smooth.

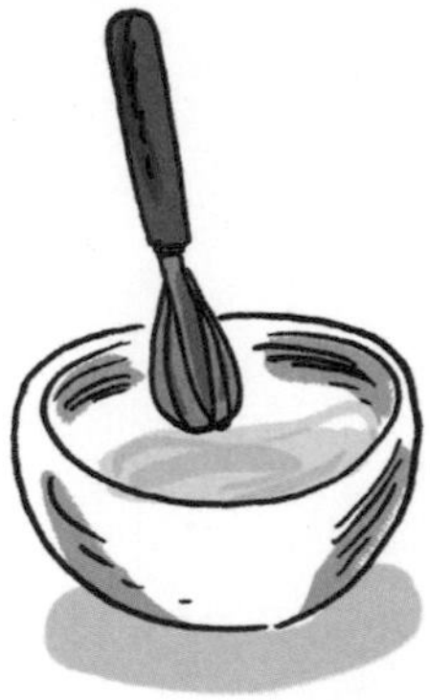

7. Add the dressing to the salad and mix well.

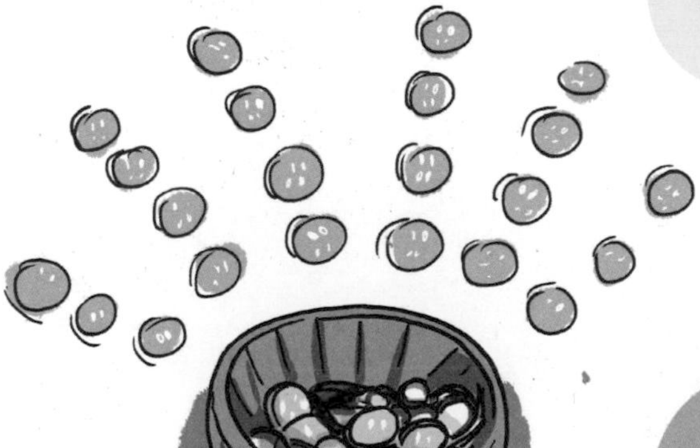

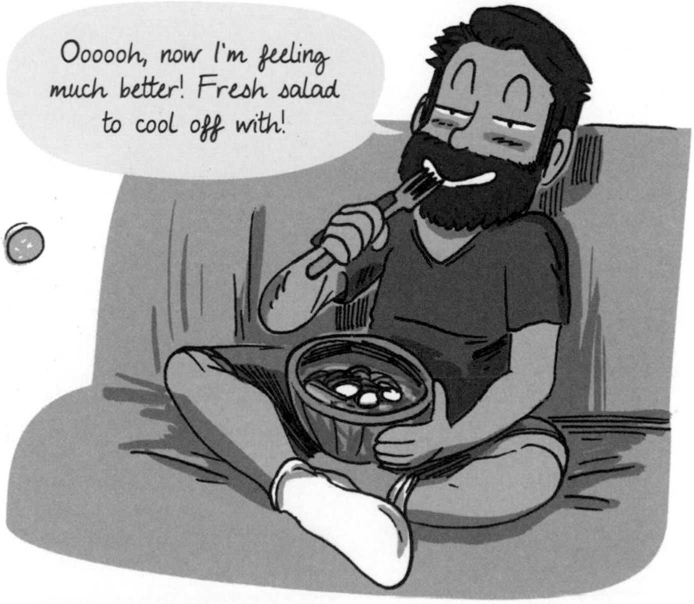
Oooooh, now I'm feeling much better! Fresh salad to cool off with!

Chapter 3

SUSHI

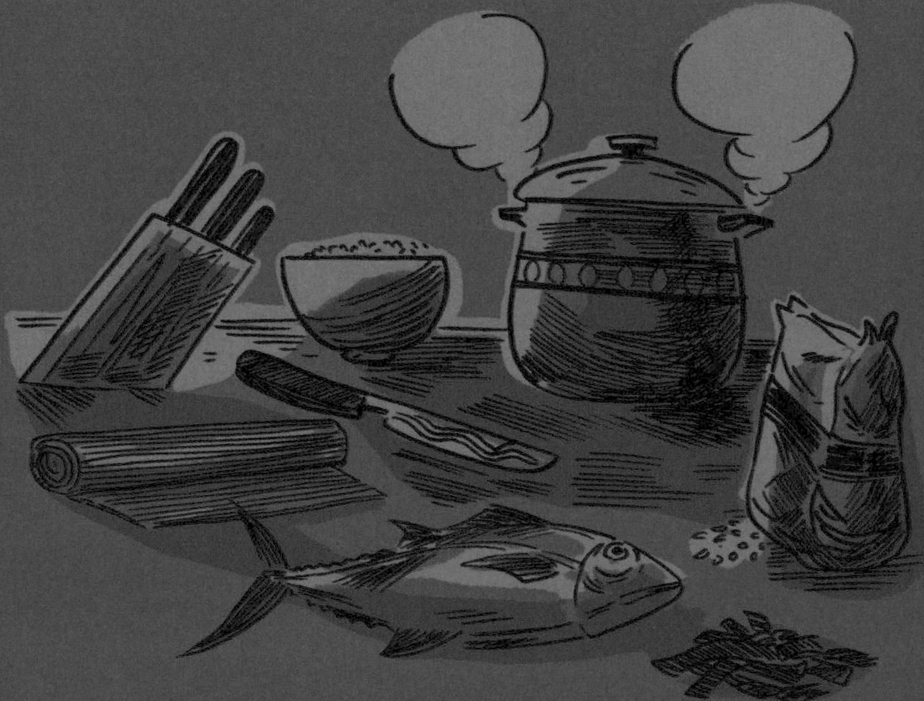

Everyone else has already talked about sushi. Now it's our turn! Sushi comes in many different shapes and sizes. We want to show you some common sushi varieties and also some very different ways of preparing sushi. You choose your favorite. Just be creative and buy top quality ingredients to make your own personal versions of these recipes. Sushi is the quintessential Japanese dish. It looks easy but it requires care and a little practice. So take your time, be patient and practice a few times to get it right!

Professor Maiko's Sushi Lecture

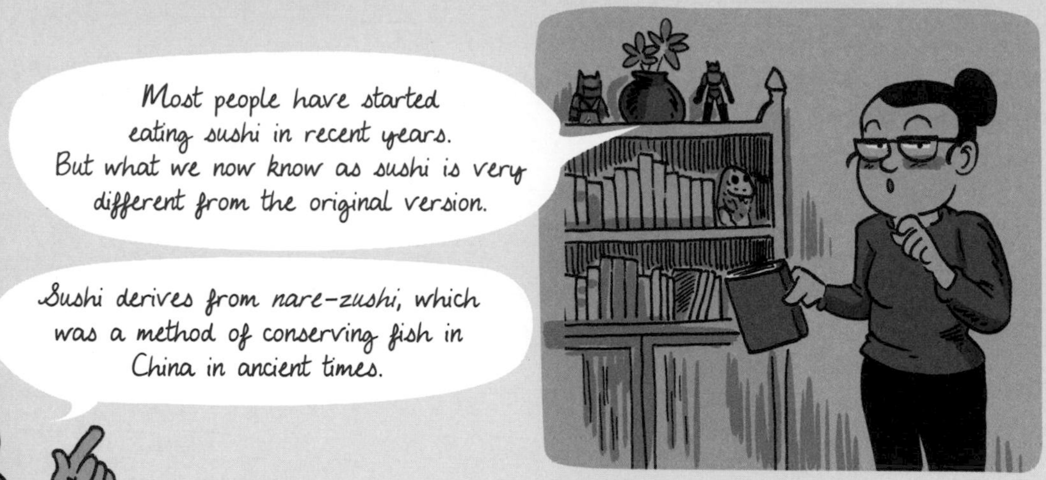
Most people have started eating sushi in recent years. But what we now know as sushi is very different from the original version.

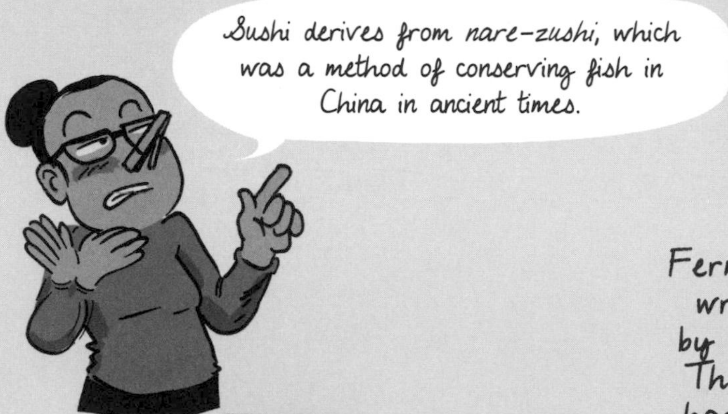
Sushi derives from *nare-zushi*, which was a method of conserving fish in China in ancient times.

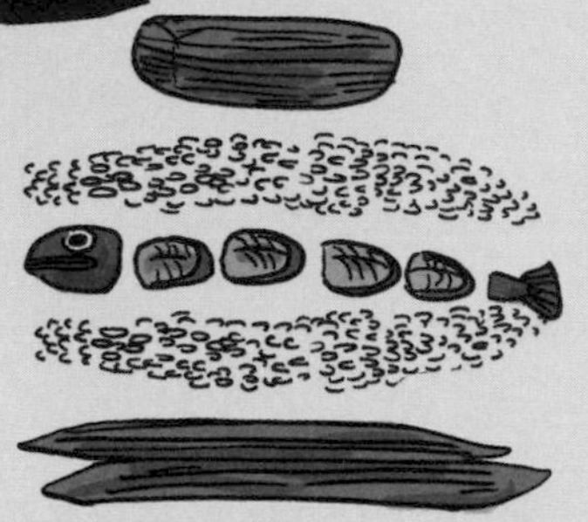
RICE VINEGAR

Fermented fish was cooked, salted and wrapped in bamboo leaves protected by rice, to allow it to be transported. The rice was discarded and the fish had a strong aroma and salty taste. In the 17th century, rice vinegar was added to the cooked rice, speeding up the process of curing the fish. At the beginning of the 19th century, a man named Yonei Hamaya had the idea of serving raw fish from Tokyo Bay over cooked rice seasoned with rice vinegar. This is how nigiri sushi started!

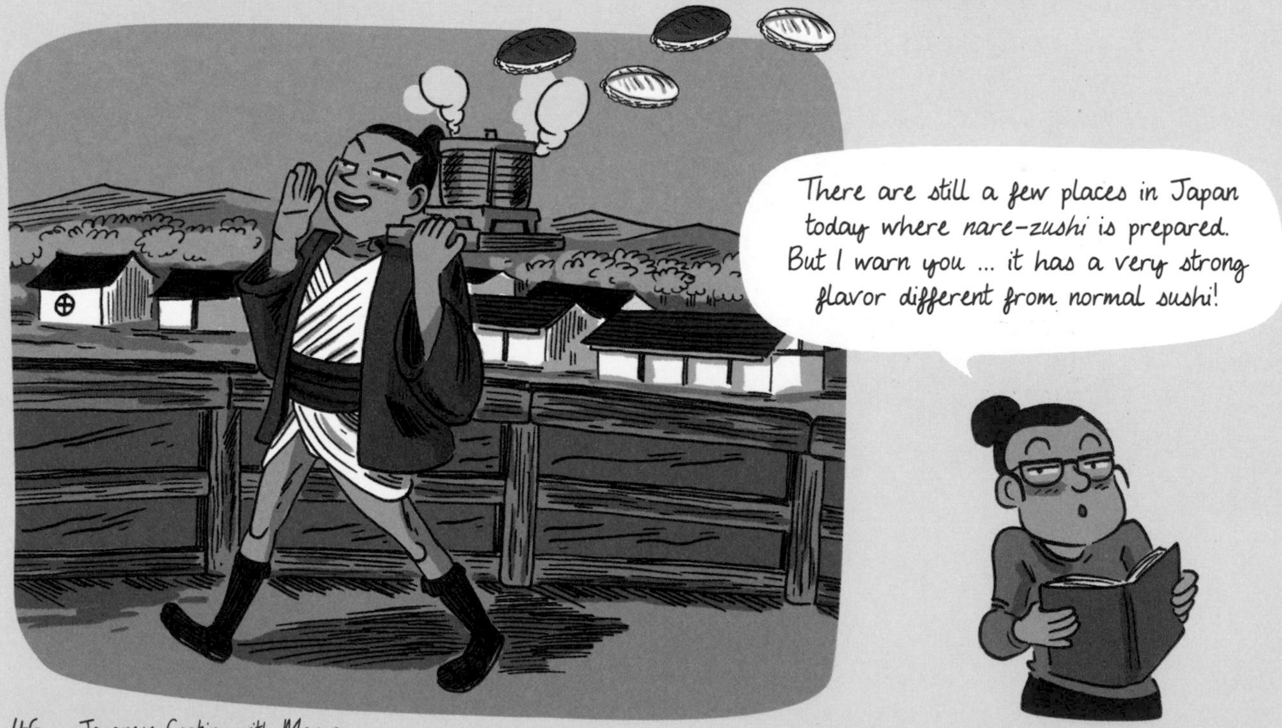
There are still a few places in Japan today where *nare-zushi* is prepared. But I warn you ... it has a very strong flavor different from normal sushi!

How to Use Chopsticks

If you learn to hold chopsticks correctly they are not difficult to use!

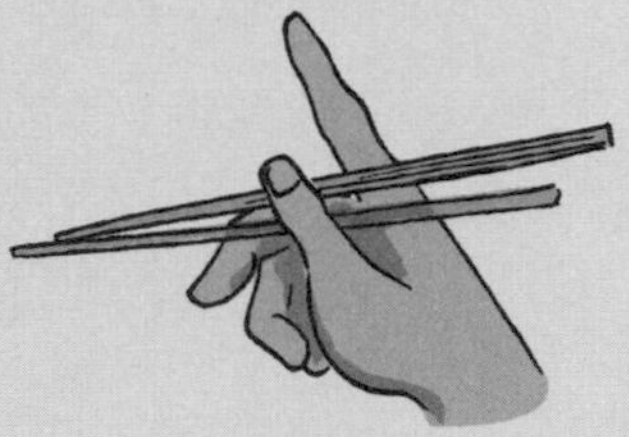

It requires a little practice to press the two sticks together supported by your fingers so the tips meet and press together.

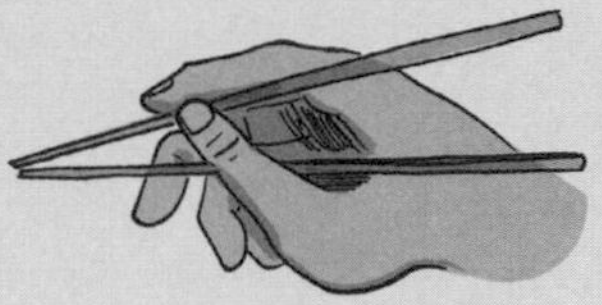

It's almost like picking up a pen to write, but you have two of them and your index finger presses them against each other.

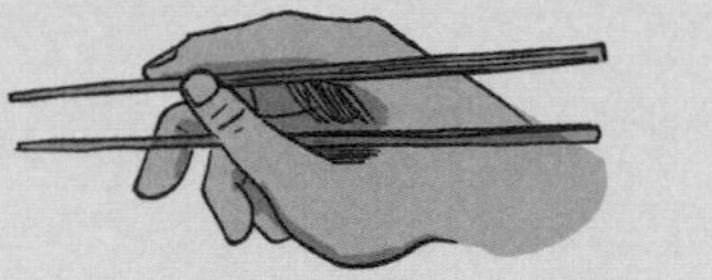

If the chopsticks are not held firmly between your thumb and index finger ... accidents can happen ... !

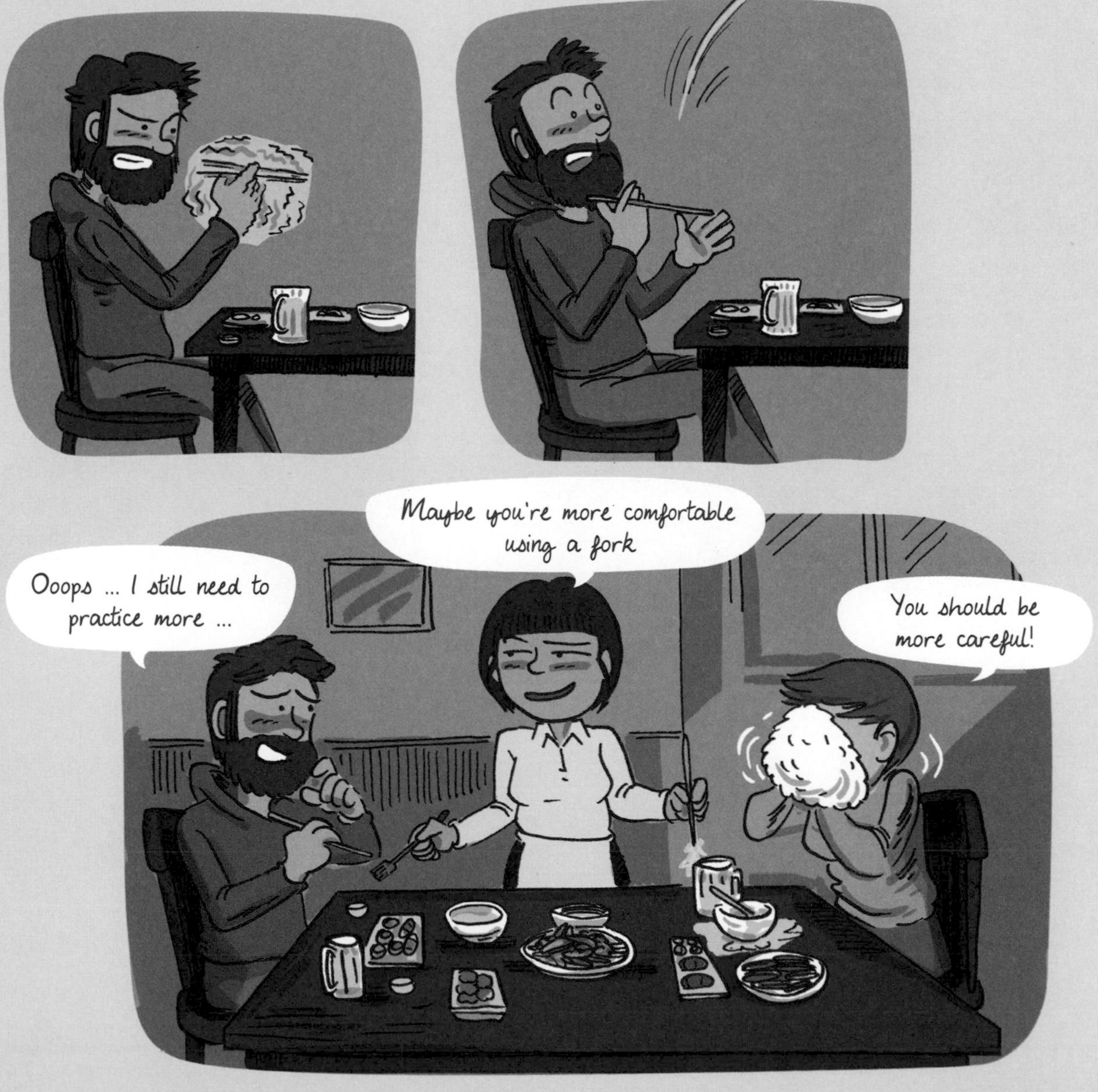
Ooops ... I still need to practice more ...
Maybe you're more comfortable using a fork
You should be more careful!

Making Sushi Rice

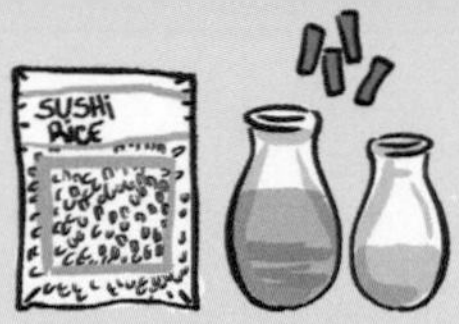
SUSHI RICE

This recipe makes around 2 cups (400 g) of cooked Sushi Rice, which is enough for one type of sushi for 4-6 people. You can make more by increasing the rice and sauce proportionately.

Makes 2 cups (400 g) of Sushi Rice
Time: 60 minutes

1 cup (200 g) uncooked sushi rice
1 cup (250 ml) water
(rice:water ratio is 1:1 by volume or 1:1.2 by weight)
3 small strips dried kombu seaweed
2 tablespoons Sushi Rice Sauce
(see **facing page**)

To wash the rice, use your open hand to stir it by making circles inside the bowl.

Gently rub the rice with your hands.

It's important not to break the grains!

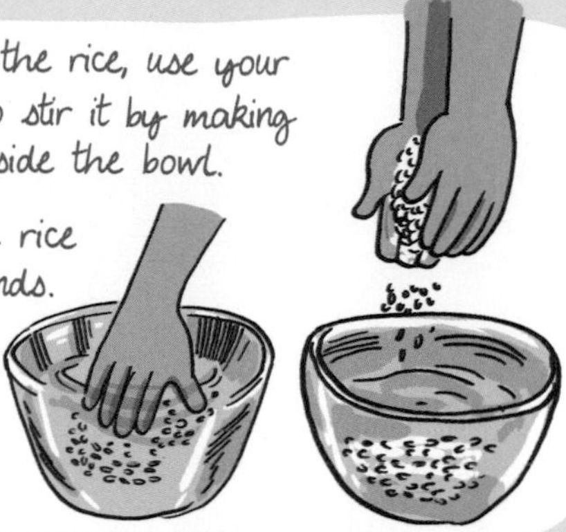

1. Wash the rice in a bowl with plenty of water. Change the water 4 or 5 times, till it runs clear.

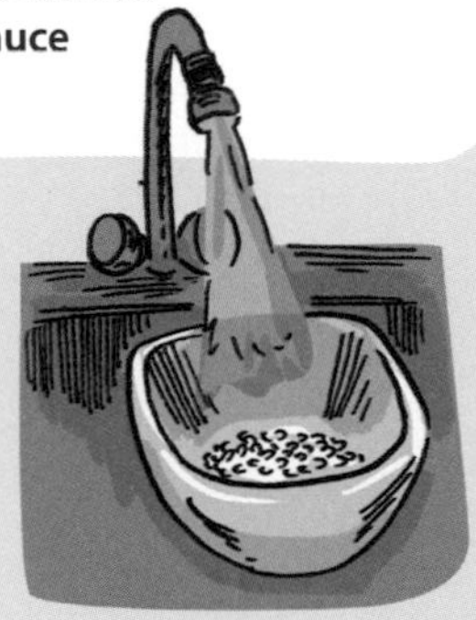

2. When the water runs clear, drain the rice and let it stand in a fine sieve for 30 minutes ...

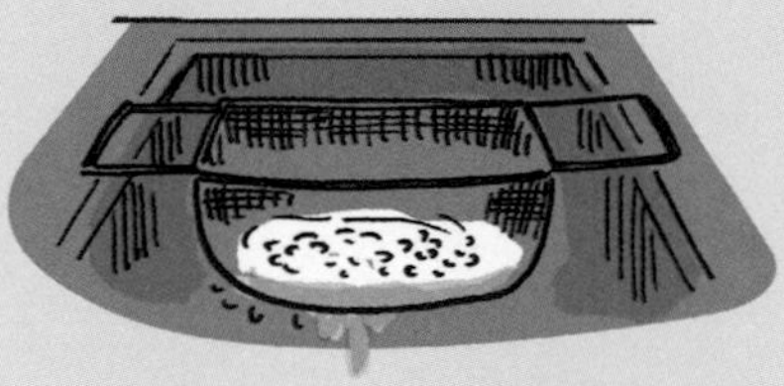

3. Put the rice in a pot with the water and kombu seaweed.

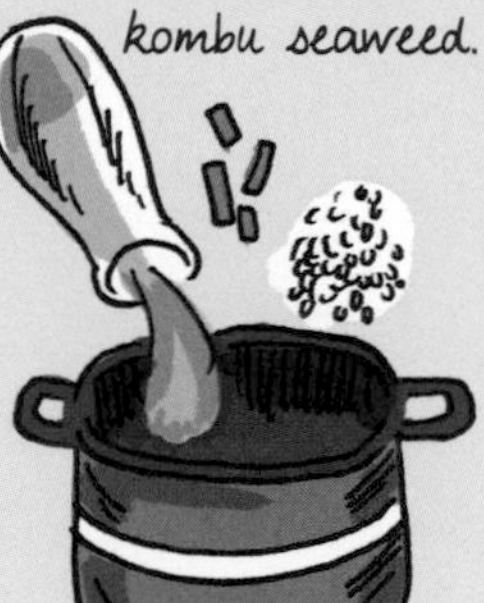

4. When it comes to a boil, turn down the heat and cook it for 15-20 minutes over low heat.

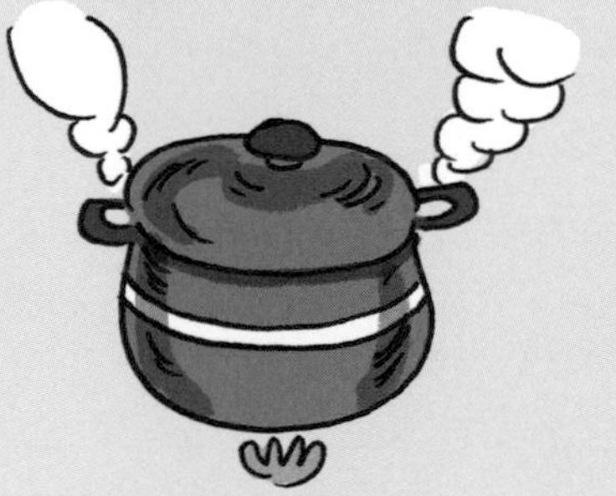

5. Then turn the heat to high for 10-15 seconds and quickly turn it off.

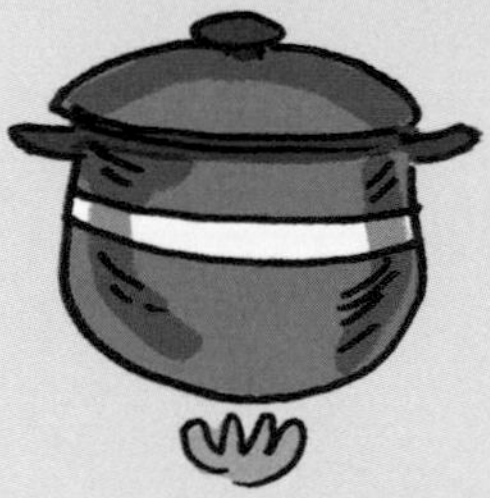

6. Remove the pot from the stove and let it sit covered for 10-15 minutes.

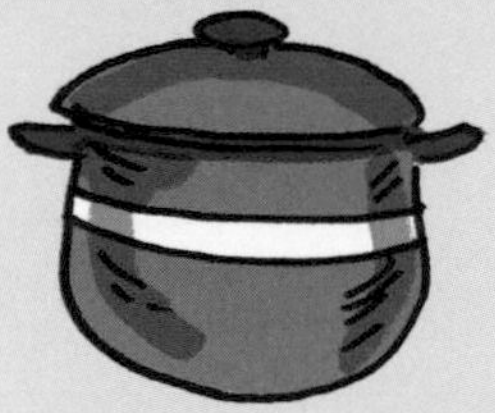

7. Transfer the cooked rice to a large glass or wooden container. (Do not use a metal pan!) Add the Sushi Rice Sauce (see facing page).

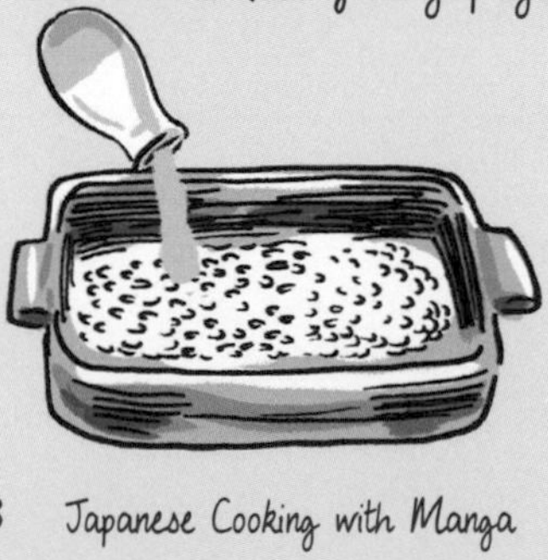

8. Mix the sauce into the rice carefully with wooden spoons, to avoid breaking up the grains. But try to break up any rice balls that form and coat the rice evenly with the Sushi Rice Sauce.

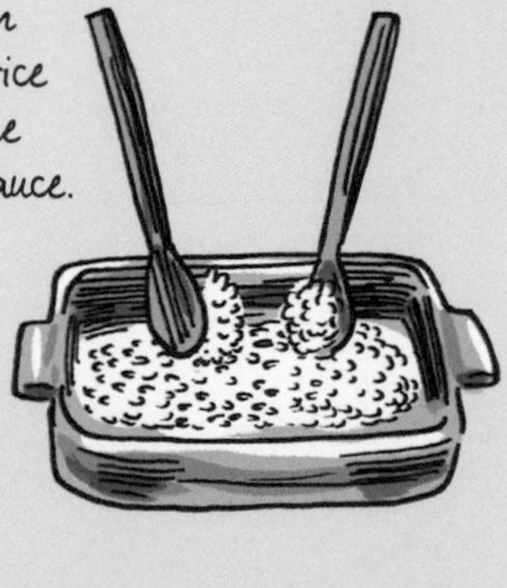

9. Spread the coated rice out in a wide glass baking dish and fan it gently to cool slowly.

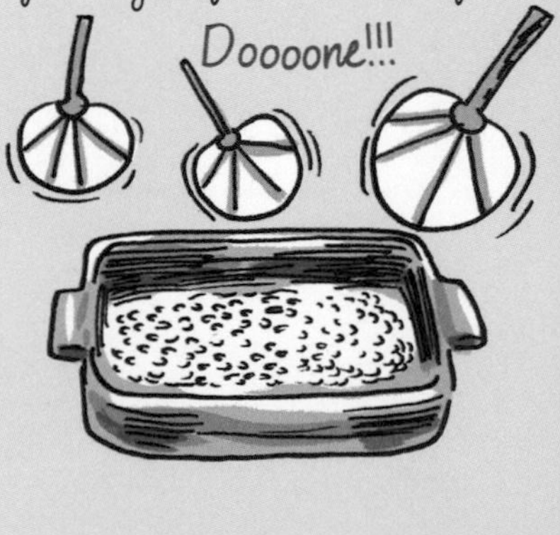
Doooone!!!

The Secret of Sushi Rice Sauce

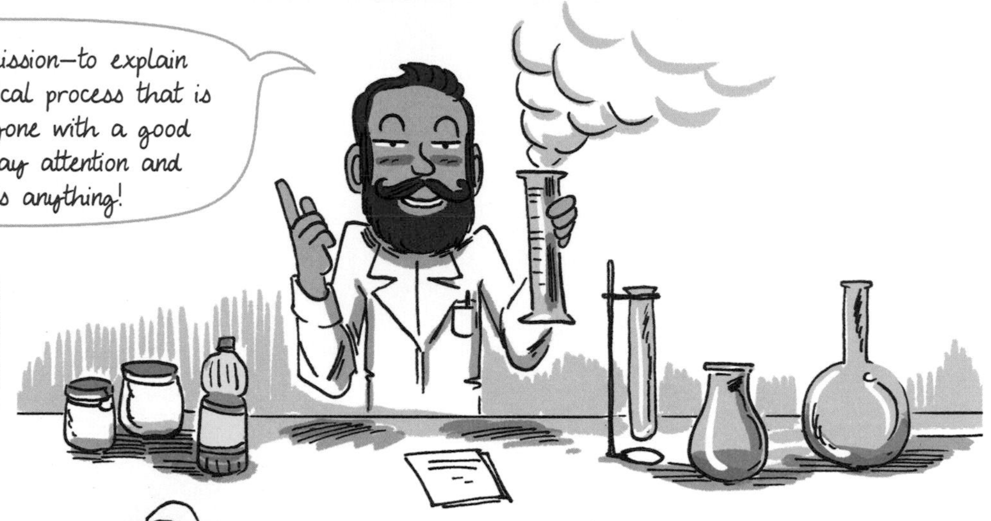
I have a new mission—to explain a top secret chemical process that is accessible to anyone with a good education. So pay attention and do not miss anything!

Makes 3 tablespoons
Time: 5 minutes

6 teaspoons rice vinegar
3 teaspoons sugar
1 teaspoon salt

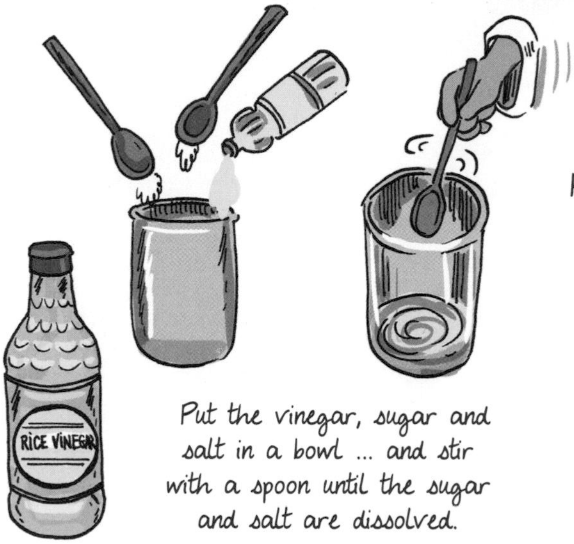
RICE VINEGAR

Put the vinegar, sugar and salt in a bowl ... and stir with a spoon until the sugar and salt are dissolved.

This recipe makes enough sauce for one portion of Sushi Rice (see recipe on facing page). If you are making different amounts of Sushi Rice, remember the ratio: 6 parts of vinegar to 3 parts of sugar to 1 part of salt. Without the appropriate amount of vinegar, the Sushi Rice will not taste right. Rice Vinegar provides the freshness and flavor needed to harmonize with the rice and other ingredients. If you cannot find rice vinegar you can use white wine or cider, but the taste will be different and you should dilute it with water 3:2.

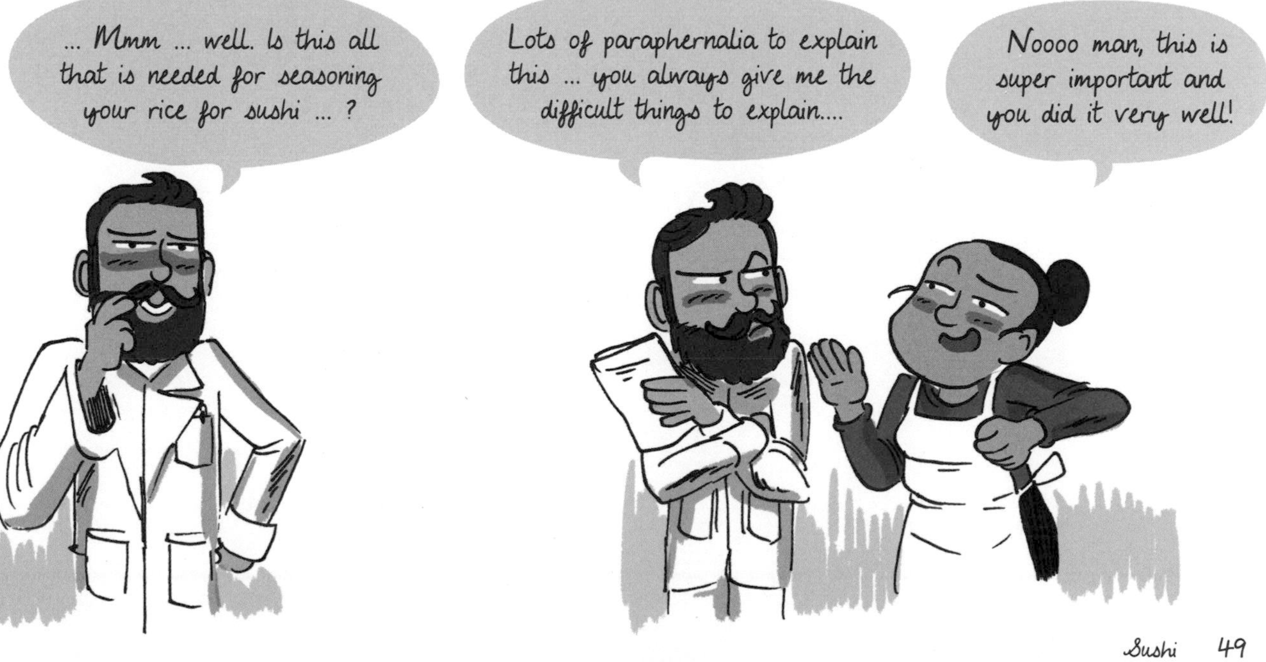
... Mmm ... well. Is this all that is needed for seasoning your rice for sushi ... ?
Lots of paraphernalia to explain this ... you always give me the difficult things to explain....
Noooo man, this is super important and you did it very well!

Buying and Cutting Fish for Sushi

The best way to buy fish is to go to a fish market. Always look for the freshest fish that's in season. Ask your friendly fishmonger for advice.

I have all kinds of fish, and the bream that just came in today looks great!

To select good fish, you have to touch and see it. If the fish is soft to the touch, it's a sign it has lost its freshness. The fish must have a bright color and firm flesh. Bright eyes are also a good sign that the fish is fresh!

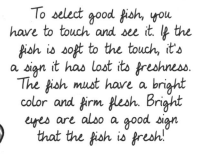

Packaged fish saves some time, but it is difficult to tell if it is really fresh.

Enlist the help of your fishmonger to clean and gut the fish!

I'll cut the head and tail off and clean it. Is that okay?

Perfect. I will fillet it and make the cuts for the sushi myself at home.

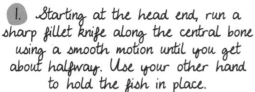

1. Starting at the head end, run a sharp fillet knife along the central bone using a smooth motion until you get about halfway. Use your other hand to hold the fish in place.

2. Turn the fish around and do the same starting from the tail end. Cut through the skin and pull the fillet away from the bone.

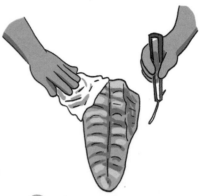

3. Once you've cut one side, do the same on the other side.

4. To remove the skin from the fillet, place the knife at the tail end between the skin and the flesh. Run the knife slowly along the fillet with the knife blade, firmly gripping the skin as you cut it away from the flesh.

5. Dry the whole fillet with paper towels. Once clean, remove any pin bones that you see with tweezers.

Now it's time to cut the fish according to the types of sushi you're going to make!

1. First cut the fillet in half lengthwise. One side will be thicker and one will be thinner.

2. Cut off the outer edges and remove them as they probably have little pin bones. This should give you two pieces with a fairly regular shape.

3. Cut the thicker part of the fillet into small slices at an angle to make the pieces for nigiri sushi.

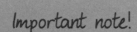

4. Use the narrower piece to cut elongated strips that can be used for maki rolls.

Important note!

Before cutting the final small pieces you will use for sushi, it is advisable to put the fish in the fridge for at least 2 hours to let them age slightly.

Hosomaki Thin Rolls

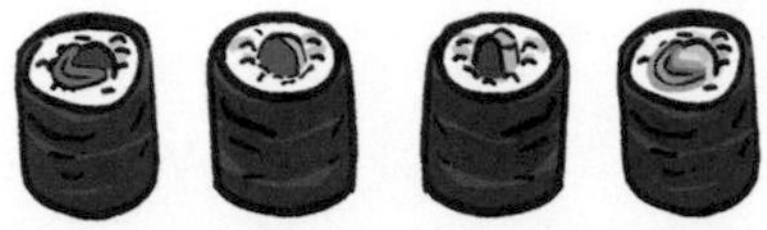

Hosomaki means "thin roll". It's a small cylinder—the classic hosomaki has a diameter of only about 1 inch (2.5 cm). It normally contains just one or two thin ingredients like tuna or salmon or cucumber or avocado. Here we show you how to make three different types! Serve with wasabi and soy sauce!

Makes 6 rolls (36 pieces)
Time: 90 minutes

- 1 portion (2 cups/400g) cooked Sushi Rice (see page 48)
- 3 sheets nori seaweed 7½ x 8¼ in (19 x 21 cm)
- 6 tablespoons Umeboshi Cream**
- 1 small ripe tomato
- ½ Japanese or baby cucumber, peeled, deseeded and sliced lengthwise
- 4 slices of fresh salmon
- ½ avocado, peeled and pitted
- 4 slices of ham
- 1 omelette (made with 2 eggs)
- Wasabi paste, to serve
- Soy sauce, to serve

**Umeboshi cream can be purchased in jars but you can make your own by blending umeboshi paste with silken tofu, olive oil and garlic until very smooth and creamy.

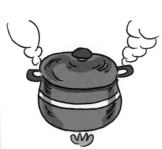

1. First prepare the Sushi Rice by following the instructions on pages 48 and 49.

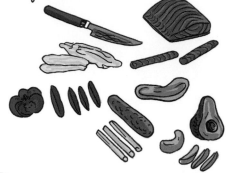

2. Prepare all the ingredients you'll need for the filling of the hosomaki. Cut them into long, even strips.

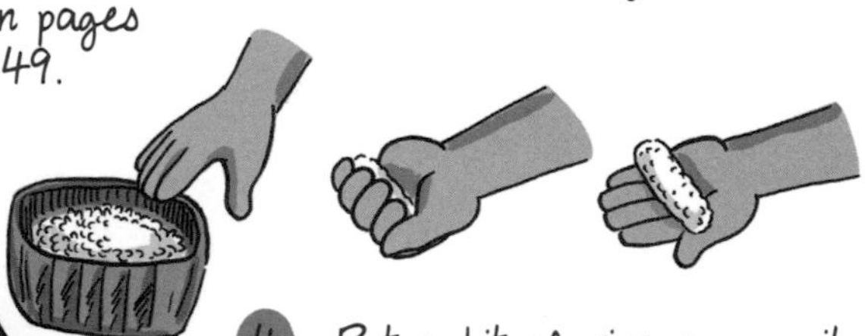

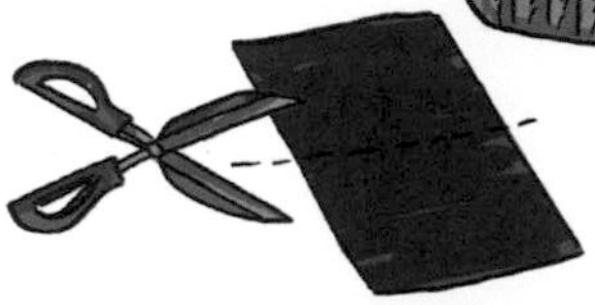

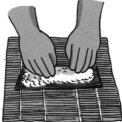

3. Cut each nori seaweed into two equal parts. One piece is used for each roll. Put it on a bamboo sushi mat.

4. Put a bit of vinegar or oil on your fingers (so the rice doesn't stick) and take a handful of rice, squeezing it into an elongated cigar shape.

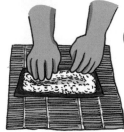

5. Place the handful of rice on the sheet of seaweed, spreading it with your fingers along the length of the seaweed.

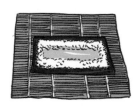

6. With your fingers make a groove in the center to place the fillings.

7. Spread the Umeboshi Cream on the rice and then place:

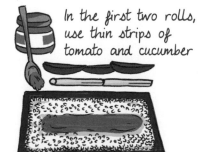

In the first two rolls, use thin strips of tomato and cucumber

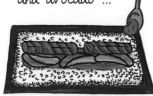

In next two rolls, put strips of salmon and avocado ...

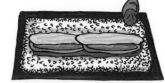

In the last two rolls, use strips of omelette and ham.

8. Now you start to roll. With one hand holding the ingredients, lift the edge of the mat with the other hand.

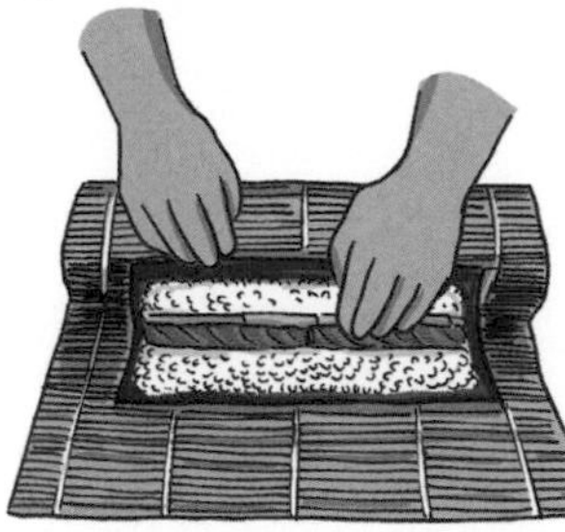

9. Wrap it tightly and press a little until a roll is formed.

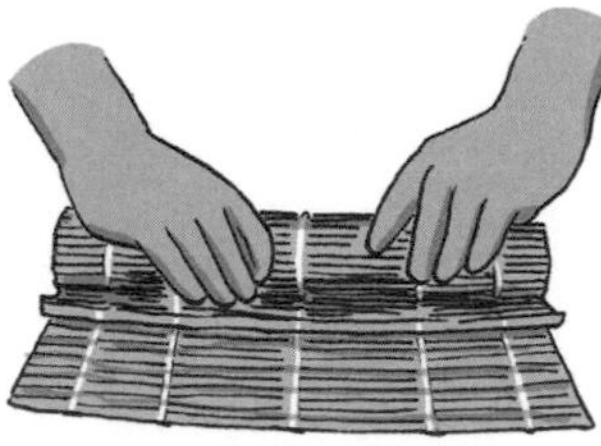

10. With your fingers holding the sides, work outward to make the shape of the roll even.

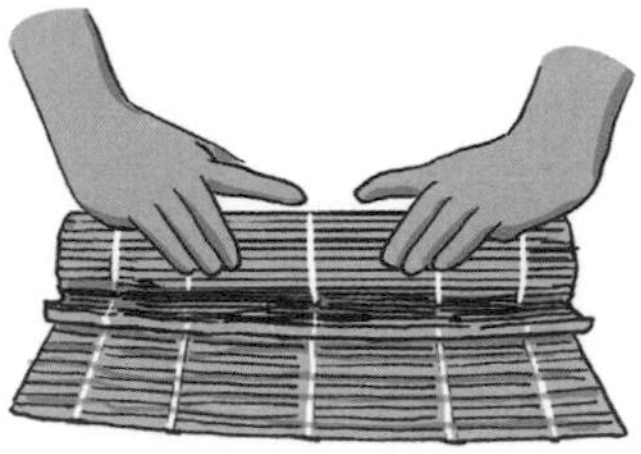

11. Take away the mat and proceed to cut the roll. First cut it in half ... and then cut each half into 3 pieces. So you get 6 hosomaki pieces from each roll you make.

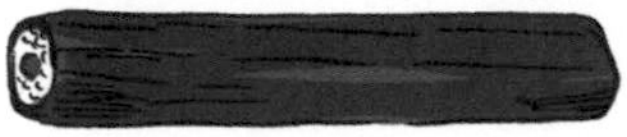

Make sure the knife is sharp and moisten it to make a smooth cut!

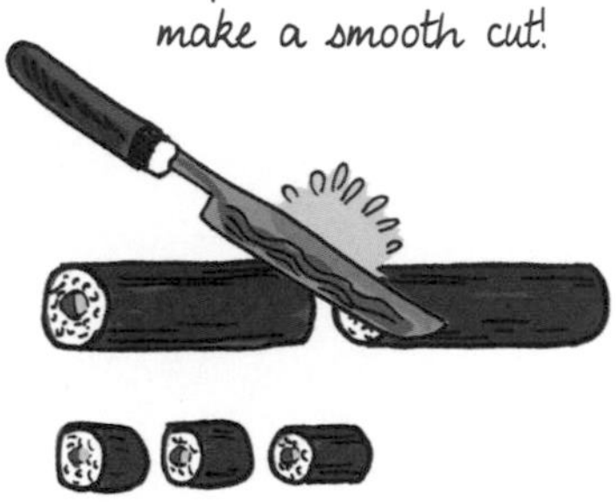

Remember you can make these rolls with any kind of ingredients you like! Fish, vegetables, etc ... Serve them with small bowls of wasabi paste and soy sauce.

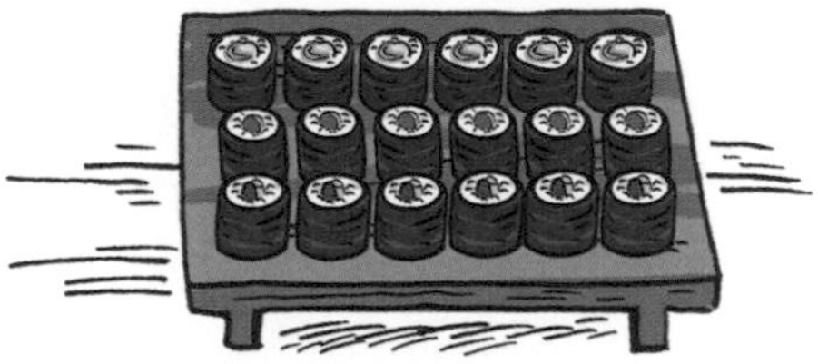

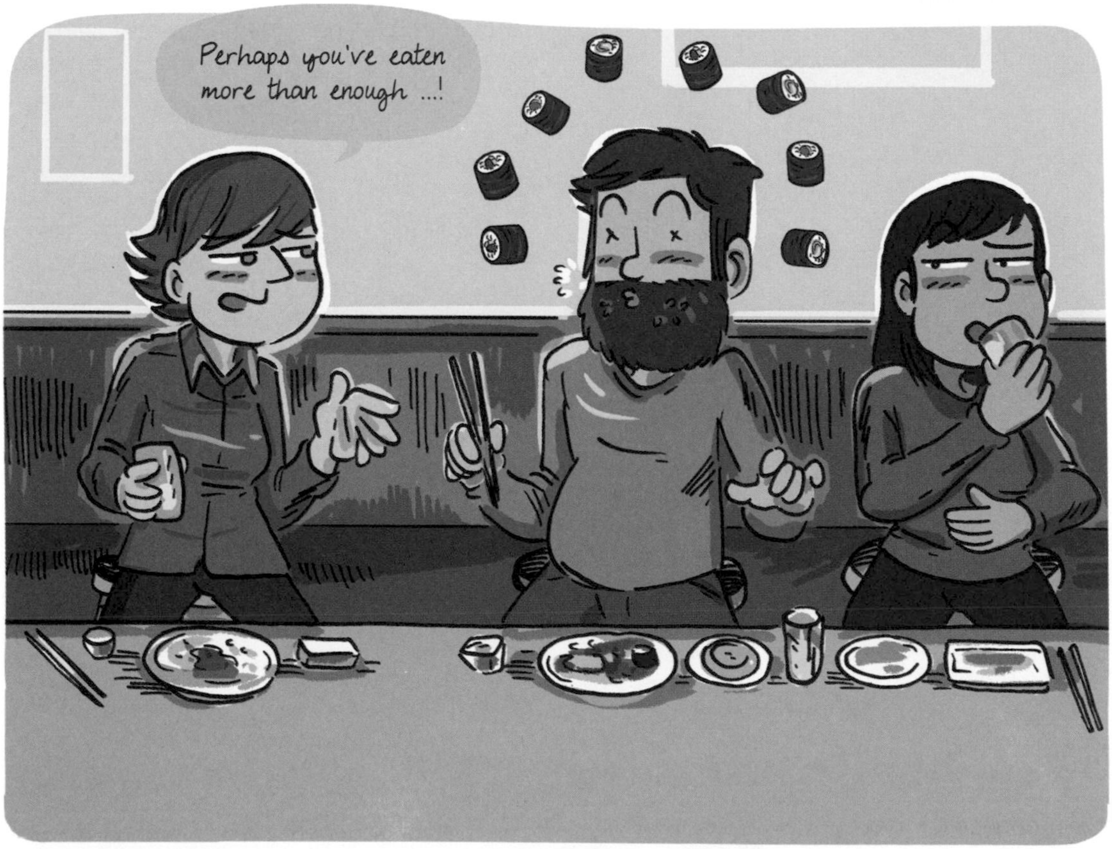
Perhaps you've eaten more than enough ...!

Futomaki Fat Rolls

Futomaki means "fat-roll" ... a larger cylindrical sushi. The classic futomaki has a diameter of around 2-2½ inches (5-6 cm). It can have three or four fillings inside. You can use raw ingredients or simple sauces and cooked items. We suggest three combos here but use your creativity! Don't forget the wasabi and soy sauce!

Makes 3 rolls / 18 pieces
Time: 90 minutes

1 portion (2 cups/400g) cooked Sushi Rice (see page 48)
3 sheets nori seaweed 7½ x 8¼ in (19 x 21 cm)
1 lettuce leaf
½ ripe tomato
1 can tuna (5 oz/150 g), drained well and flaked, mixed
   with 2 tablespoons mayonnaise
2 long strips of fresh tuna
½ avocado, peeled and pitted
½ Japanese cucumber, peeled, deseeded and sliced
   lengthwise
3 slices cooked ham
1 omelette (made with 2 eggs), sliced thinly
Wasabi paste, to serve
Sushi soy sauce (page 14), to serve

> The main difference between the futomaki and hosomaki is the larger size. This allows you to include more ingredients inside.

1. First prepare the Sushi Rice by following the instructions on pages 48 and 49.

2. Prepare the ingredients you are going to use for the fillings. Cut the vegetables in strips, mix the canned tuna with the mayonnaise and cut the fresh tuna into long, thin strips.

> Take your time in each step of the process. Good organization and following each step carefully will help you make neater and more tasty rolls.

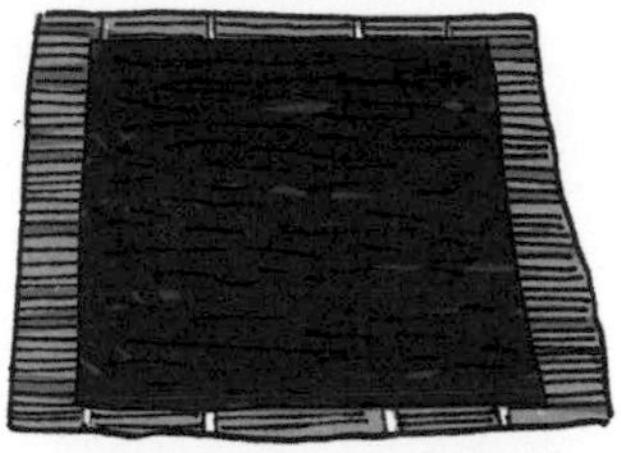

3. Place a full sheet of seaweed on a sushi mat, shiny side down. Dip your hands in rice vinegar and place a large handful of the Sushi Rice on the sheet of seaweed. Leave about a 1/2 in (1.5 cm) strip along the top of nori farthest away from you. Spread the rice out to cover the rest of the nori sheet.

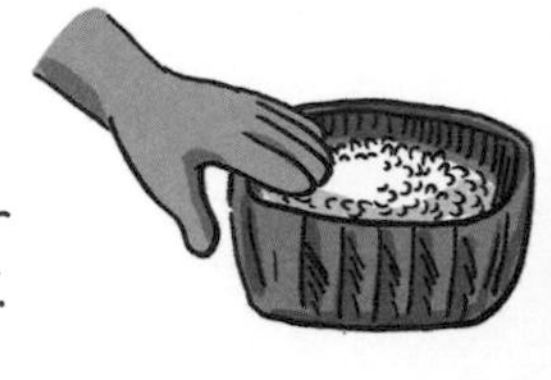

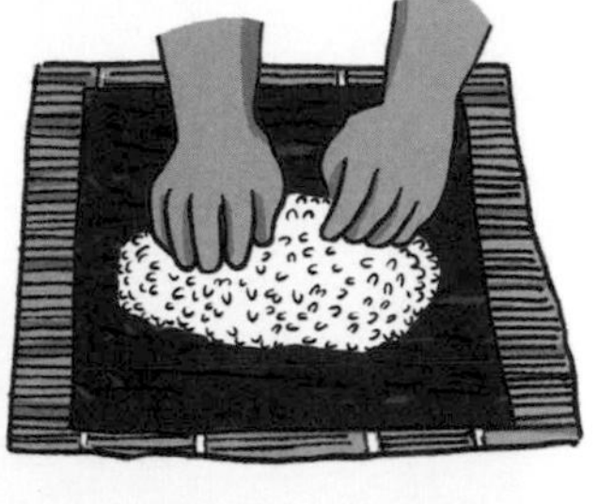

4. Place the ingredients on the bottom half of the rice nearest to you. For this roll we use lettuce, tomato and the tuna salad mixture.

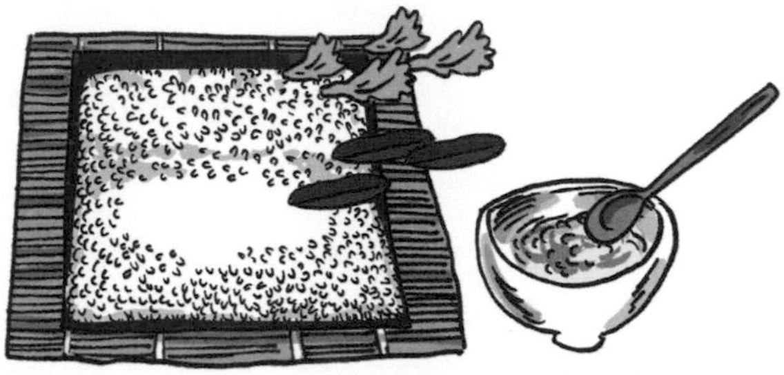

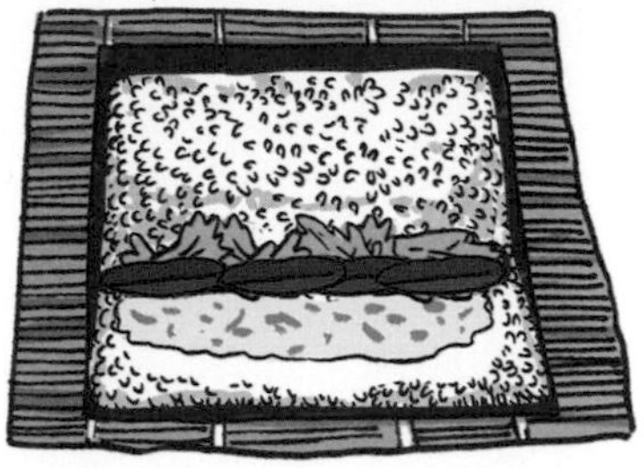

5. Now you start to roll. With one hand holding the ingredients, lift the edge of the mat with the other hand.

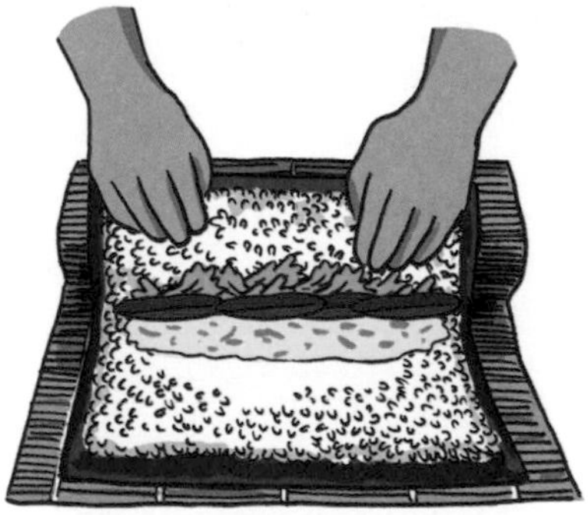

6. Wrap it tightly around the ingredients and press it down a little to shape it into a roll.

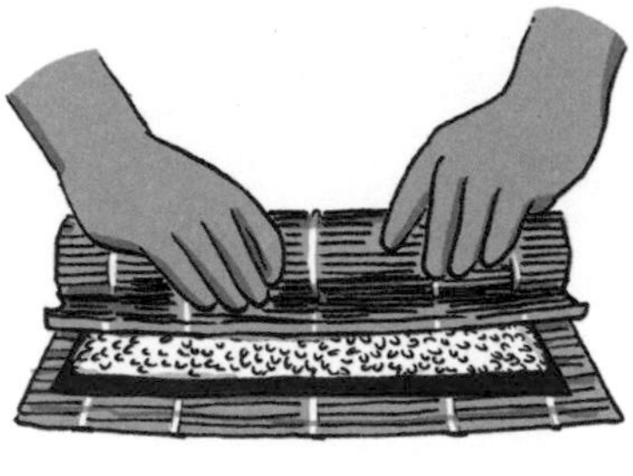

7. With your fingers holding the mat, work outward to make the shape of the roll even.

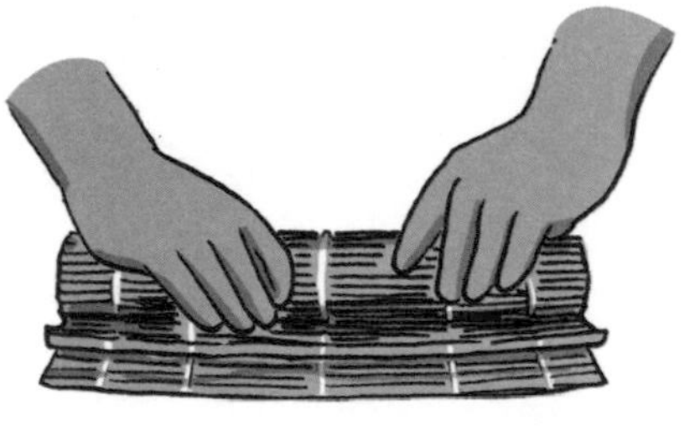

A second roll can be made using the fresh tuna, avocado and deseeded cucumber. Deeeliciousssssss!!!!

Make another one with the cucumber, ham and omelette. Wowwwww!!!!!! Be creative!

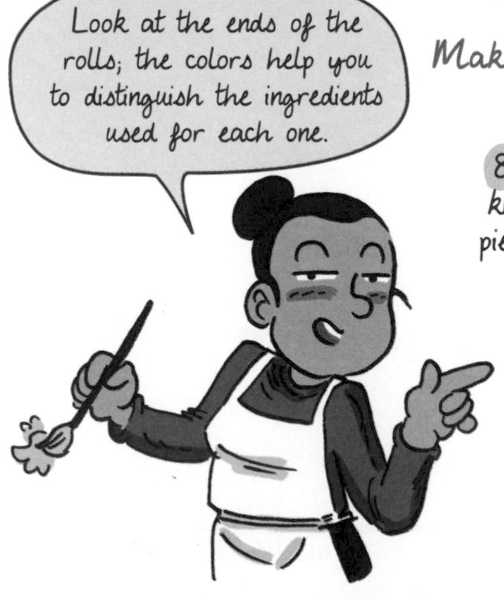
Look at the ends of the rolls; the colors help you to distinguish the ingredients used for each one.

8. With a sharp moistened knife, cut the rolls into equal pieces—5 to 6 pieces for each roll. Voila the futomaki!!

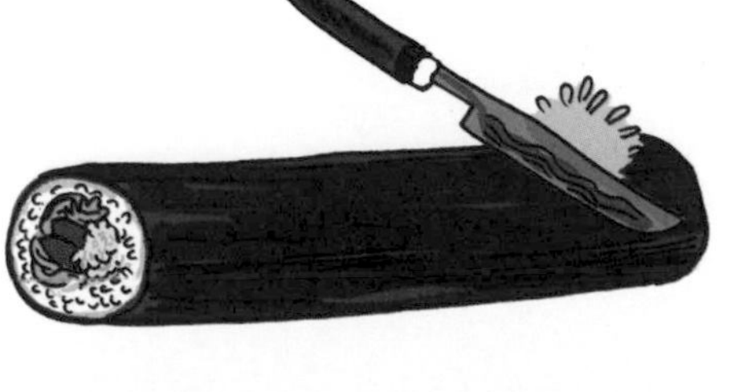

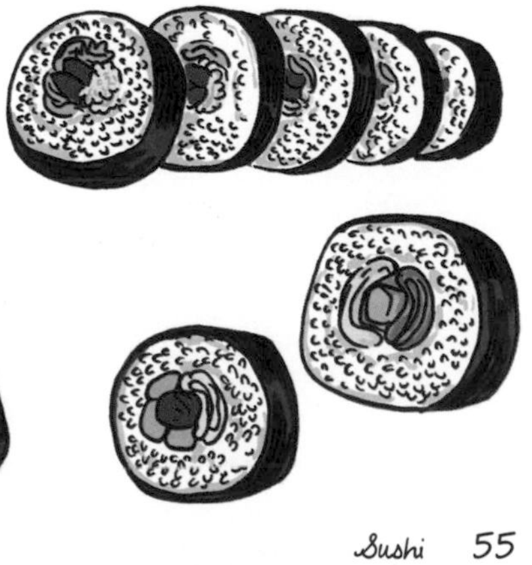

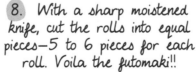

Uramaki "Inside-Out" California Rolls

These can be made with two or three or more fillings. You can use any ingredients you want like herbs, fish or something crunchy. Serve with wasabi and soy sauce!

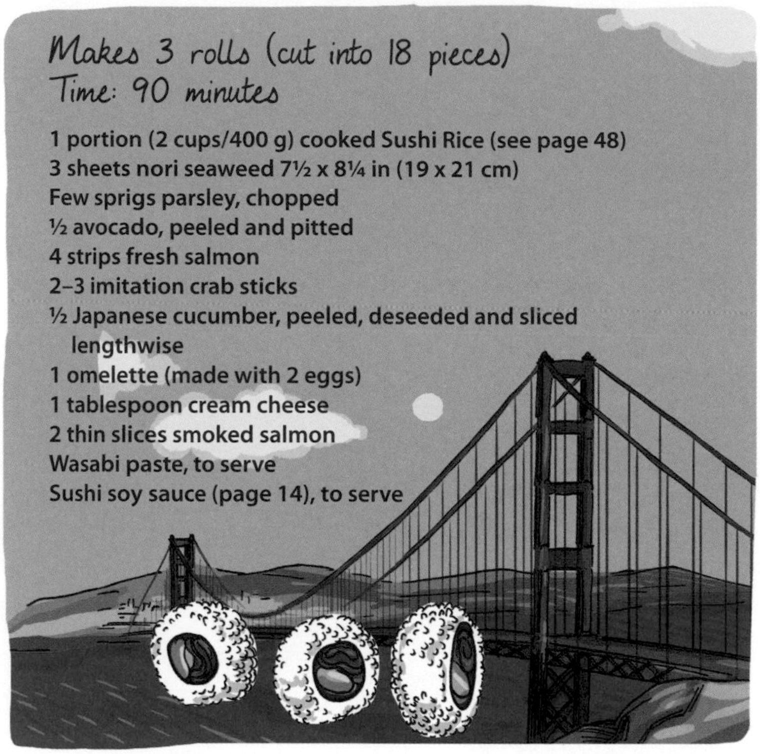

Makes 3 rolls (cut into 18 pieces)
Time: 90 minutes

1 portion (2 cups/400 g) cooked Sushi Rice (see page 48)
3 sheets nori seaweed 7½ x 8¼ in (19 x 21 cm)
Few sprigs parsley, chopped
½ avocado, peeled and pitted
4 strips fresh salmon
2–3 imitation crab sticks
½ Japanese cucumber, peeled, deseeded and sliced lengthwise
1 omelette (made with 2 eggs)
1 tablespoon cream cheese
2 thin slices smoked salmon
Wasabi paste, to serve
Sushi soy sauce (page 14), to serve

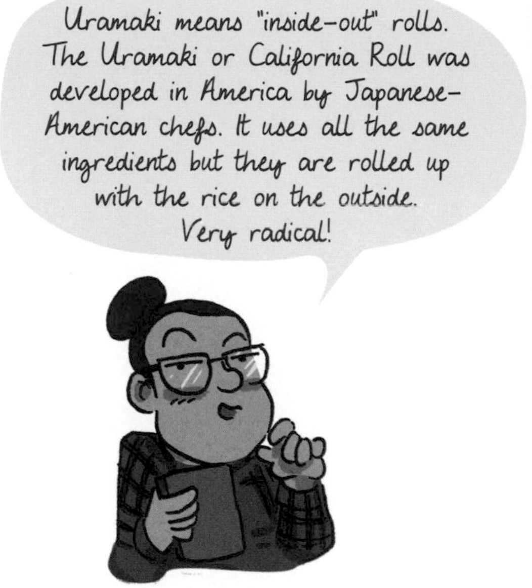
Uramaki means "inside-out" rolls. The Uramaki or California Roll was developed in America by Japanese-American chefs. It uses all the same ingredients but they are rolled up with the rice on the outside. Very radical!

1. Prepare the Sushi Rice by following the instructions on pages 48 and 49.

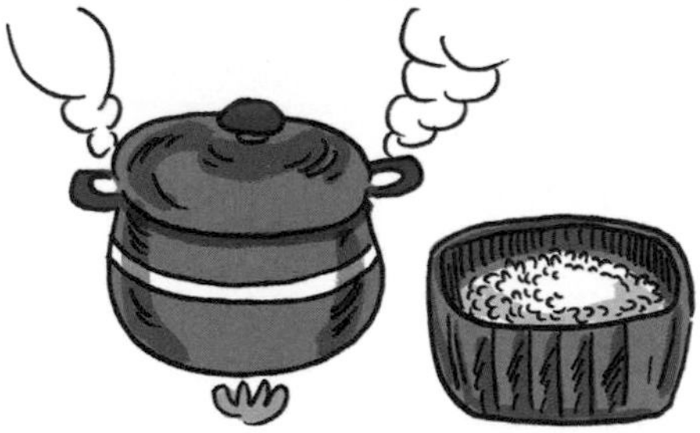

2. Cut the avocado and fresh salmon into 4 long narrow strips.

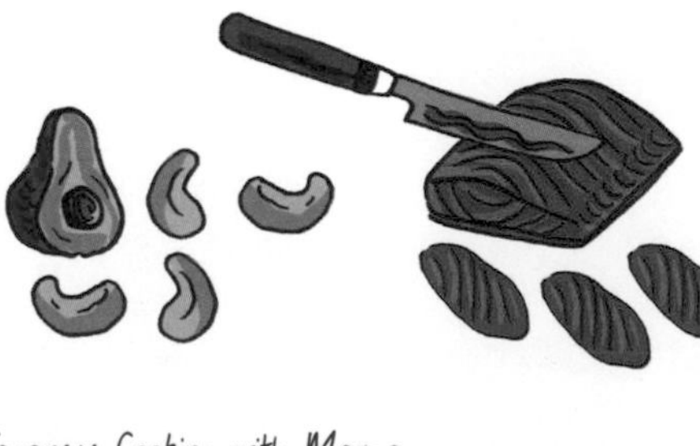

Do the same with the cucumber and omelette.

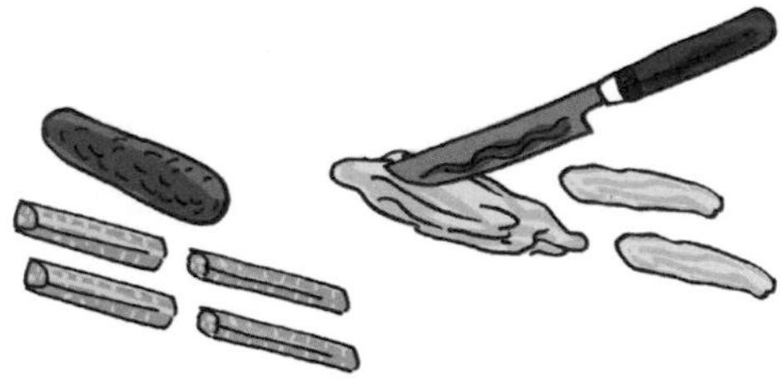

3. Wrap the bamboo sushi mat with a sheet of plastic cling wrap so the plastic completely covers the mat.

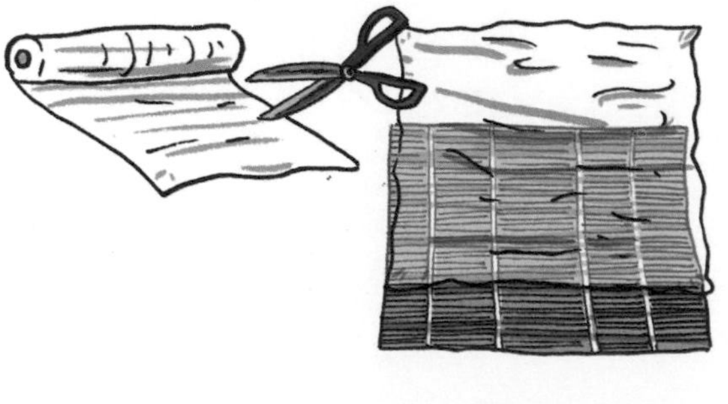

4. Place a sheet of seaweed on the plastic-covered mat, shiny side down. Wet your fingers with rice vinegar and place a large handful of Sushi Rice on the sheet of seaweed, spreading it out with your fingers so it covers the entire seaweed surface.

5. Now sprinkle the chopped parsley over the rice.

6. Flip the nori seaweed and Sushi Rice over so that the nori seaweed is facing upward and the rice is on the plastic wrap. Prepare one roll with avocado and salmon and another with imitation crab sticks, cucumber and omelette. A third roll can be made with smoked salmon and cream cheese (not shown here).

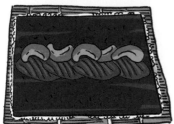 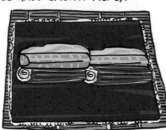

7. Now start to roll. With one hand holding the ingredients, lift the edge of the mat with the other hand.

8. Wrap it tightly around the fillings and press it a little to shape it so a roll is formed.

9. With your fingers holding the sides, work outward to make the shape of the roll even, then remove the plastic-covered mat.

10. With a sharp moistened knife, cut each roll into six equal pieces. Enjoy your California Rolls with wasabi and sushi soy sauce!

Nigiri Sushi

Nigiri is the most common type of sushi served in restaurants. They come in different sizes, but it is better to keep them small so you can eat them in one bite!

Nigiri are small hand-pressed pieces of sushi. Nigiri sushi is actually the original type of sushi and consists of a mound of Sushi Rice pressed into a small oval, with a topping. They can be topped with anything—fresh tuna, salmon, cooked prawns or even vegetables, cheese or BBQ pork. You can also wrap them with a strip of nori seaweed to enclose the toppings. Here we show you how to make them, and give you some ideas for ingredients you can use, but you should try other ones too!

Makes around 20 pieces
Time: 90 minutes

1 portion (2 cups/400 g) cooked Sushi Rice (see page 48)
20 toppings of your choice (see below)
- **4 pieces fresh or smoked salmon**
- **4 pieces sliced cheese**
- **4 slices avocado**
- **4 spears poached asparagus**
- **4 slices ham or turkey ham**

First, prepare all the ingredients you plan to use. Here are some ideas, but you can use just about anything provided it is cut to the right size!
To make good nigiri you need to take your time and don't rush. Careful preparation of the rice and toppings is essential!

Cut the fish into even rectangular pieces, around $2\frac{1}{2} \times 1\frac{1}{4}$ in (6 x 3 cm). Cut the vegetables into regular and elongated pieces also.

Here are some examples of toppings you can use for Nigiri Sushi: each topping should be cut to around $2\frac{1}{2} \times 1\frac{1}{4}$ inches (6 x 3 cm).

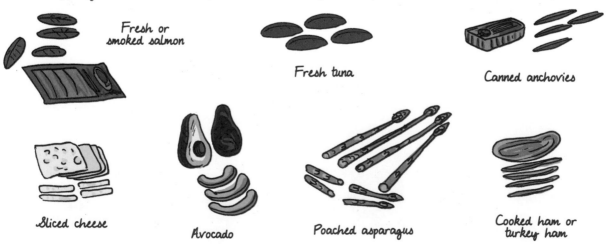

Fresh or smoked salmon
Fresh tuna
Canned anchovies
Sliced cheese
Avocado
Poached asparagus
Cooked ham or turkey ham

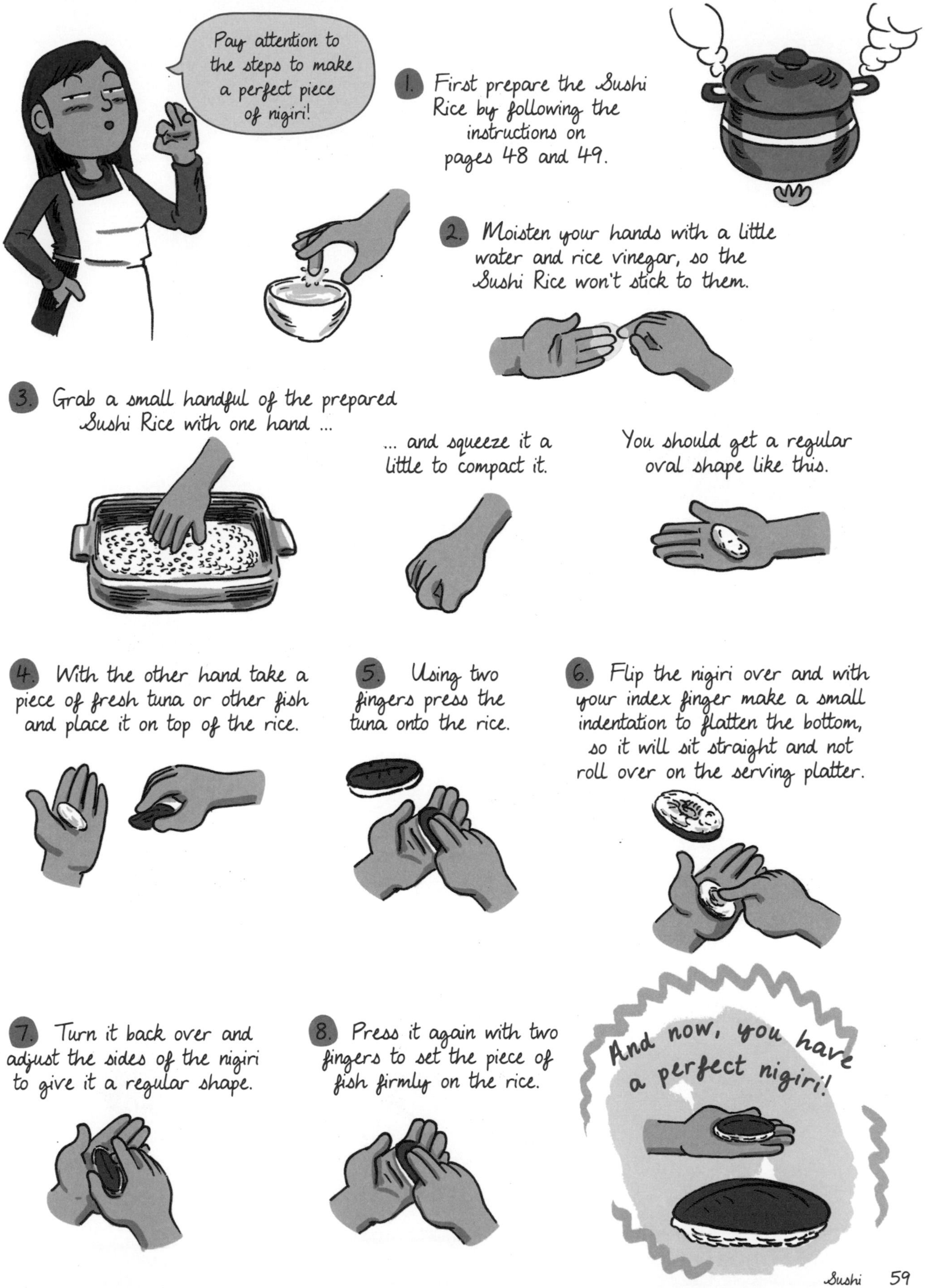

Pay attention to the steps to make a perfect piece of nigiri!
1. First prepare the Sushi Rice by following the instructions on pages 48 and 49.
2. Moisten your hands with a little water and rice vinegar, so the Sushi Rice won't stick to them.
3. Grab a small handful of the prepared Sushi Rice with one hand ...
... and squeeze it a little to compact it.
You should get a regular oval shape like this.
4. With the other hand take a piece of fresh tuna or other fish and place it on top of the rice.
5. Using two fingers press the tuna onto the rice.
6. Flip the nigiri over and with your index finger make a small indentation to flatten the bottom, so it will sit straight and not roll over on the serving platter.
7. Turn it back over and adjust the sides of the nigiri to give it a regular shape.
8. Press it again with two fingers to set the piece of fish firmly on the rice.
And now, you have a perfect nigiri!

Here are various types of nigiri you can make ...

Tuna nigiri

Seabream nigiri

Salmon nigiri

Anchovy nigiri

Now I'll show you how to use strips of nori seaweed to hold fish or other ingredients on the rice.

9. Using scissors, cut the nori into even strips, about 1/2 x 3½ in (1 x 9 cm).

10. Moisten the ends of the strip so they will stick together.

11. Secure the topping to the rice with the nori strips.

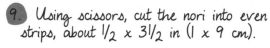

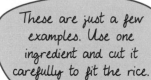

Smoked salmon nigiri

Edam cheese nigiri

These are just a few examples. Use one ingredient and cut it carefully to fit the rice.

Be creative and try different kinds of toppings!

Avocado nigiri

Poached asparagus nigiri

Cooked ham nigiri

"Battleship" Nigiri Sushi

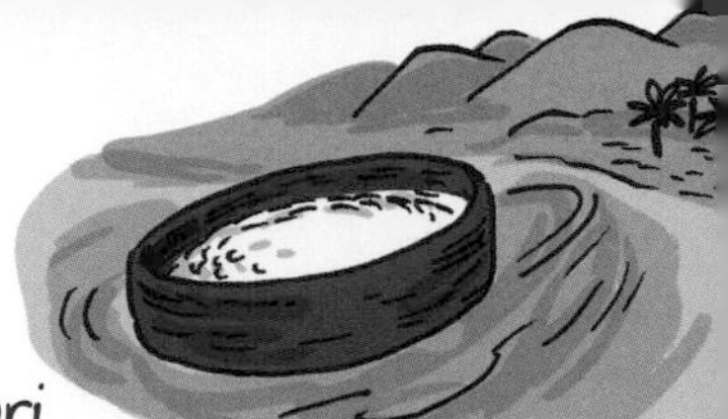

Gunkan is a special kind of nigiri where a horizontal band of nori seawood surrounds the rice and the topping. It was invented to hold loose ingredients like fish roe or tuna salad. Gunkan in Japanese literally means "warship".

Makes 20 pieces
Time: 90 minutes

- 1 portion (2 cups/400 g) cooked Sushi Rice (see page 48)
- 4 sheets nori seaweed 7½ x 8¼ in (19 x 21 cm)
- 4 tablespoons fish roe
- ½ avocado, pitted and sliced
- 4 pieces cooked ham or turkey ham
- 1–2 radishes, sliced
- 8 slices sashimi tuna
- 1 omelette (made with 2 eggs)
- ½ can tuna (2 oz/60 g) mixed with 1 tablespoon mayonnaise
- Wasabi paste, to serve
- Sushi soy sauce (page 14), to serve

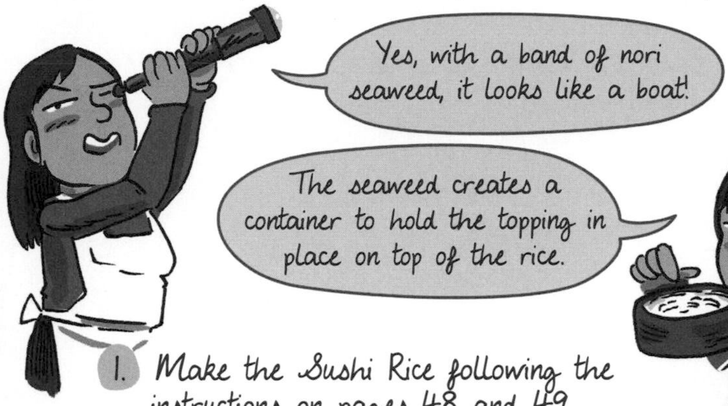
Yes, with a band of nori seaweed, it looks like a boat!

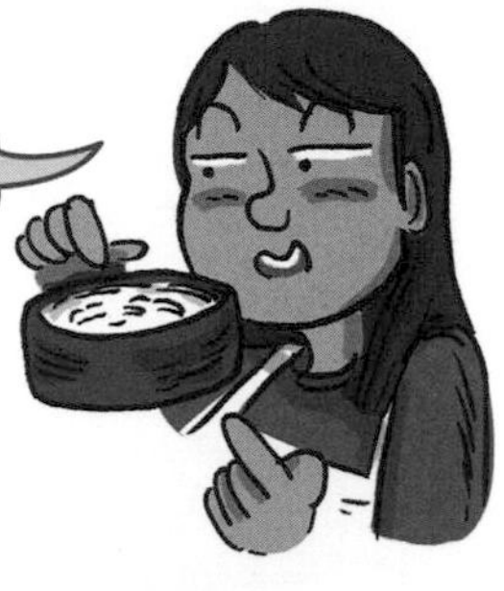
The seaweed creates a container to hold the topping in place on top of the rice.

1. Make the Sushi Rice following the instructions on pages 48 and 49.

2. Cut each sheet of seaweed with scissors into 5 regular strips that are 1½ x 8¼ in (4 x 20 cm).

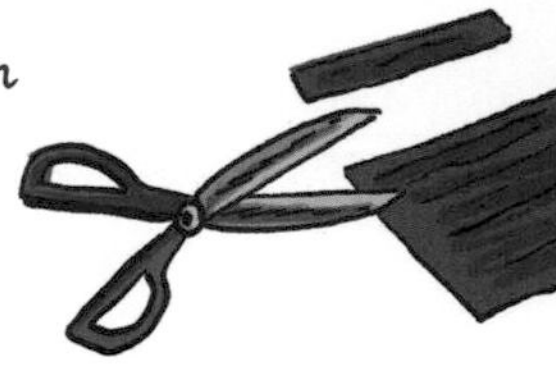

3. Cut all the ingredients into elegant pieces that will fit onto the rice inside the seaweed band.

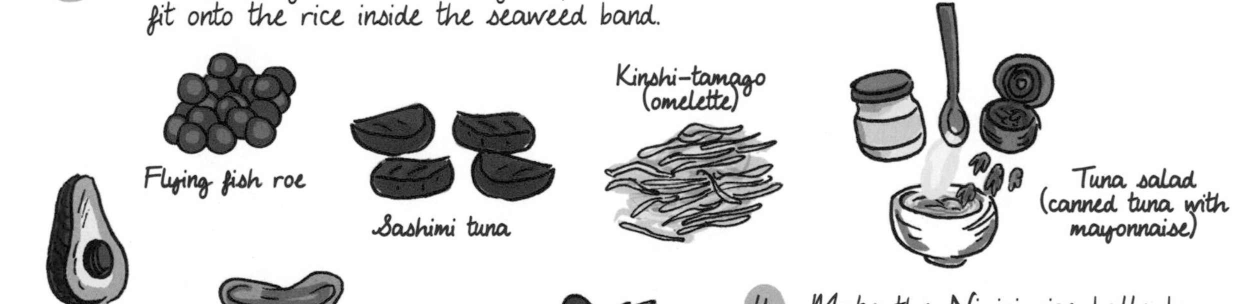
Flying fish roe
Sashimi tuna
Kinshi-tamago (omelette)
Tuna salad (canned tuna with mayonnaise)

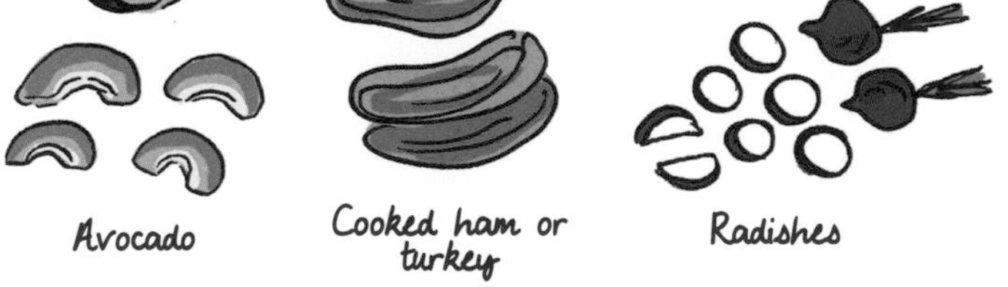
Avocado
Cooked ham or turkey
Radishes

4. Make the Nigiri rice balls by following the instructions on page 59. Use one strip to wrap round each nigiri rice ball.

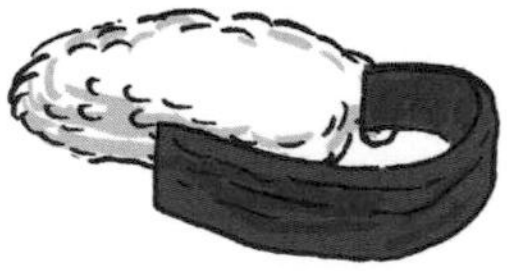

Here are some examples of Gunkan nigiri. Look how pretty they are!

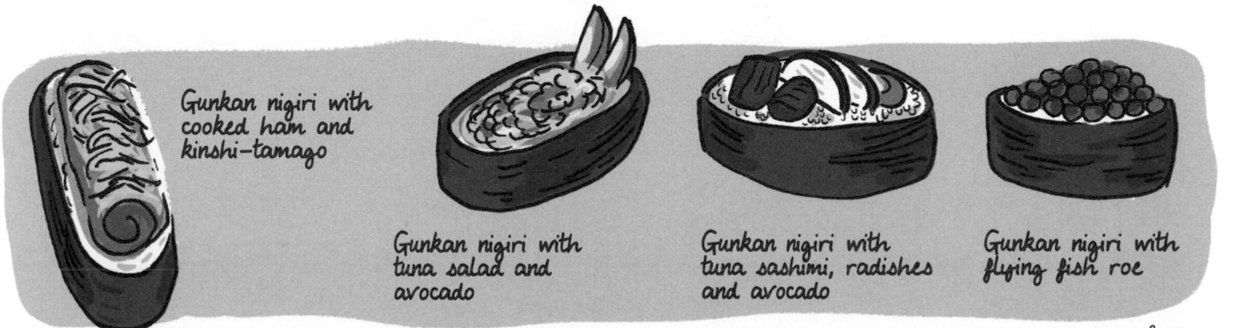
Gunkan nigiri with cooked ham and kinshi-tamago
Gunkan nigiri with tuna salad and avocado
Gunkan nigiri with tuna sashimi, radishes and avocado
Gunkan nigiri with flying fish roe

Hand-rolled Temaki Sushi Cones

Temaki means "handrolled". Temaki Sushi cones are made by placing Sushi Rice and fillings on a sheet of seaweed and rolling it up in a cone shape. Each person normally rolls their own Temaki, and that's why they are great for parties or large groups. All you need to do is prepare the Sushi Rice, nori seaweed and fillings. If you have more people coming, you can double the recipe!

Makes 12 cones—enough for 4-6 people

Time: 60 minutes

- 2 portions (4 cups/800 g) cooked Sushi Rice (see page 48)
- 12 sheets nori seaweed, 7½ x 8¼ in (19 x 21 cm)
- 6 radishes, washed and sliced
- 2 Japanese cucumbers, peeled and cut into long strips
- 12 slices fresh or smoked salmon
- 1 omelette (made with 2 eggs), cut into thin strips
- 1 small packet cream cheese
- 1 can tuna (4 oz/120 g), drained well, flaked and mixed with 2 tablespoons mayonnaise
- Sushi soy sauce (page 14), to serve
- Wasabi paste, to serve
- Pickled ginger, to serve

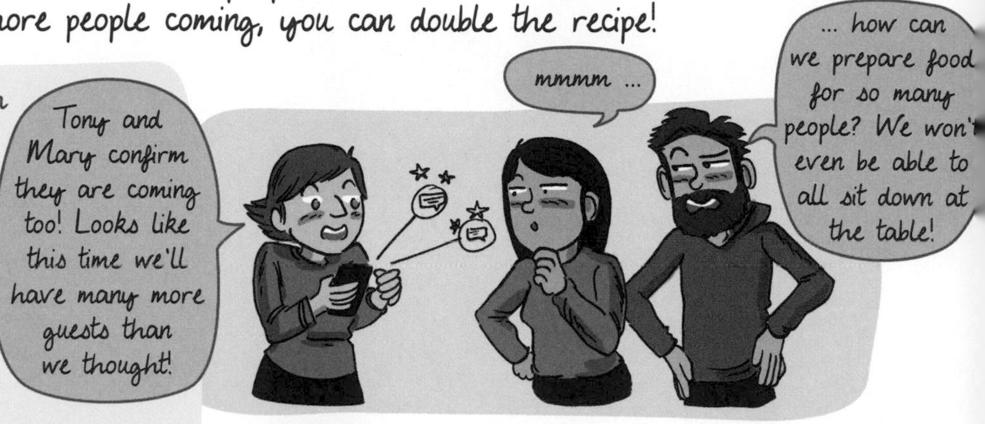

Tony and Mary confirm they are coming too! Looks like this time we'll have many more guests than we thought!
mmmm ...
... how can we prepare food for so many people? We won't even be able to all sit down at the table!

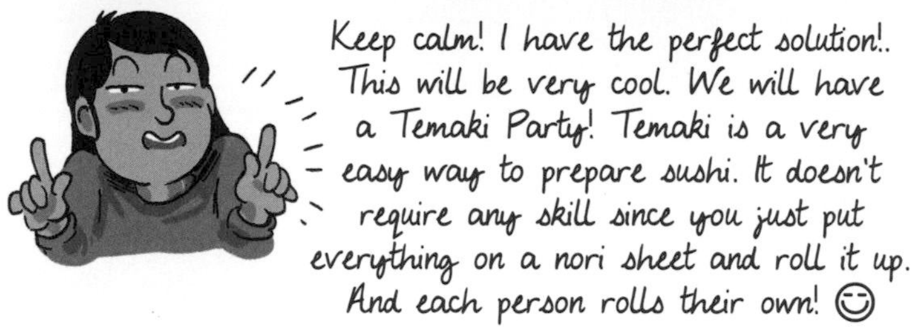

Keep calm! I have the perfect solution!. This will be very cool. We will have a Temaki Party! Temaki is a very easy way to prepare sushi. It doesn't require any skill since you just put everything on a nori sheet and roll it up. And each person rolls their own! ☺

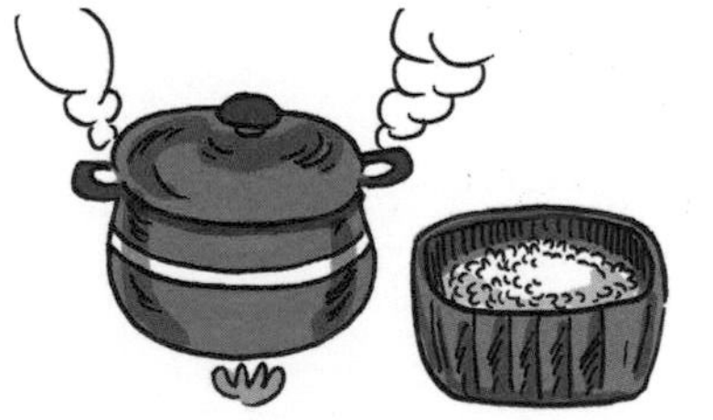

1. First prepare the Sushi Rice by following the instructions on pages 48 and 49. Allow approx. 150g cooked rice per person.

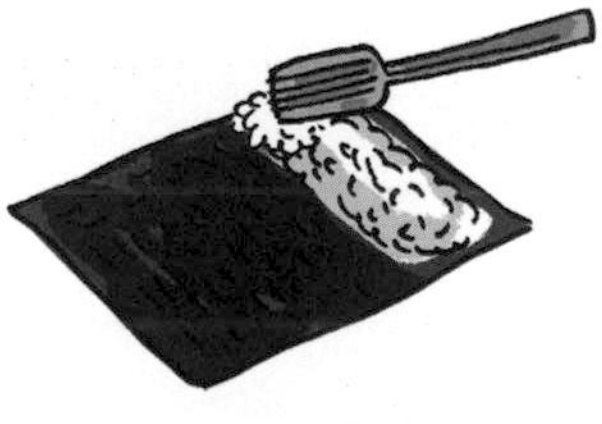

2. Each person should take a sheet of seaweed, place it shiny side down, and spread some rice on one side of the seaweed.

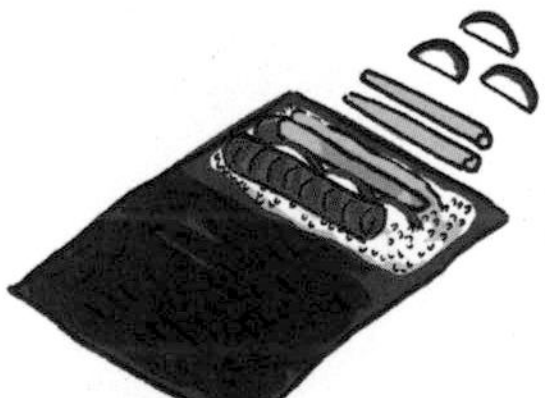

3. Place the fillings (preferably 2-3 kinds) vertically across the middle of the rice.

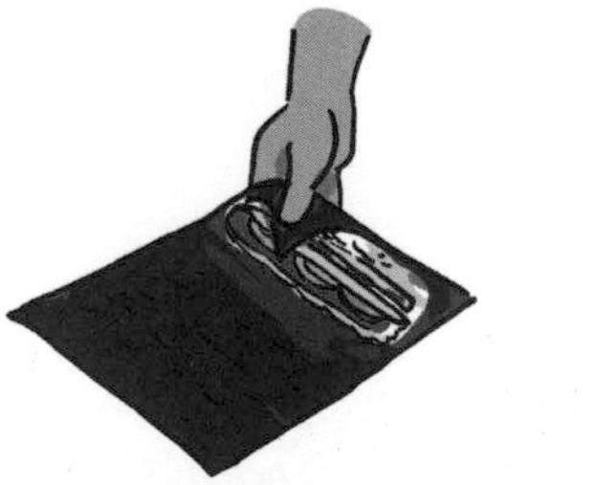

Here we suggest slices of radish, cucumber and fresh salmon, all cut into even, elongated strips.

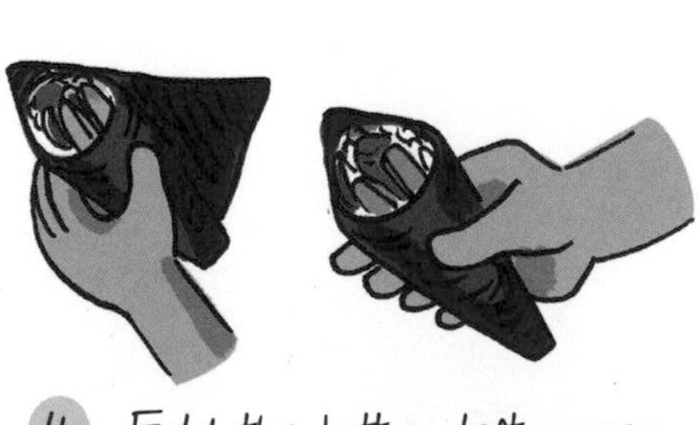

4. Fold the bottom left corner of the nori over the fillings at an angle and begin rolling to form a cone.

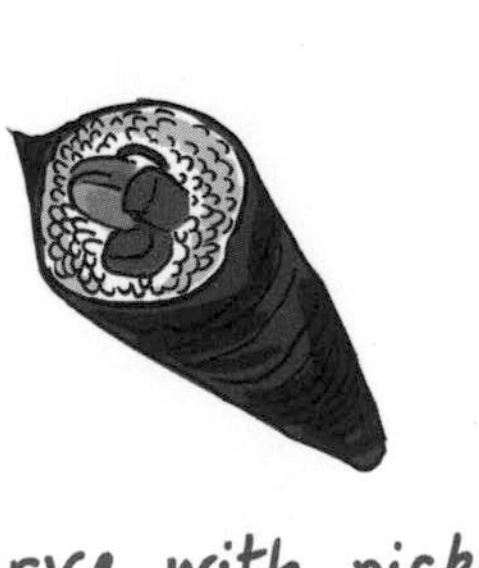

Serve with pickled ginger, wasabi, and soy sauce as condiments.

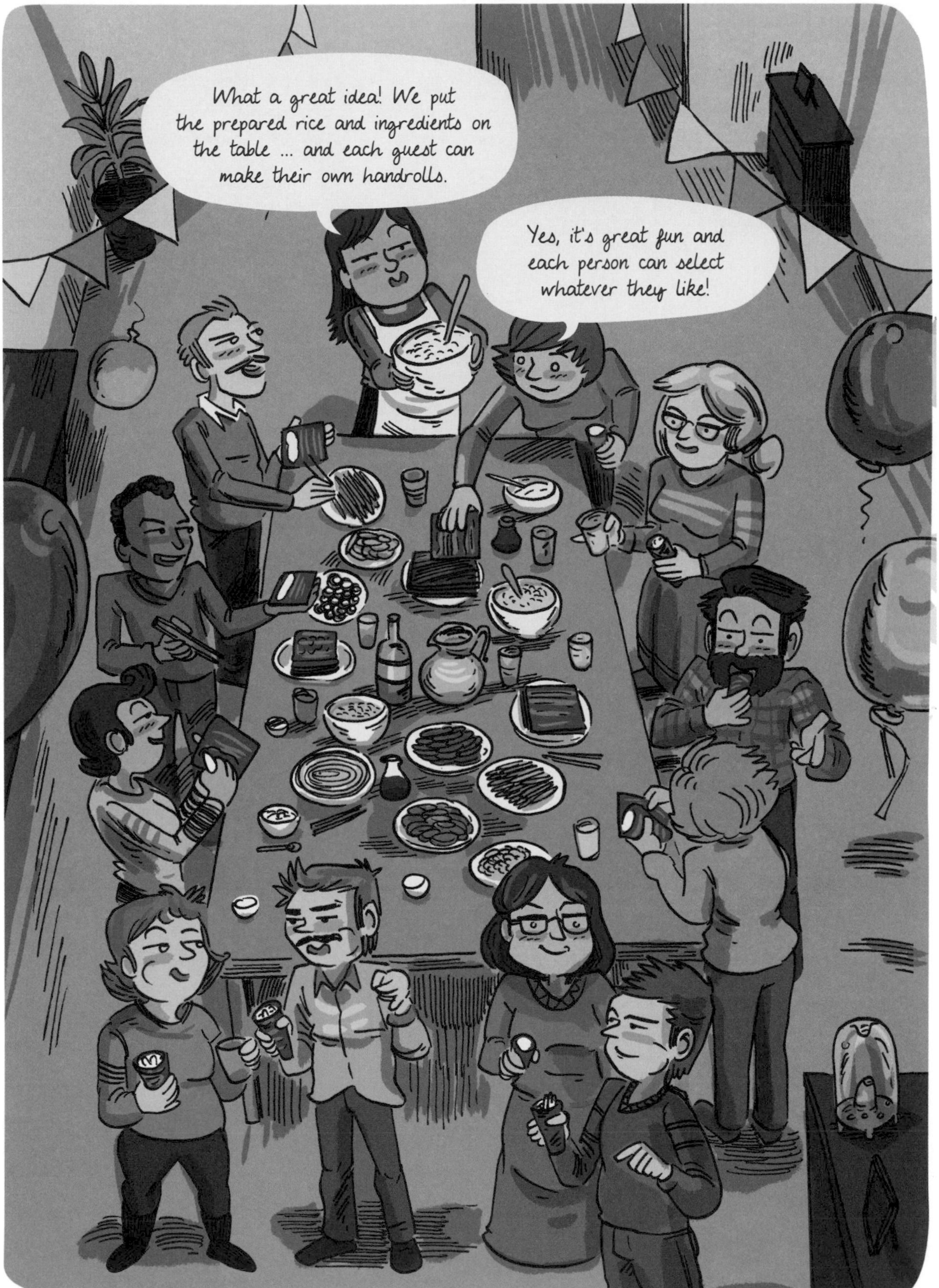
What a great idea! We put the prepared rice and ingredients on the table ... and each guest can make their own handrolls.
Yes, it's great fun and each person can select whatever they like!

Chirashi Sushi

Chirashi means "scattered". Chirashi Sushi is a bowl of sushi rice with other ingredients scattered on top of the rice. The great thing about Chirashi Sushi is that you can add as many different ingredients as you like and you just slice them up quickly. So it's very easy! Here we give you some suggestions, but use your imagination and come up with your own versions.

Serves 4-6
Time: 1 hour

2 portions (4 cups/800 g) cooked Sushi Rice (see page 48)
1 omelette (made with 2 eggs), cut into fine strips
2 avocadoes, pitted and cut in thin slices
1 packet thinly sliced smoked salmon
1 tomato, thinly sliced
Wasabi paste, to serve
Sushi soy sauce (page 14), to serve
Pickled ginger, to serve

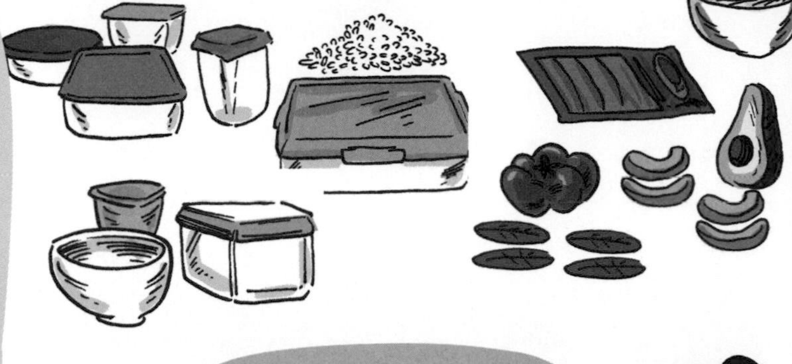

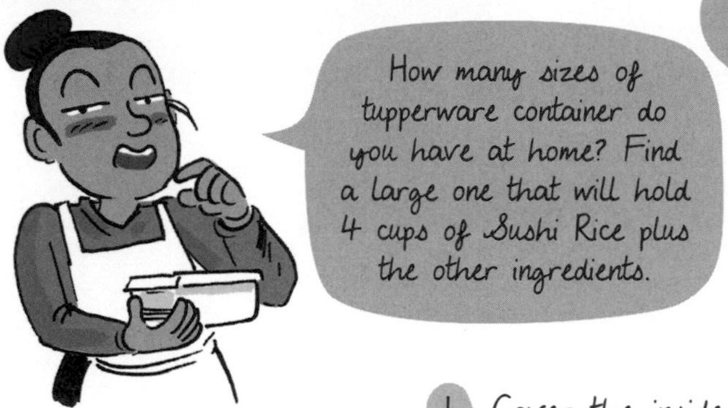
How many sizes of tupperware container do you have at home? Find a large one that will hold 4 cups of Sushi Rice plus the other ingredients.

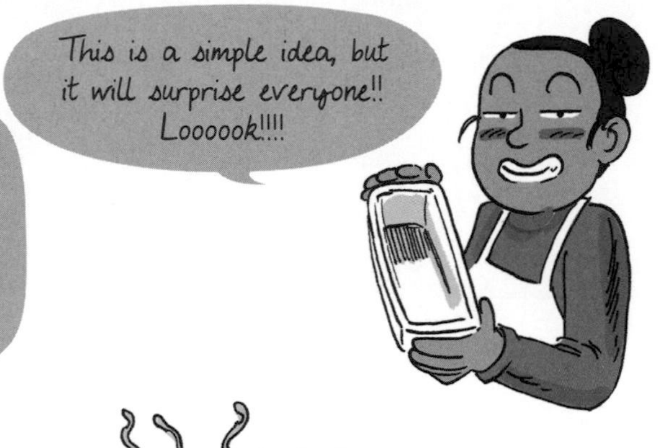
This is a simple idea, but it will surprise everyone!! Looooook!!!!

An empty tupperware works as a mold to create the Chirashi Sushi.

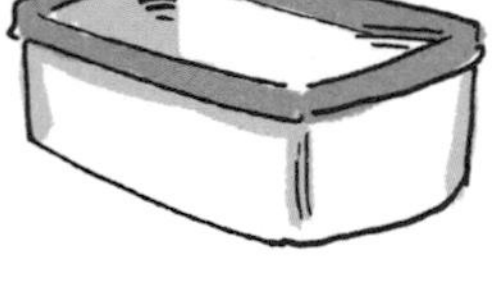

1. Cover the inside of the tupperware with cling wrap.

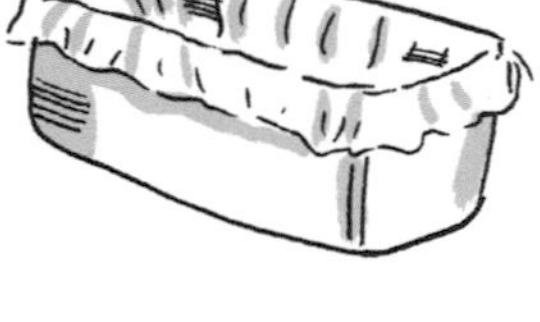

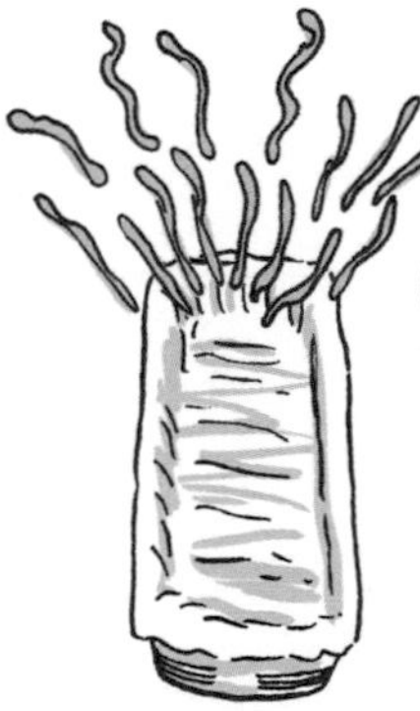

2. First scatter the omelette strips on the bottom of the tupperware.

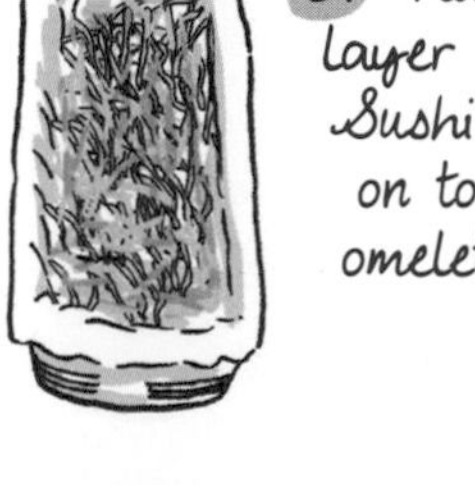

3. Add one thin layer of cooked Sushi Rice rice on top of the omelette strips.

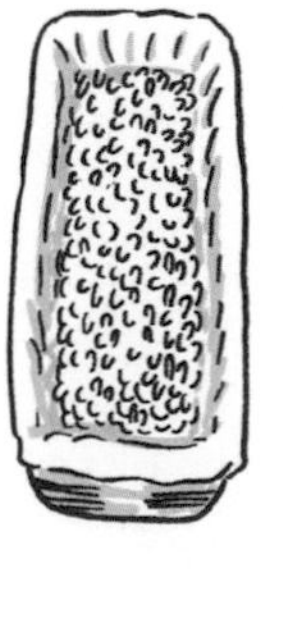

4. Spread out the rice evenly.

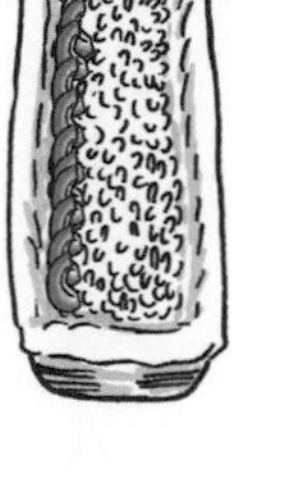

5. Next place slices of avocado on top of the rice.

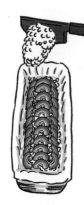

6. Add more cooked rice on top of the avocado and spread it out evenly.
You can go on adding as many layers you want and varying the ingredients depending on the depth of the mold.
7. Now find a plate that has about the same diameter as the mold.
8. Put the plate on top of the mold, hold both of them together firmly with two hands and flip them so the mold is now on top and the plate is on the bottom.
9. Put the plate on the table and remove the mold. The cling wrap will ensure that the rice does not stick to the mold. Then remove the cling wrap.
10. Slice up the tomato, smoked salmon and the remaining avocado ...
11. ... and use them to garnish the top of the Chirashi. It will look like a layer cake and everyone will wonder what it is!
Slice it carefully with a very sharp knife and serve it with wasabi, sushi soy sauce and pickled ginger slices.
Presentation is very important in Japanese cooking, so take your time with this last step! It looks really beautiful and tastes sooo gooooood!!!

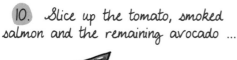

Beautiful Temari Sushi

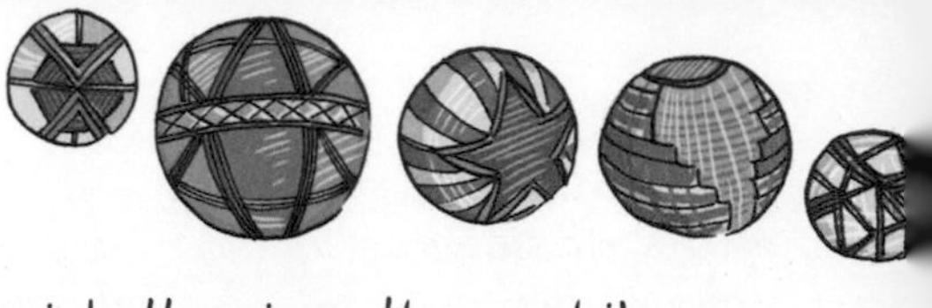

Temari Sushi is named after colorful Japanese temari balls since the sushi's round shape and colorful toppings resemble them. Temari sushi basically consists of a ball of sushi rice with toppings of your choice. Colors are important so select your ingredients with this in mind.

Makes around 12 pieces
Time: 1 hour

1 portion (2 cups/400 g) cooked Sushi Rice (see page 48)
2 sheets nori seaweed 7½ x 8¼ in (19 x 21 cm)
Topping ingredients to your taste: cheese slices, radishes, boiled shrimp, fresh tuna or salmon slices, omelette, avocado, ham ….

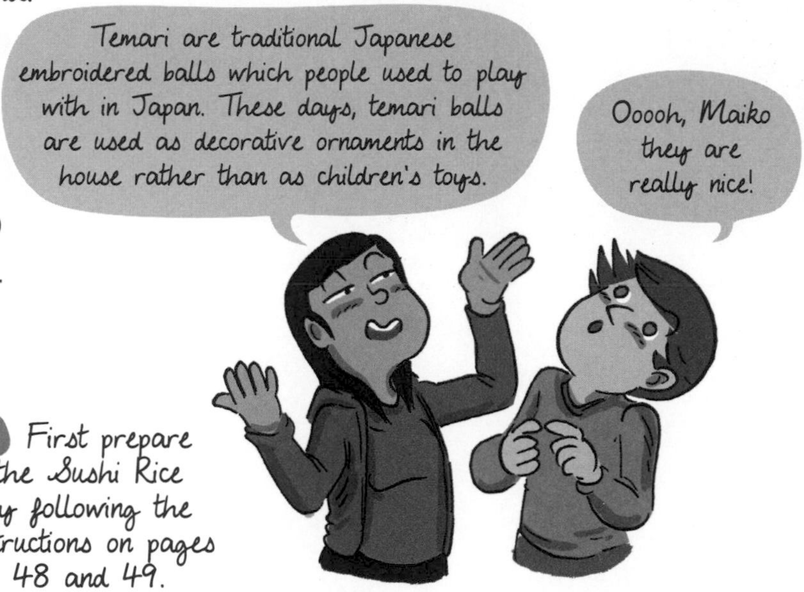
Temari are traditional Japanese embroidered balls which people used to play with in Japan. These days, temari balls are used as decorative ornaments in the house rather than as children's toys.
Ooooh, Maiko they are really nice!

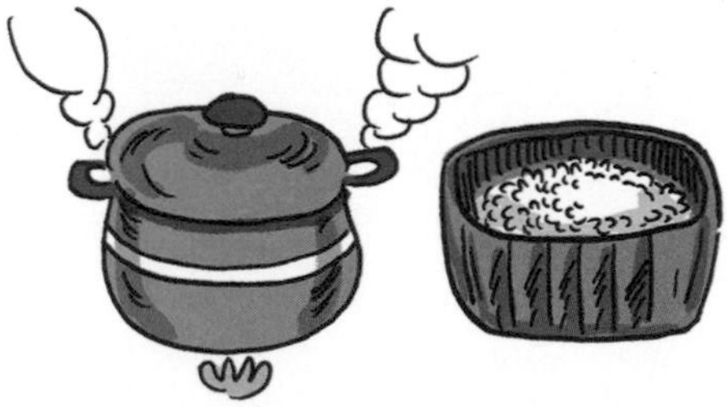

1. First prepare the Sushi Rice by following the instructions on pages 48 and 49.

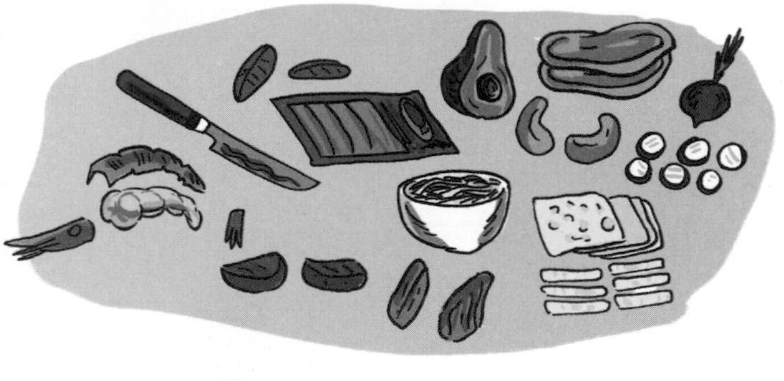

2. Select the ingredients you want to create interesting patterns on the sushi.

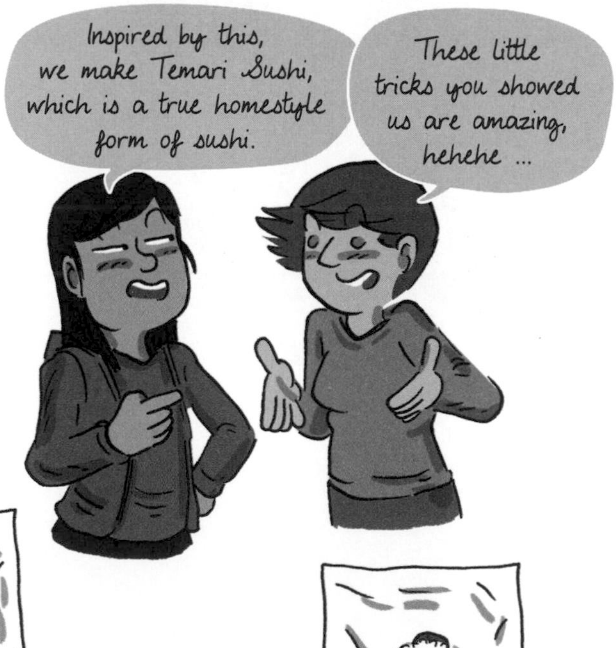
Inspired by this, we make Temari Sushi, which is a true homestyle form of sushi.
These little tricks you showed us are amazing, hehehe …

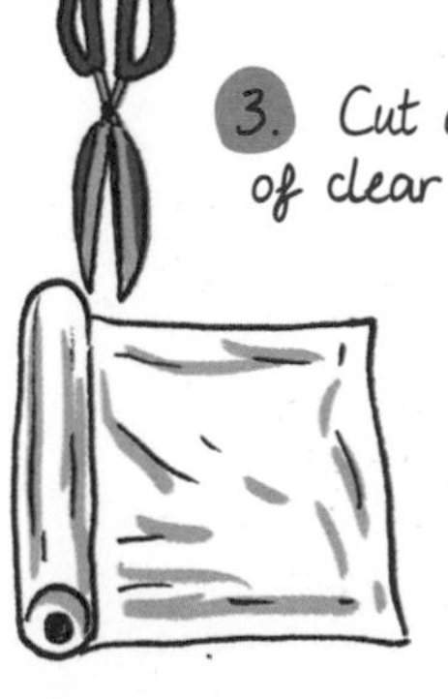

3. Cut a square piece of clear plastic wrap.

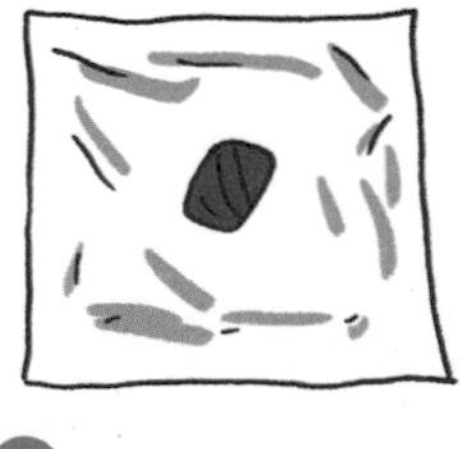

4. First, place the main ingredient in the middle of the plastic sheet. Here, we are using a piece of smoked salmon.

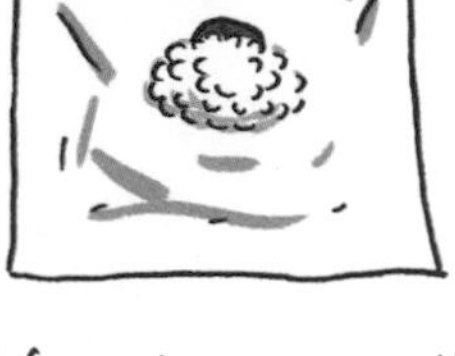

5. Now place a small scoop of rice on the salmon.

6. Pull the 4 corners of the plastic wrap up around the sushi to enclose it completely.

7. Turn it over and hold it with one hand. Use your other hand to twist the wrap tightly to create a perfectly round ball shape.

8. Remove the plastic from the ball and you'll have a perfect Temaki Sushi ball.

That's all there is to it! The important thing to remember is to place the toppings in reverse order from top to bottom.

The fun part of making temari is using scissors, tweezers and nori to create lots of different shapes and patterns!

For example:

2 strips of seaweed to make an X + omelette + cooked ham + rice on top. Here is what you get!

9. Here are some other interesting combinations you can try:

Seaweed dots + radish slices + cheese dots + rice

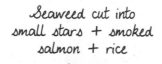

Seaweed cut into small stars + smoked salmon + rice

Cooked and peeled prawns cut in half + sliced cheese + rice

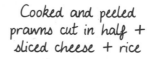

Seaweed strip + fresh tuna + avocado slice + omelette strips + rice

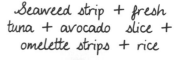

Chapter 4

VEGETABLES & TOFU

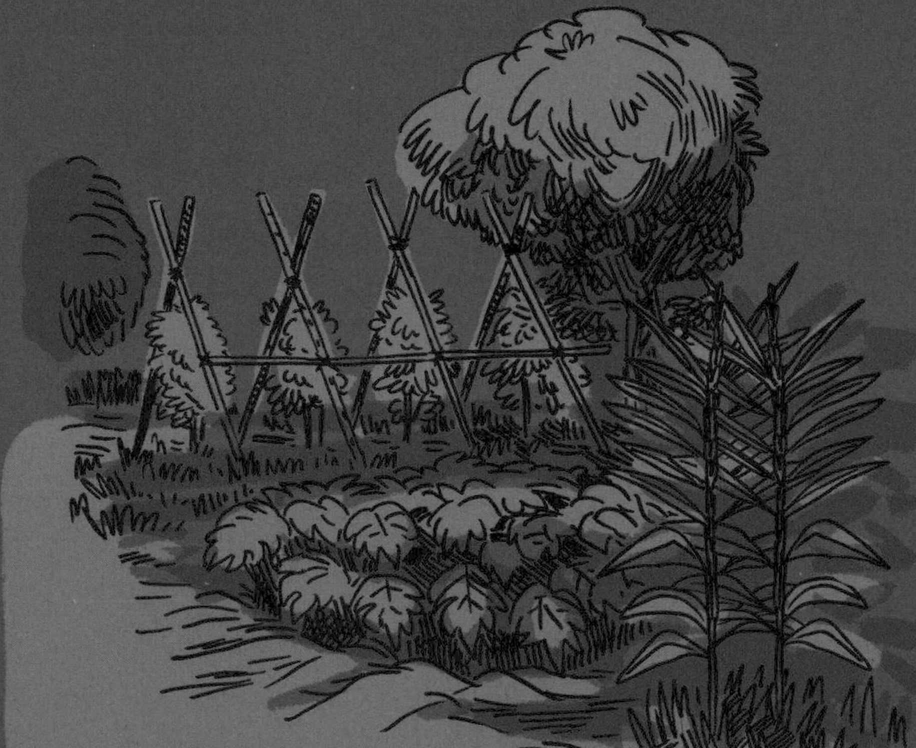

After a long day in the garden picking vegetables, we are inspired to prepare some delicious Japanese-style dishes using our freshly-picked veggies ... which you can also buy from your local farmers' market. Using fresh seasonal ingredients is one of the secrets of Japanese cuisine. Fresh vegetables add quality to your diet and they also make your recipes suuperr tastyyyy!!!! Moreover, they are better for your health. So, are you ready to head to your local farmers' market?

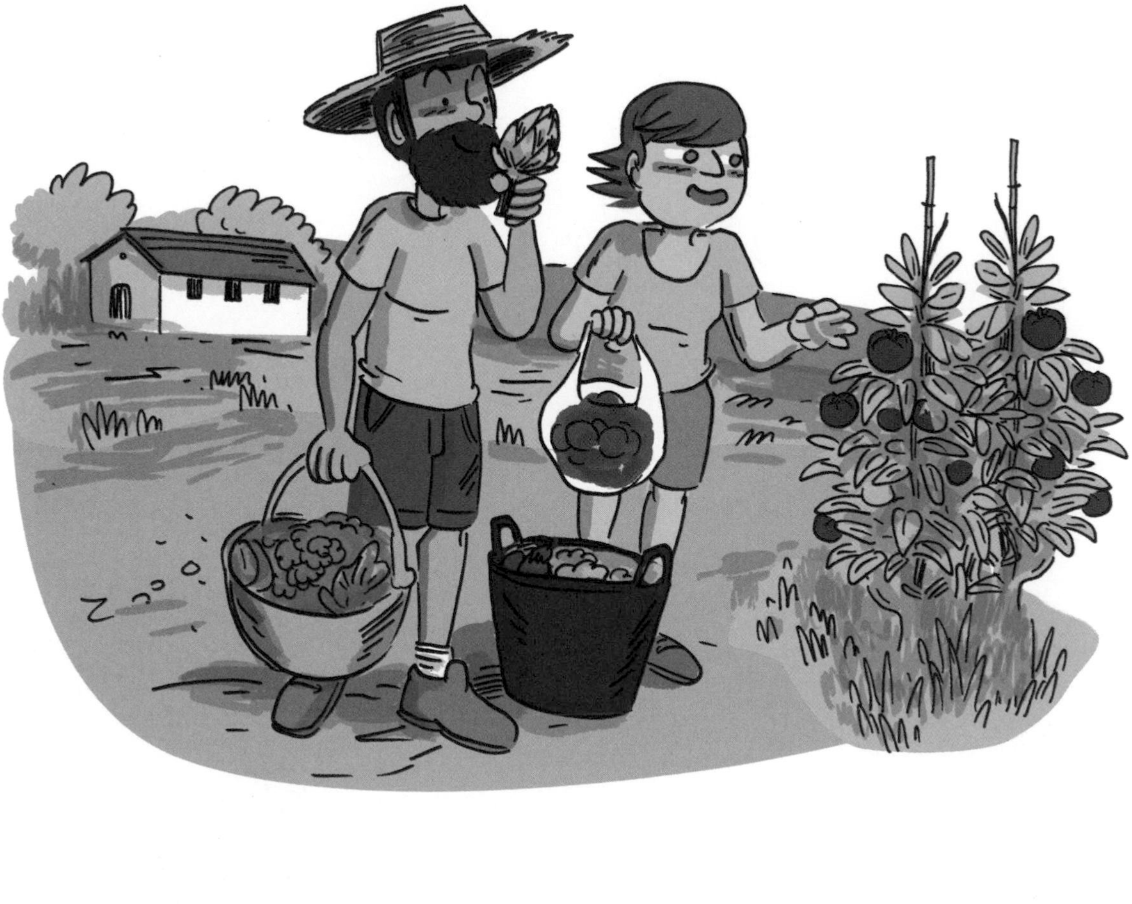

Baked Eggplant Slices with Miso Topping

These delicious and tender eggplant slices are topped with a salty and sweet miso topping called dengaku. It takes its name from the spring rice harvest celebration in Japan. This recipe is very easy to prepare and is perfect as an appetizer or when you have to cook for a lot of people, since you can prepare it in advance.

Serves 2-3
Time: 30 minutes

1 large eggplant
Olive oil, for brushing

Dengaku Sauce

½ cup (100 g) miso paste
2 tablespoons sugar
2 tablespoons mirin
2 tablespoons sake or white wine
1 tablespoon black or white sesame
   seeds, to sprinkle on top (optional)
Salt, to taste
Olive oil, to brush on the eggplant

If you prefer, you can use zucchini instead of eggplant. The secret is in the sauce! And it's so easy to make!

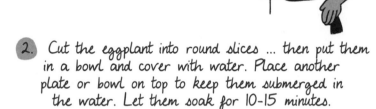

1. Preheat the oven to 360°F (180°C).

2. Cut the eggplant into round slices ... then put them in a bowl and cover with water. Place another plate or bowl on top to keep them submerged in the water. Let them soak for 10-15 minutes.

3. Make the Dengaku Sauce by adding the miso, sugar, mirin and sake or white wine to a saucepan and heating it over medium heat.

4. Stir all the ingredients well until it begins to boil and then remove it from the heat.

5. Remove the eggplant slices from the water and drain well. Make shallow cross hatch cuts on the top of each slice.

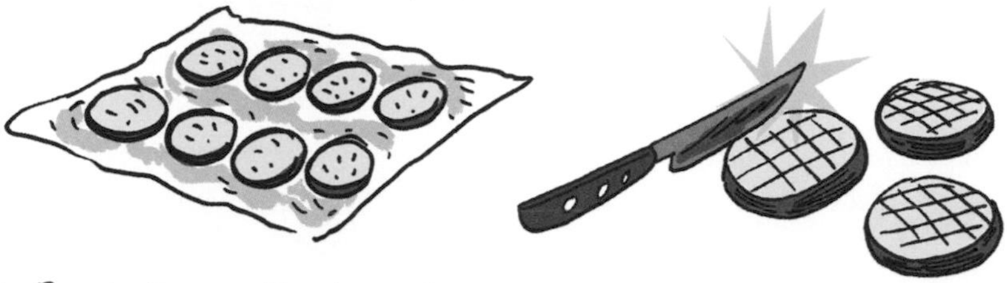

6. Sprinkle a little salt on top of each slice.

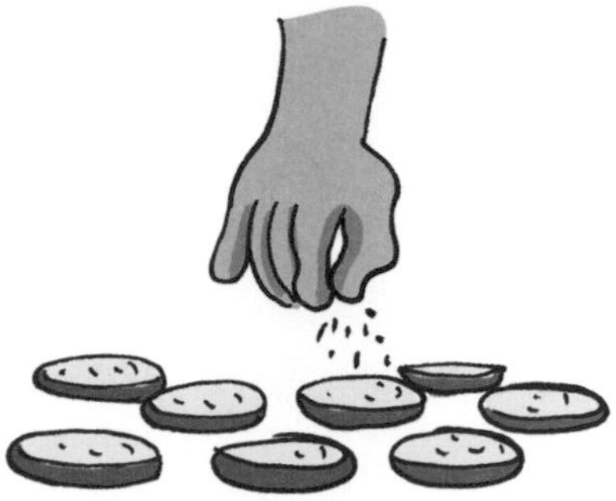

7. Brush them with olive oil and place them on a baking tray lined with baking paper or foil.

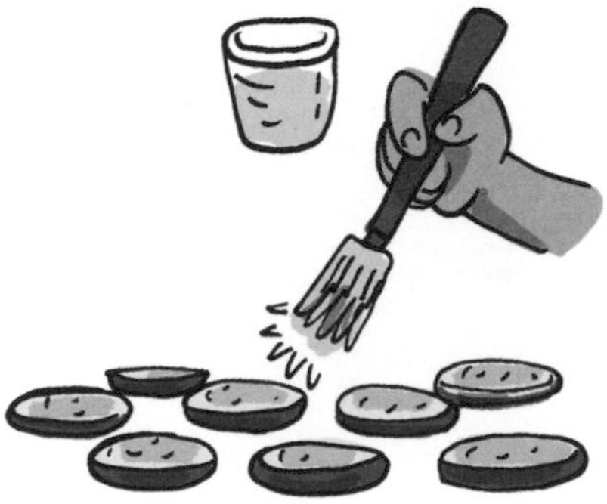

8. Bake in the oven at 360°F (180°C) for about 15 minutes until lightly browned.

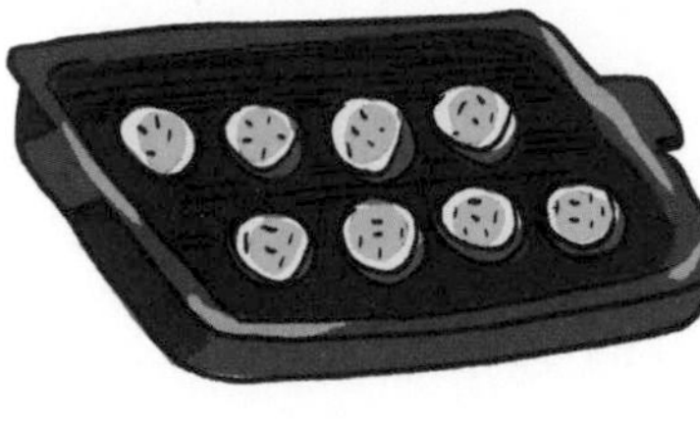

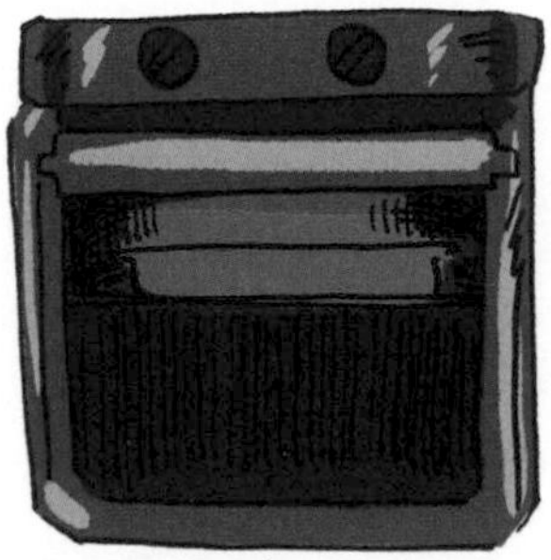

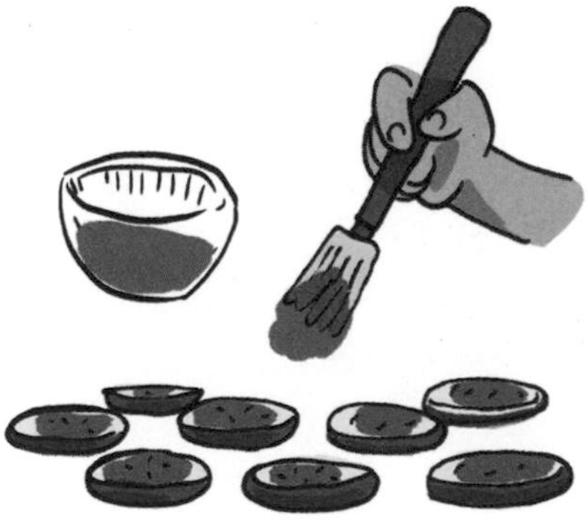

9. Take them out and spread the Dengaku Sauce over them (using a brush) then put them back into the oven to bake for another 5 minutes.

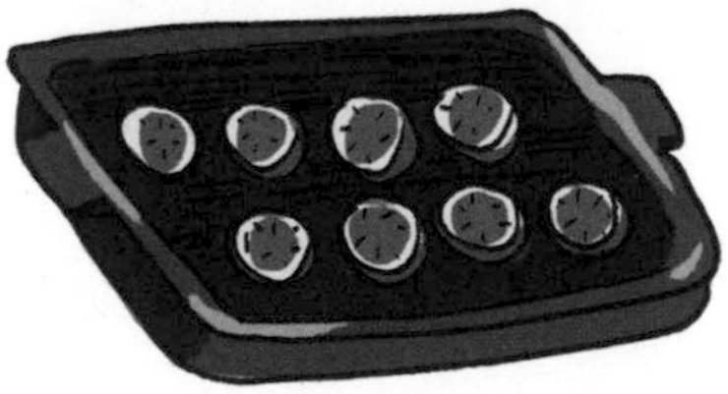

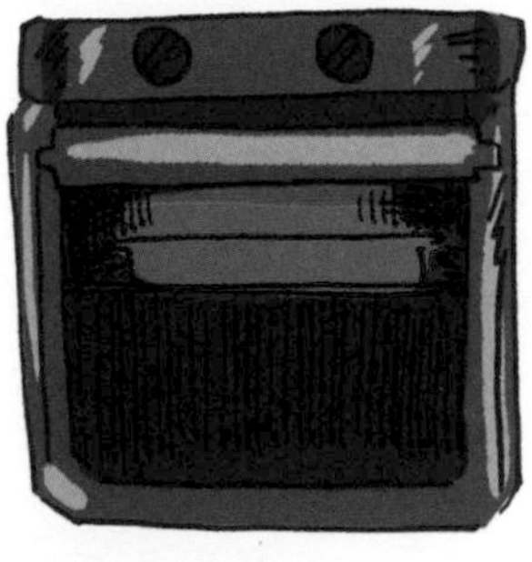

10. As a final touch, sprinkle some sesame seeds on top!

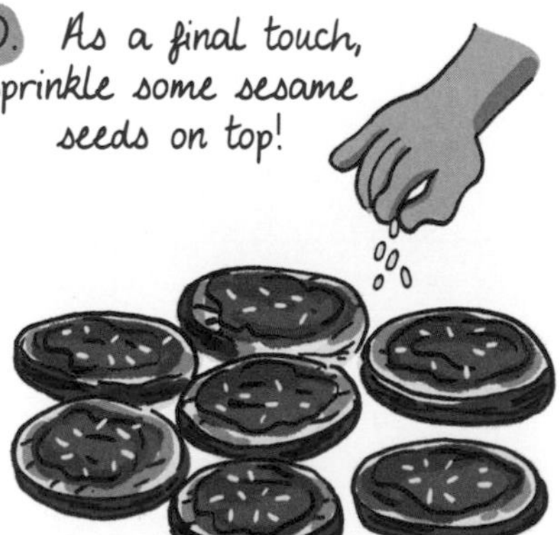

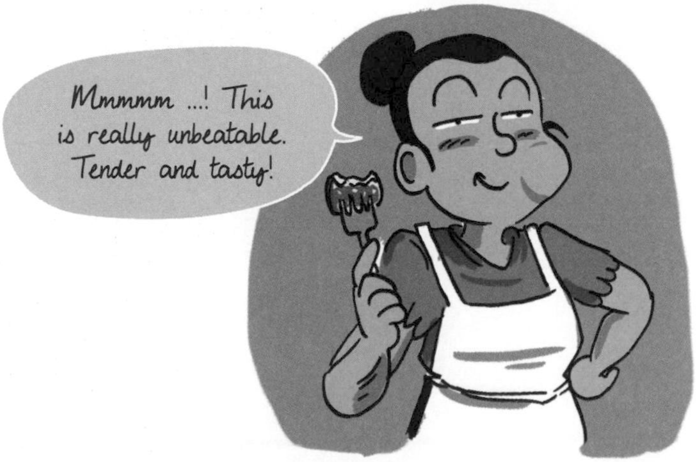
Mmmmm ...! This is really unbeatable. Tender and tasty!

Tofu & Smoked Salmon Quiche

Quiche is a classic French dish but it originated in Germany, in the medieval kingdom of Lothringen. The word "quiche" is from the German "Kuchen" which means cake. Quiche can be served for breakfast, lunch or as an appetizer for dinner. The Japanese bring a special touch to this open pie. This recipe calls for smoked salmon and spinach but you can also use ham or asparagus.

Serves 4
Time: 40 minutes

1½ packets silken tofu (around 1 lb (450 g)
1 packet of frozen or fresh puff pastry sheet dough (½ lb/250 g)
7 oz (200 g) smoked salmon
1 bunch spinach leaves, washed and stems removed
7 oz (200 g) button mushrooms
Oil, for frying
½ cup (150 g) grated parmesan cheese
2 tablespoons miso paste
¼ cup (60 ml) fresh cream
4 eggs

1. Preheat the oven to 400°F (200°C).

2. Press the tofu by putting it on a plate and placing a heavy plate or bowl on top of it and allowing all the water to drain off.

3. Spread a sheet of puff pastry dough onto a large baking dish.

4. Sliced the salmon, spinach, and mushrooms. Slice the tofu into small cubes. Put them all in a skillet with a bit of oil.

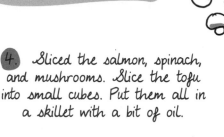

5. Fry for 5 minutes over medium heat until the spinach and mushrooms are soft and then pour the mixture on top of the pastry dough.

6. Add the grated cheese, miso, cream and eggs to a mixing bowl.

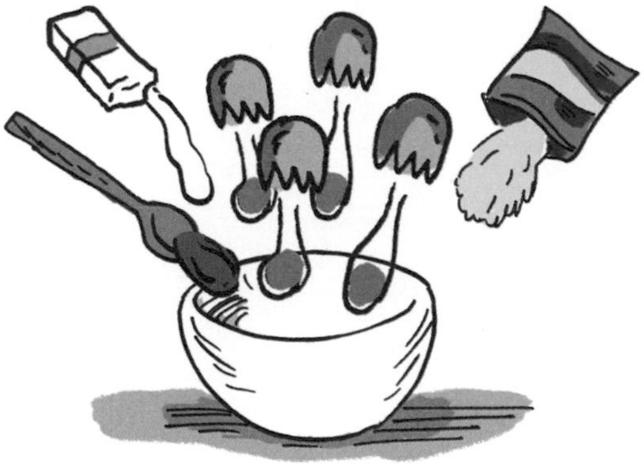

7. Combine them to form a smooth mixture.

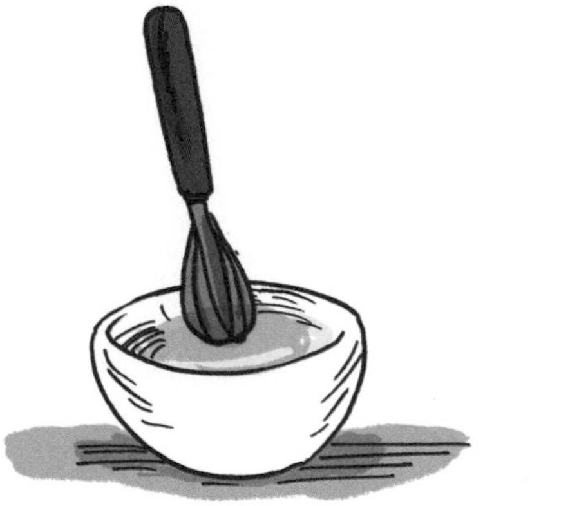

8. Pour the mixture over the other ingredients and spread it evenly.

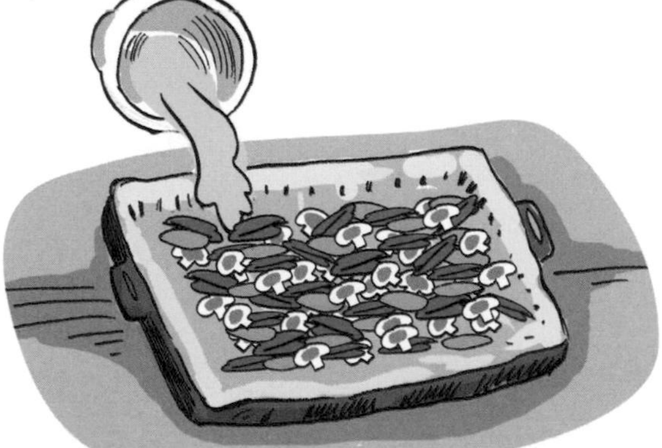

9. Bake at 400°F (200°C) for 20-30 minutes or until golden brown.

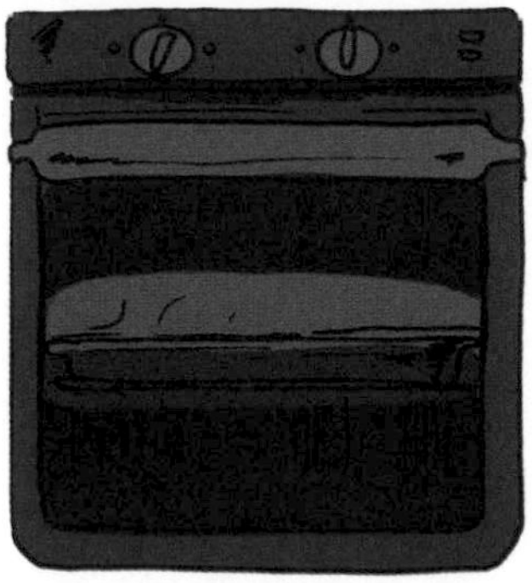

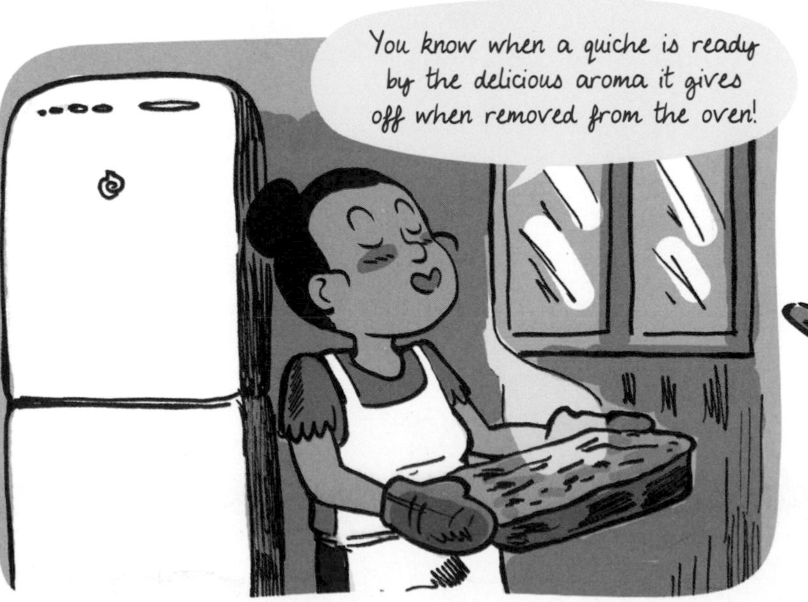
You know when a quiche is ready by the delicious aroma it gives off when removed from the oven!

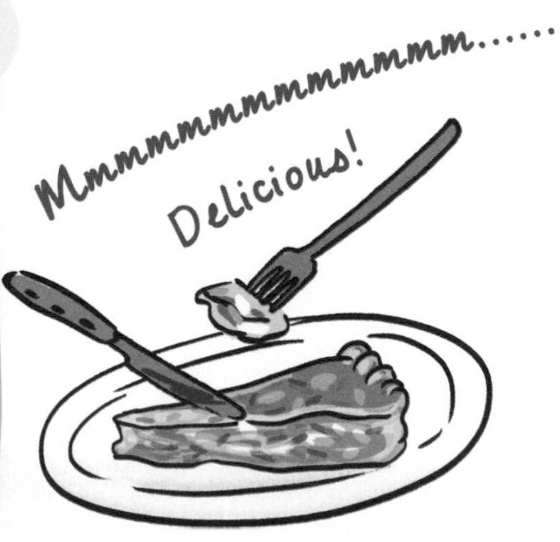
Mmmmmmmmmmmmmm......
Delicious!

Soy Braised Vegetables Kinpira Gobo

Kinpira Gobo is a dish of vegetables braised in a sweet soy gravy. The name Kinpira comes from a legendary muscleman, and it indicates how nutritious the dish is. Normally it is served as a sidedish along with grilled meats, rice and miso soup.

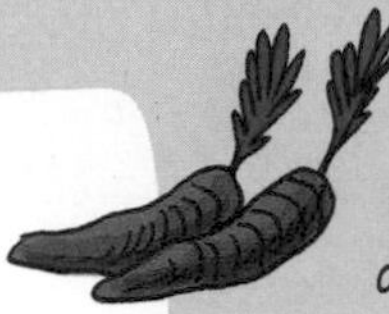

Serves 2
Time: 20 minutes

2 green peppers, deseeded
2 large carrots, peeled
1 tablespoon sesame oil
1 small red pepper (optional)
Salt, to taste
1 cup (250 ml) water
2 tablespoons soy sauce
1 tablespoon mirin
1 tablespoon white sesame seeds

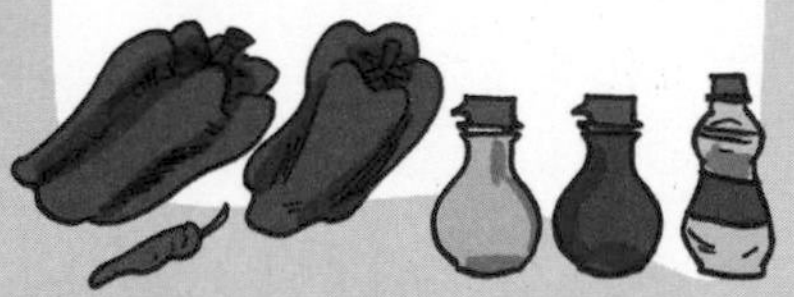

1. Cut the green peppers and carrots into even strips.

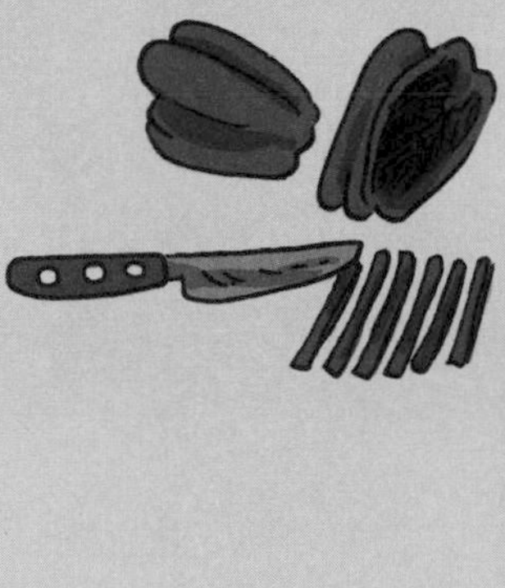

2. Place the sesame oil and the red pepper in a pot over medium heat.

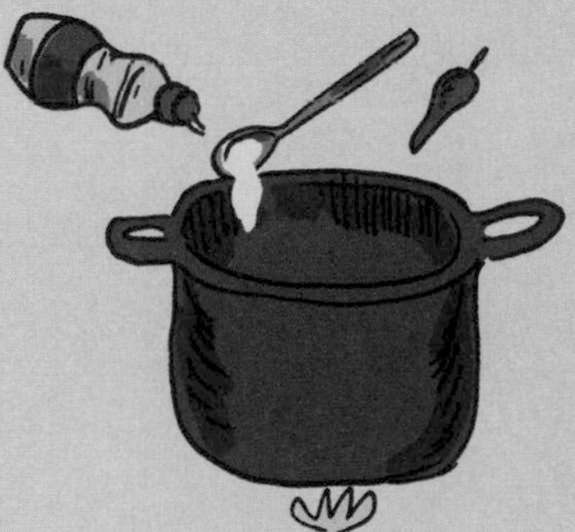

3. When the oil is hot, add the vegetables ...

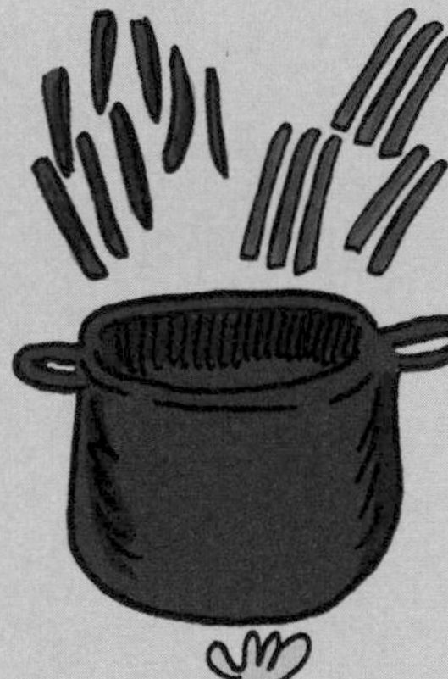

Add a pinch of salt and stir.

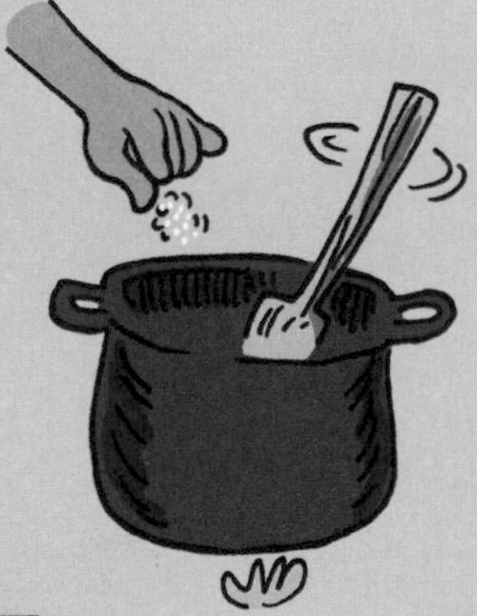

4. Stir-fry the vegetables for about 5 minutes then add the water.

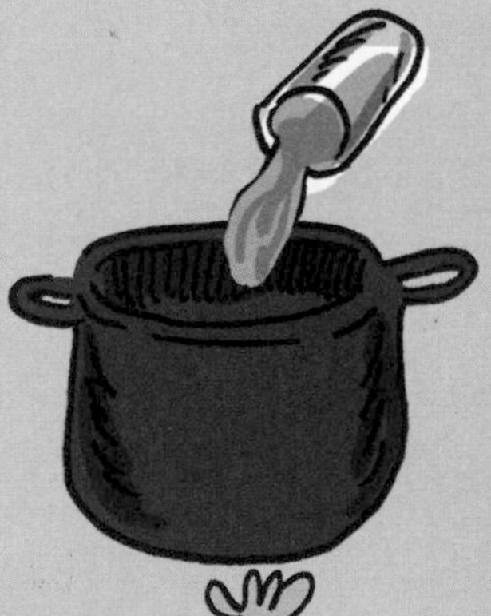

5. Let the vegetables simmer around 10 minutes with the pot covered.

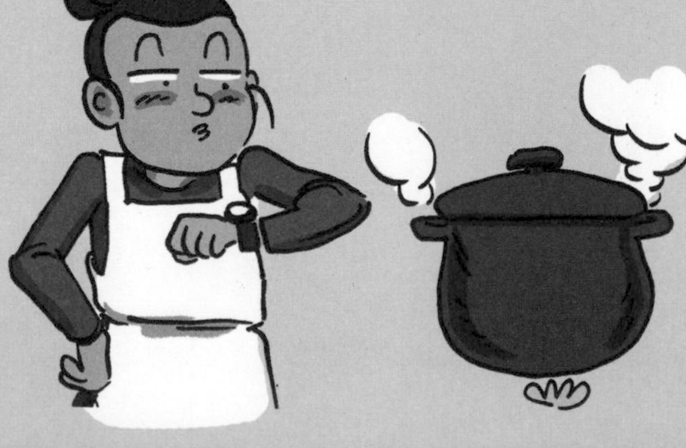

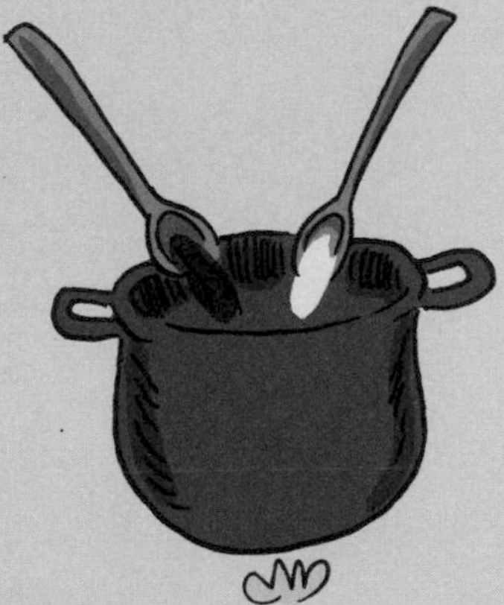

6. When the vegetables are cooked, add the soy sauce and mirin.

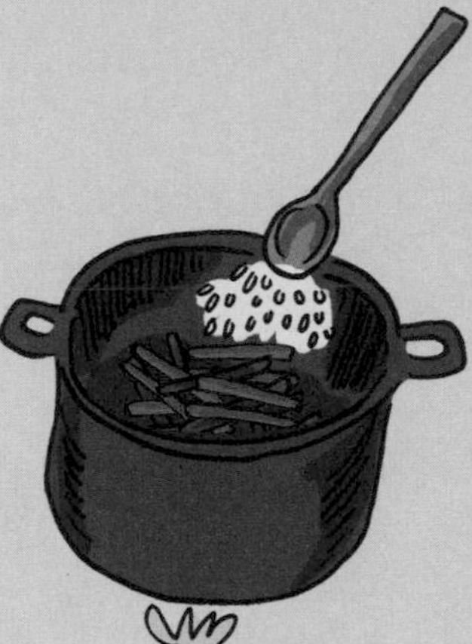

7. Now add a tablespoon of white sesame seeds ... and stir well!

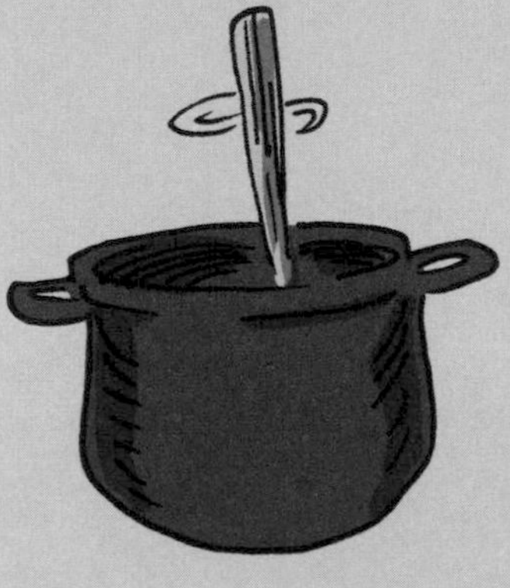

Ready to serve! This vegetable sidedish is perfect with either meat or fish or on its own with rice.

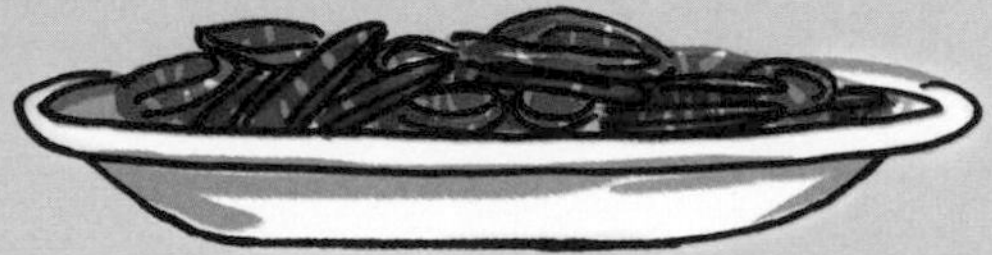

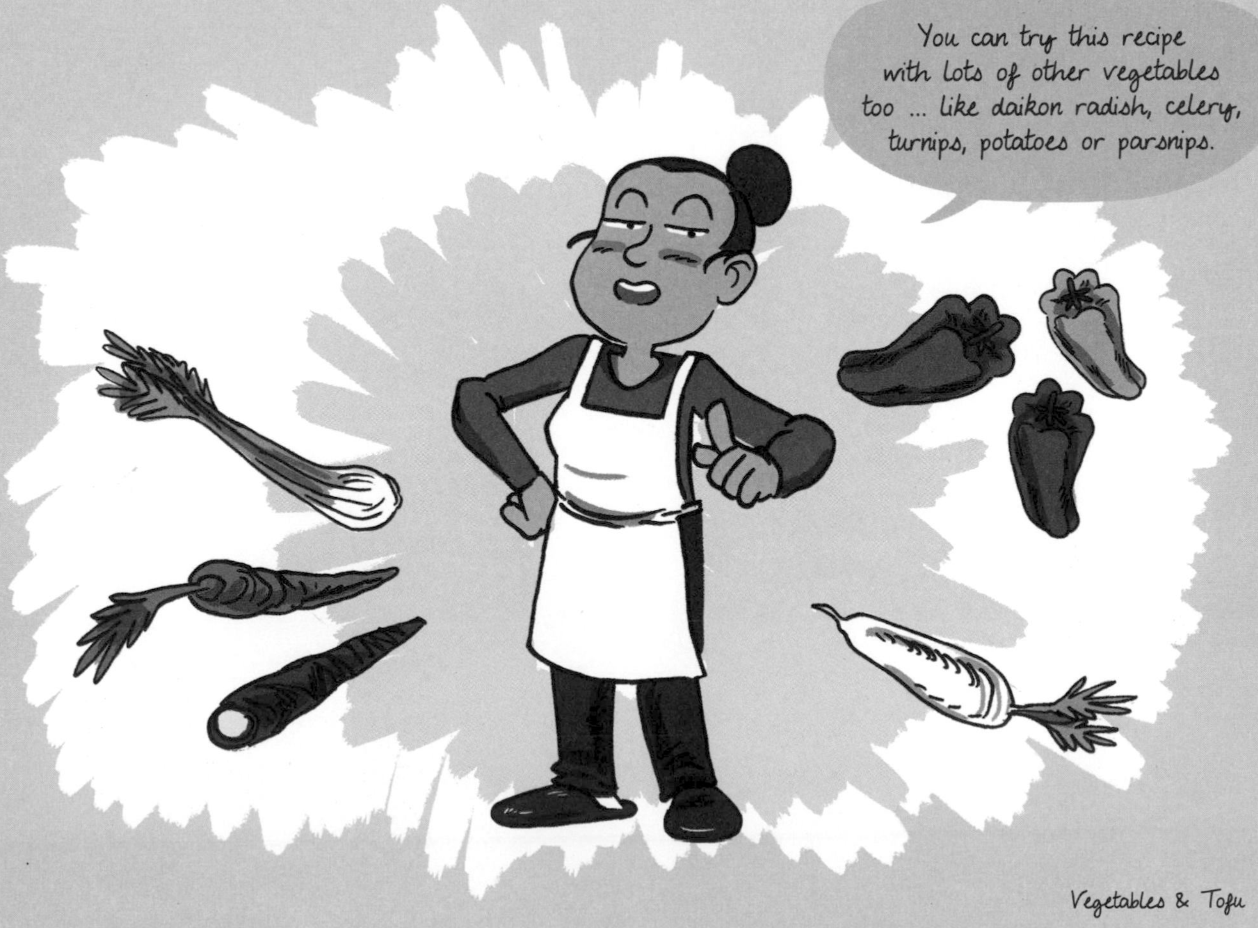
You can try this recipe with lots of other vegetables too ... like daikon radish, celery, turnips, potatoes or parsnips.

Tofu Mayonnaise

Mayonnaise is an ancient Mediterranean olive oil sauce with egg. It originated in the town of Maho, in the Balearic Islands. We make a Japanese version that is much healthier by changing the eggs and oil to tofu which may sound odd but it has a similar appearance, taste and texture to real mayo!

Makes 1½ cups (350 g)
Time: 40 minutes

1 packet silken tofu (around 12 oz/ 340g)
1 tablespoon mirin
Juice of 1 lemon
Salt, to taste

1. Drain the tofu by setting it on a plate under a tupperware full of water to press the water out.

Come on, cut it out! You will NEVER get me to like tofu.

2. Put the tofu, the mirin and lemon juice in a beater cup (or you can use a blender or food processor).

3. Give it some beater love and add salt to taste.

4. Recycle an empty mayo jar and fill it with your tofu version. Don't tell anyone!

5. Let it chillax for at least 30 minutes in the fridge. It will get smooth as silk.

There's no way you can make me change my mind....

Burgers with tofu mayo aren't a bad idea, huh?
Right! Universal smoothness!

Japanese Potato Croquettes

Potato croquettes are very popular in Japan where they are widely sold in supermarkets and butcher shops, as well as in specialty korokke shops. These are made with potatoes and a few other ingredients that are mixed together then fried. They are normally served with Steak Sauce or tomato ketchup. Deliciousss!!!

Serves 2-4 (8 croquettes)
Time: 45 minutes

4 potatoes (1¼ lbs/600 g)
1 small carrot
1 small onion
½ cup (75 g) fresh or frozen peas
4 tablespoons grated cheese
Salt and pepper, to taste
Sunflower oil, for frying
1 cup (150 g) flour
2 eggs, beaten
3 cups (300 g) panko breadcrumbs
Steak Sauce or ketchup, to serve

1. Boil the potatoes in a pot for about 20 minutes until cooked.

2. Drain and let them cool a bit, then remove the skins.

3. Mash the potatoes in a bowl with a fork.

4. Chop the carrot and onion into small pieces and fry them with a bit of oil for 15 minutes until browned.

5. Pour the fried mixture over the mashed potatoes.

6. Blanch the peas and add them to the bowl along with the grated cheese. Add salt and pepper to taste.

7. Mix all the ingredients to form a smooth consistency.

 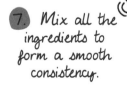

8. Once the mixture has cooled, take a handful and shape it into a patty. Continue until all of the mixture is formed into patties.

9. Dredge each croquette in the flour, beaten egg and breadcrumbs.

10. Fry the croquettes a few at a time in a pot with 2 in (5 cm) of sunflower oil for about 2-3 minutes on each side until golden brown. Once done, leave them on paper towels to drain the oil!

Big, crispy croquettes accompanied by a fresh salad and Steak Sauce or ketchup.

Sauteed Daikon Slices

Daikon is a star veggie in Japanese cuisine. It can be eaten raw in salads or cooked in soups and meat stews. It tastes a little bit spicy and is also ideal for grilling as a simple appetizer or sidedish to accompany other dishes.

Serves 2
Time: 20 minutes

1½ lbs (650 g) fresh daikon
(2 or 3 depending on size)
2 cloves garlic, crushed
4 tablespoons soy sauce
4 tablespoons mirin
1 teaspoon wasabi paste
Butter, to fry

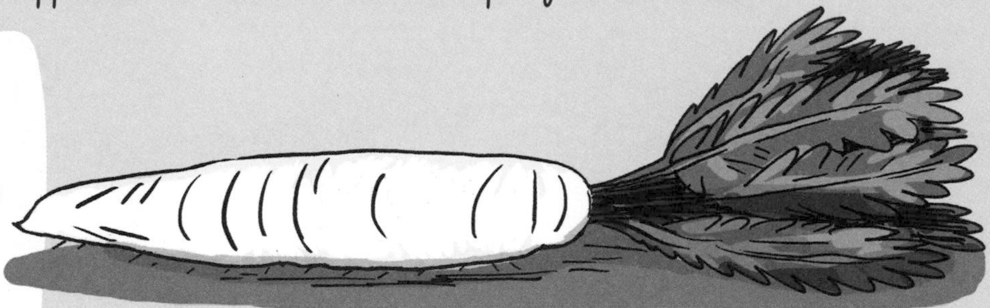

1. Peel the daikon and slice them into thick rounds. Place in a pot, cover with water and boil them for 10 minutes. Then drain them on paper towels.

2. Add the crushed garlic, soy sauce, mirin and wasabi paste to a bowl and mix well.

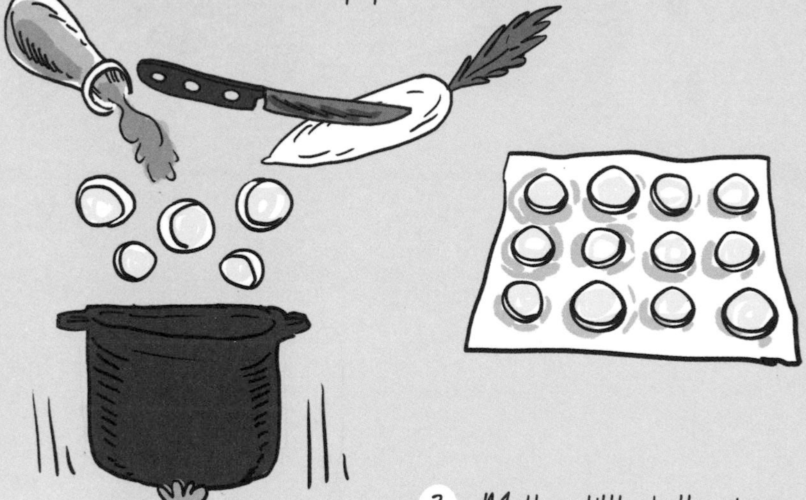

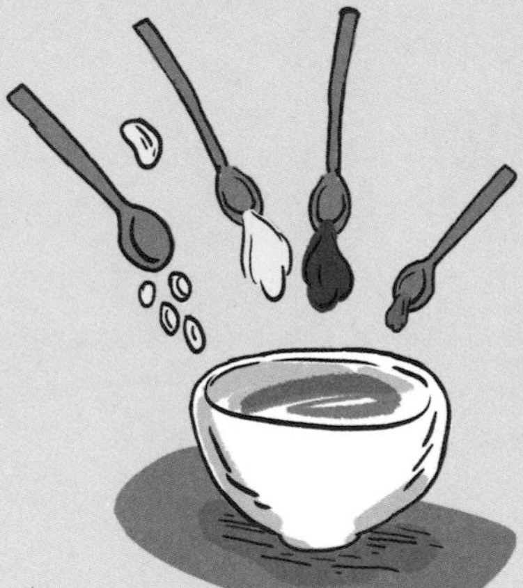

3. Melt a little butter in a large skillet.

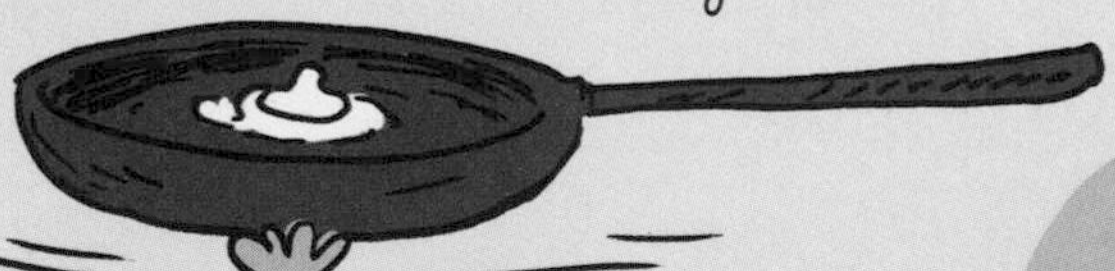

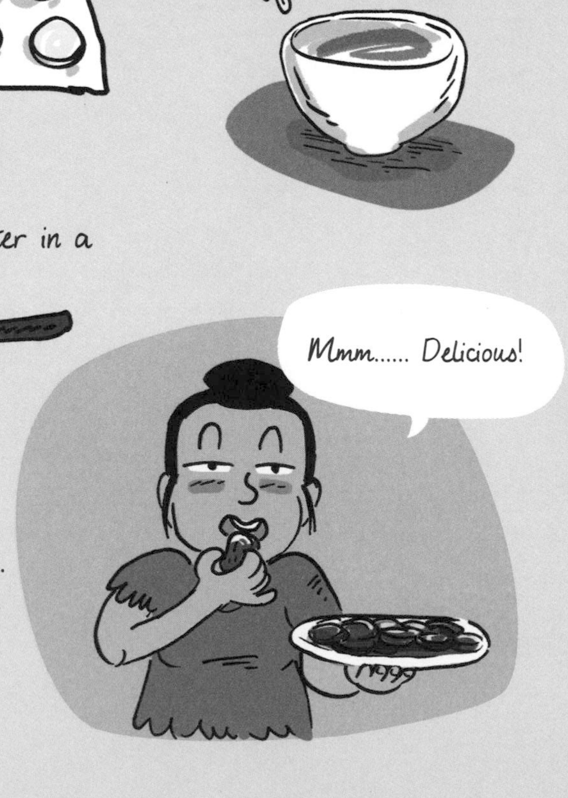
Mmm...... Delicious!

4. Sauté the daikon slices and add the sauce. Cook until reduced, about 7 minutes.

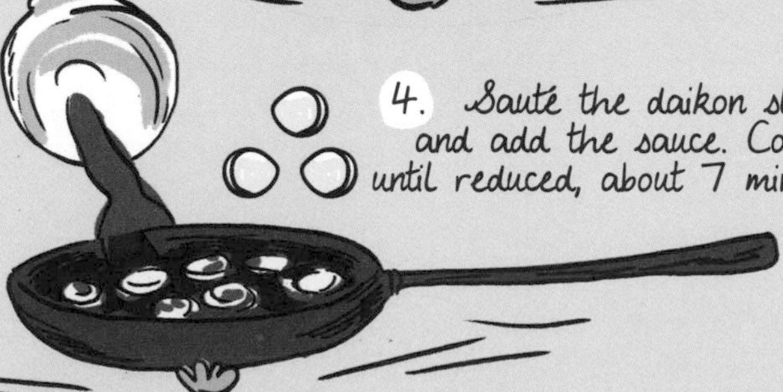

Professor Maiko's Japanese History Lecture

Hello, dear friends! I wanted to pause for a minute between recipes to share some history with you; something that is key to understanding the peculiarities of Japanese cuisine!

For centuries, traditional Japanese cuisine evolved mainly thanks to Korean and Chinese influences. But in the 16th century, European missionaries and traders brought new ingredients (potatoes, tomatoes...) and new techniques, such as deep-frying.

In the mid 19th century, the Meiji Revolution set off the beginning of the Modern Age, during which the country became totally open to European influences. This meant that new ingredients, new recipes and new habits blended with the older traditional ones.

Every dish, no matter how simple it looks to us, has an interesting story. Something as common as an egg omelette represented a big change for Japanese cuisine.

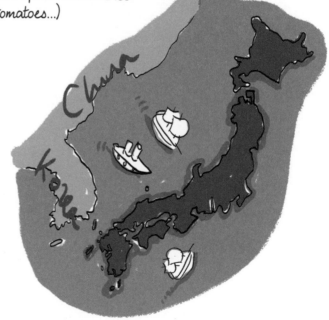

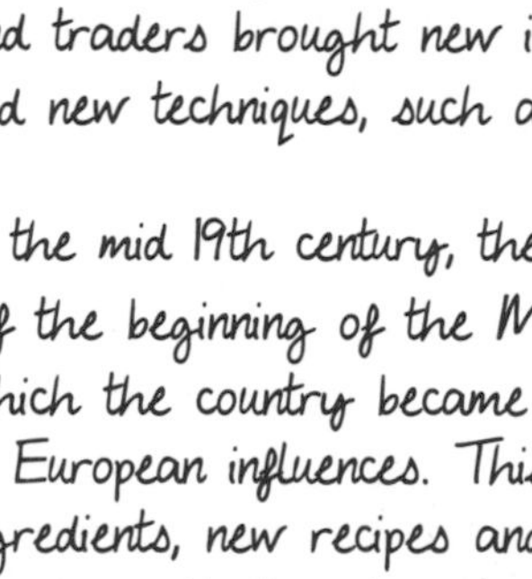

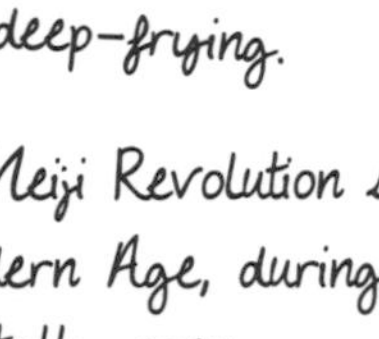

At Gourmand Gohan we aim to present Japanese food in its broadest context, showing you all the countless variations from traditional to contemporary.
We also highlight the importance that learning is key, and trying new ideas and flavors to discover something amazing that you never knew about before!

Chapter 5

MEAT & CHICKEN

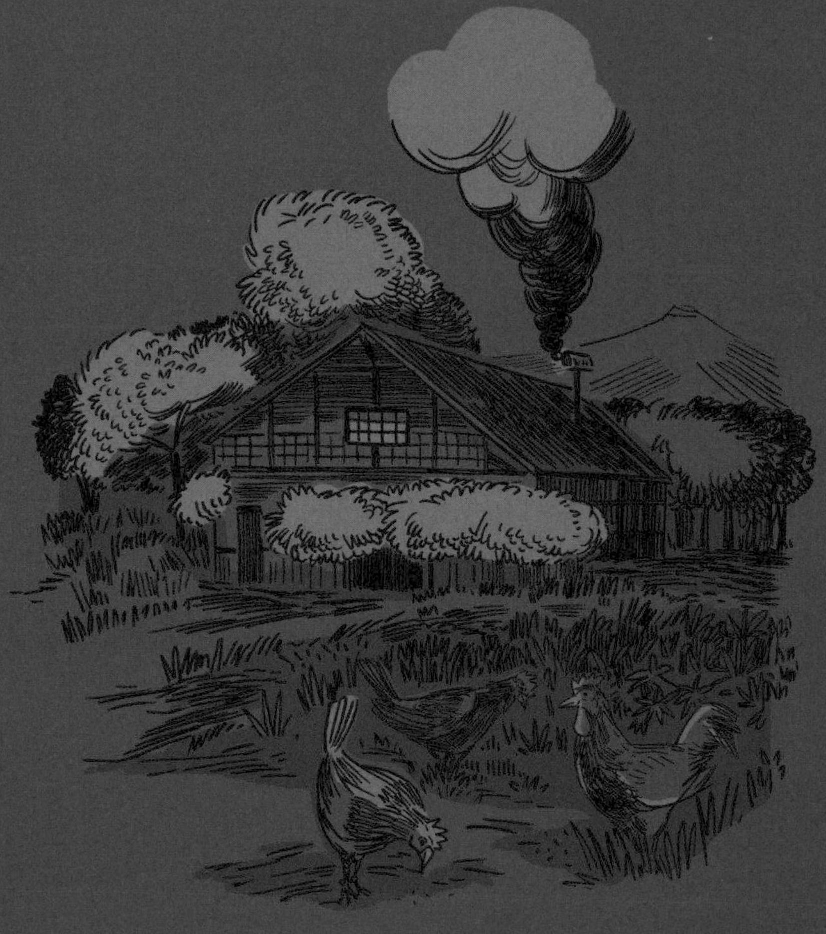

There are lots of tasty homestyle recipes to show you in this chapter!
Meat and poultry dishes from Japan are not very well known,
but they are really, really good ... especially the chicken and
pork recipes. Roasted, fried, battered, marinated, or in a rich broth ...
these dishes are perfect for cold winter days.
Take your time and make these dishes with love,
and you will agree 100%!

Japanese Fried Chicken Nuggets Tori Karaage

Chef Maiko has shown you many different recipes... Japanese classics and new creations of her own ... but now she's gonna show you how to cook an old family recipe. Traditions must be carried on! These are the famous Japanese chicken nuggets ... perfect paired with beer or with rice. The key is to marinate the chicken in a characteristic Japanese sauce before frying them. Easy and tasty!

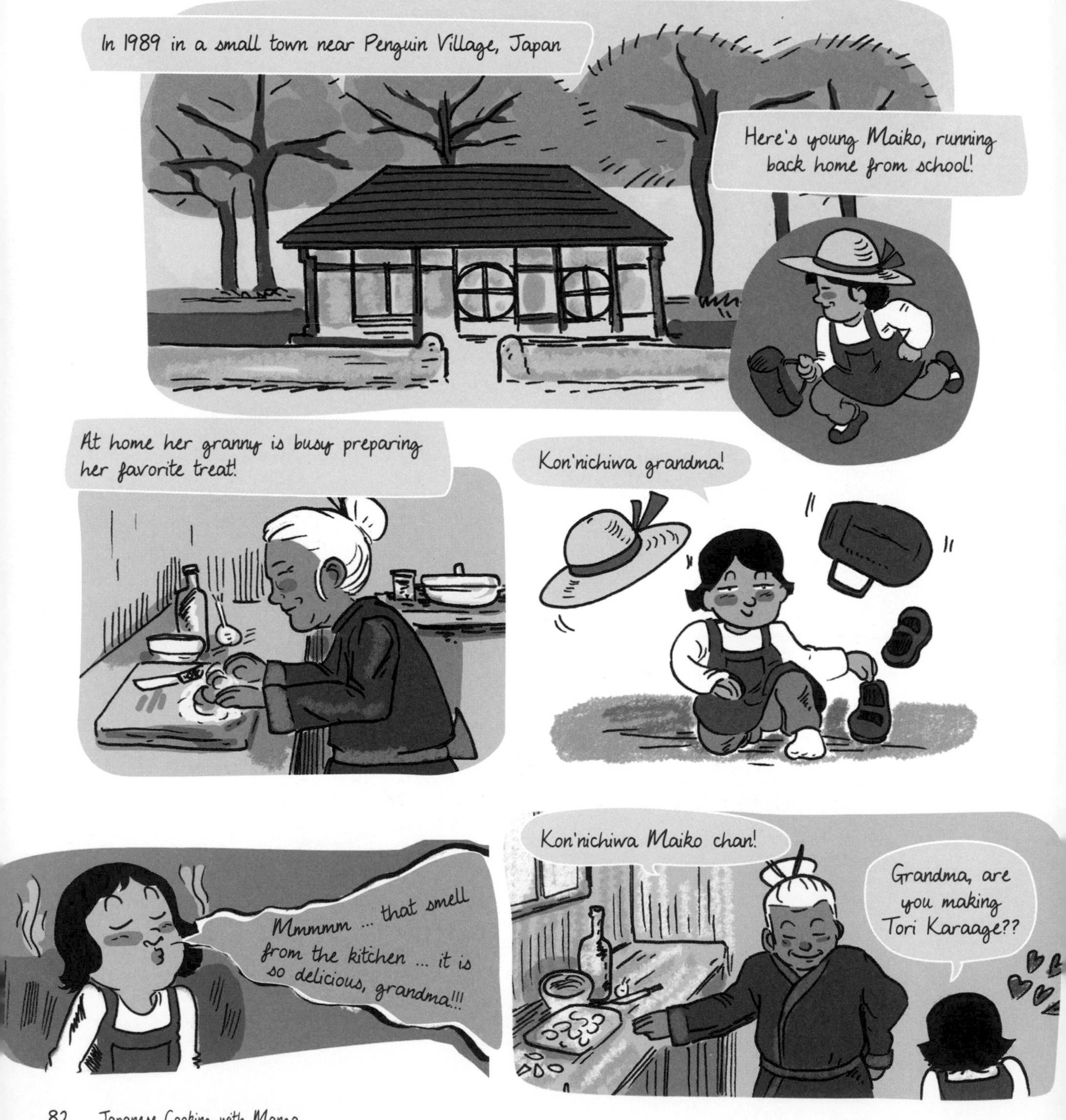

In 1989 in a small town near Penguin Village, Japan
Here's young Maiko, running back home from school!
At home her granny is busy preparing her favorite treat!
Kon'nichiwa grandma!
Mmmmm ... that smell from the kitchen ... it is so delicious, grandma!!!
Kon'nichiwa Maiko chan!
Grandma, are you making Tori Karaage??

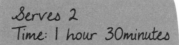

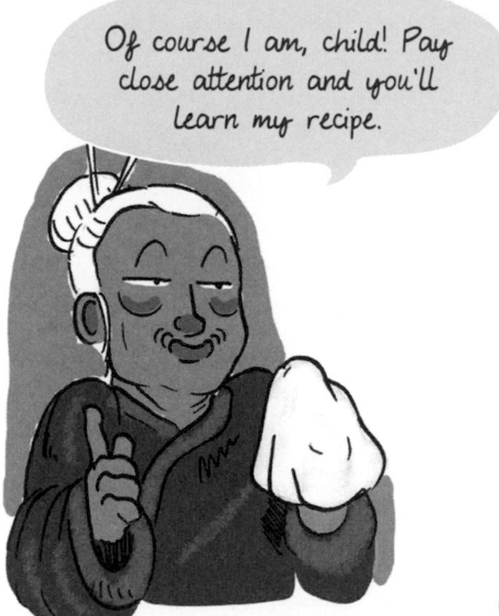
Of course I am, child! Pay close attention and you'll learn my recipe.

Serves 2
Time: 1 hour 30minutes

4 chicken thighs
½ cup (125 ml) soy sauce
½ cup (125 ml) sake or white wine
2 cloves garlic, sliced
1 tablespoon freshly grated ginger
1 small onion, chopped
Salt, to taste
Flour, to coat the chicken
Sunflower oil, to fry

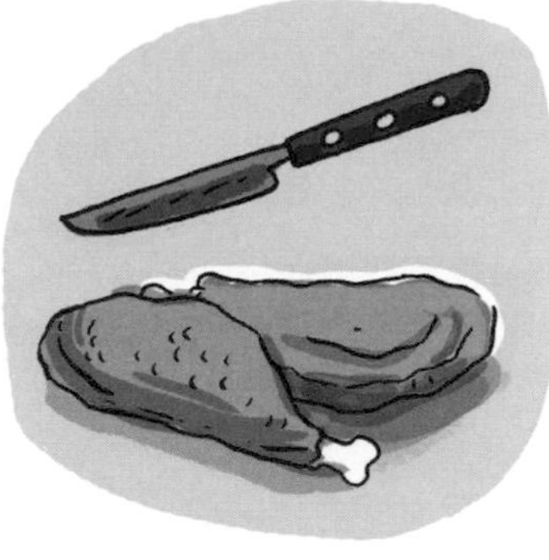

1. Debone the chicken thighs and cut the meat into small, bite-sized chunks.

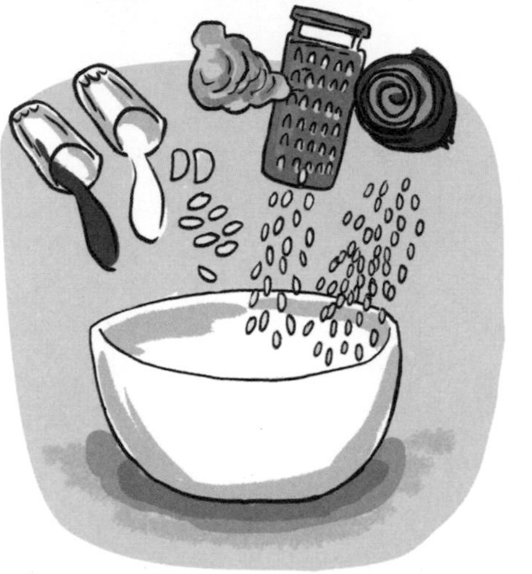

2. Combine the soy sauce, sake, sliced garlic, ginger, onion and salt in a large mxing bowl.

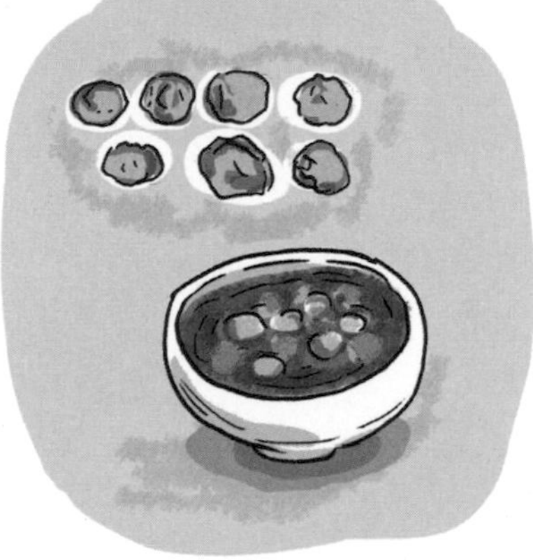

3. Marinate the chicken pieces in the mixture for an hour.

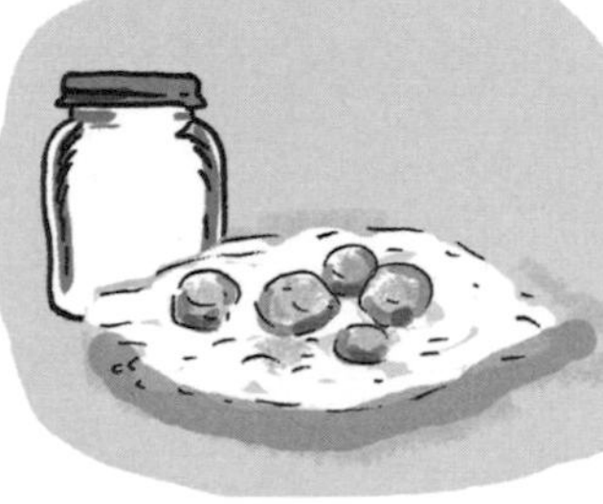

4. Coat the chicken pieces in the flour ...

5. And finally fry them in a deep skillet with about 1½ in (4 cm) of oil for 3-5 minutes (until they turn golden brown).

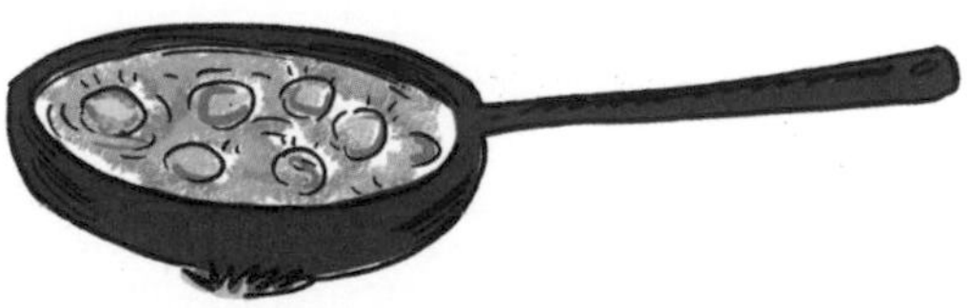

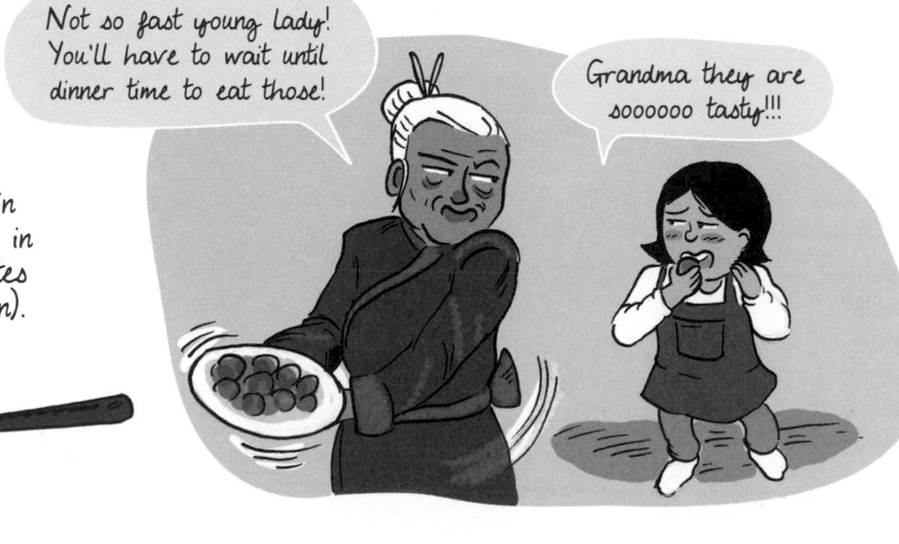
Not so fast young lady! You'll have to wait until dinner time to eat those!
Grandma they are soooooo tasty!!!

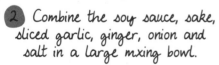

Chicken & Tofu Burgers

Tofu is a basic and versatile ingredient in Japanese cooking. It can be eaten raw with grated ginger and soy sauce or cooked with meat, eggs, vegetables or a sauce. The delicate taste and soft texture can add new dimensions to your dishes. This recipe shows you how to create a very special burger that is healthier than a regular burger!

Moshi moshi?

Maiko, my roommate says he will join us for dinner but let me warn you he's not the kind of person who likes to try new things.

Serves 3-4
Time: 30 minutes

1 packet firm tofu (around 12 oz/ 340g)
2 scallions (spring onions)
1 lb (450 g) ground chicken
3 eggs
3 tablespoons panko breadcrumbs
2 tablespoons miso paste
3 tablespoons ketchup
Oil, for frying

I brought some burgers!

See? I told you Maiko would cook something that you would like.

1. Put the tofu on a plate and place a tupperware full of water on top of it to press out the water. Allow it to drain until all the water is pressed out (around 15 minutes).

2. Thinly slice the green part of the scallions, soak it in water for about 10 minutes and drain well.

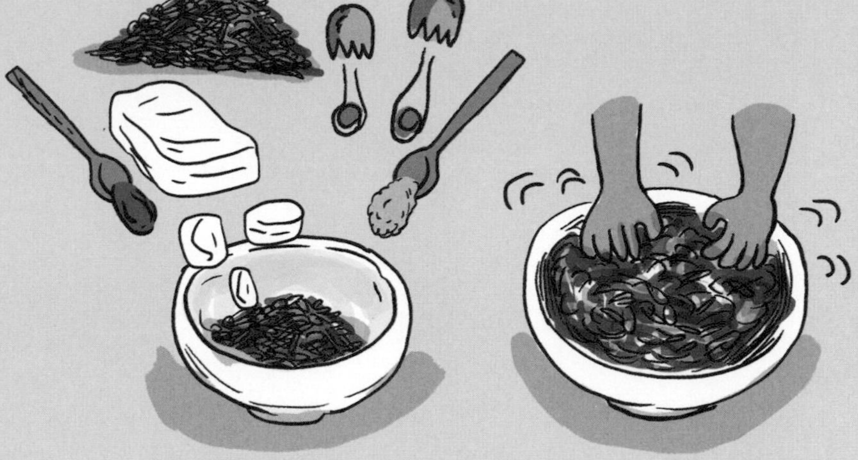

3. Put the ground chicken in a large mixing bowl. Add the tofu, scallion, eggs, breadcrumb, miso and ketchup and mix well using your hands.

4. Grab a handful of the mixture and shape it into a ball.

5. Then flatten it.

6. Shape it into a burger patty or any other shape … use your imagination!

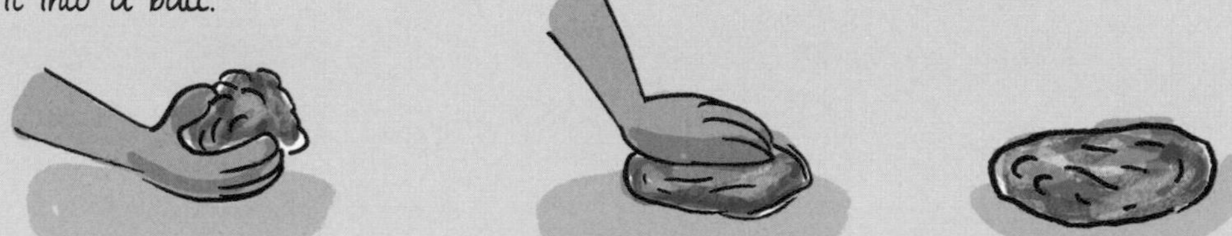

7. Repeat until all the mixture is used.

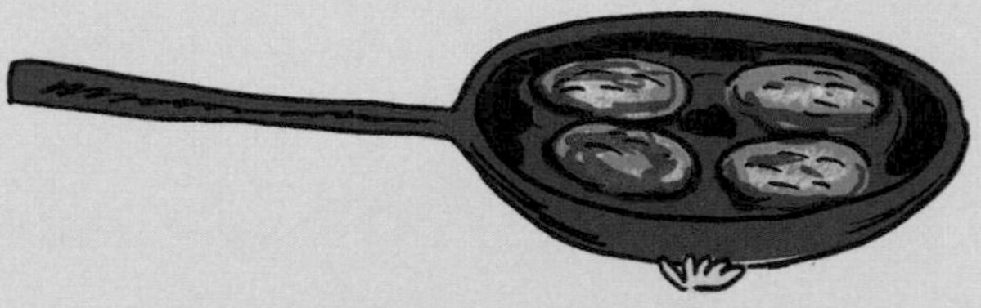

8. Fry the patties in a skillet with a little oil for 5-10 minutes until lightly browned on both sides … and

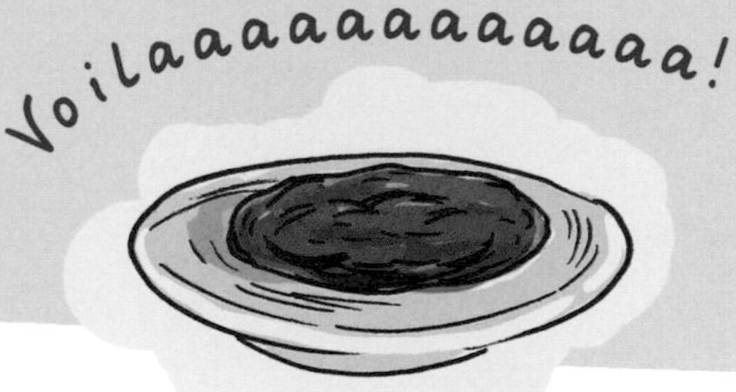
Voilaaaaaaaaaaaa!

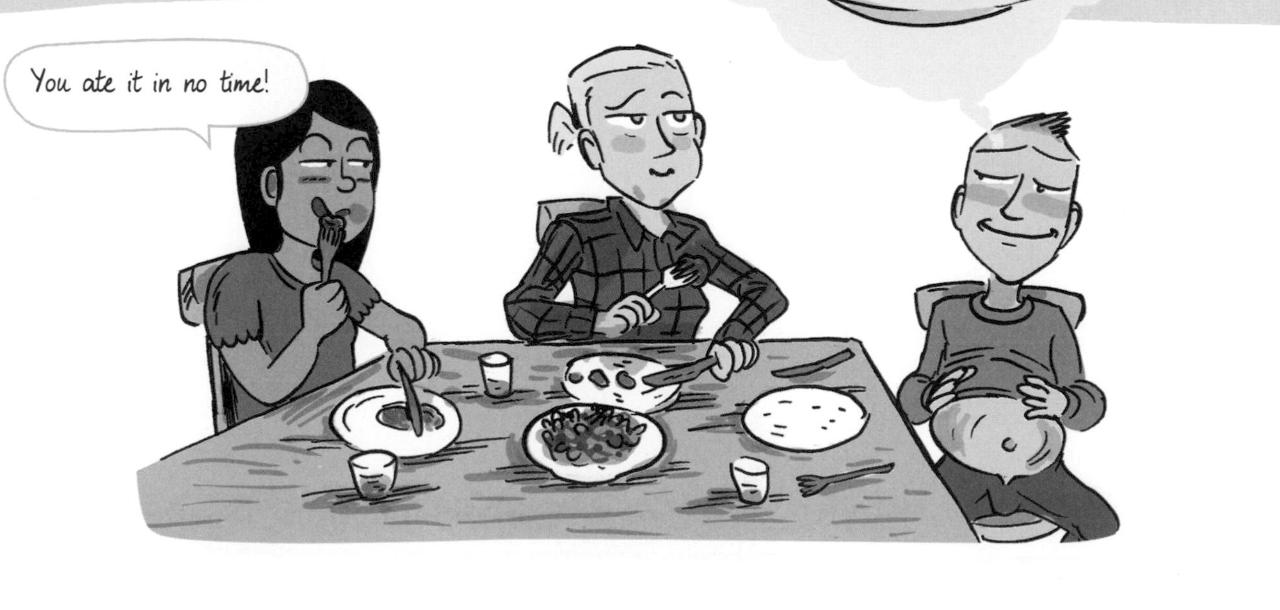
You ate it in no time!

Fragrant Pork Loin with Miso

Pork loin appears in many Japanese recipes. This preparation is very simple; the key is to give the dish a special aroma. In this case we'll add some tea leaves instead of herbs to create a unique flavor.

Serves 4-6
Time: 50 minutes

2 lbs (900 g) pork loin
Salt and pepper, to taste
2 baby leeks (green bits only), sliced
2 cloves garlic
2 cups (500 ml) water
1 teaspoon unflavored black tea leaves (jasmine or oolong)
Oil, for frying

Sauce
2 tablespoons miso paste
2 tablespoons mirin
2 tablespoons sake or white wine

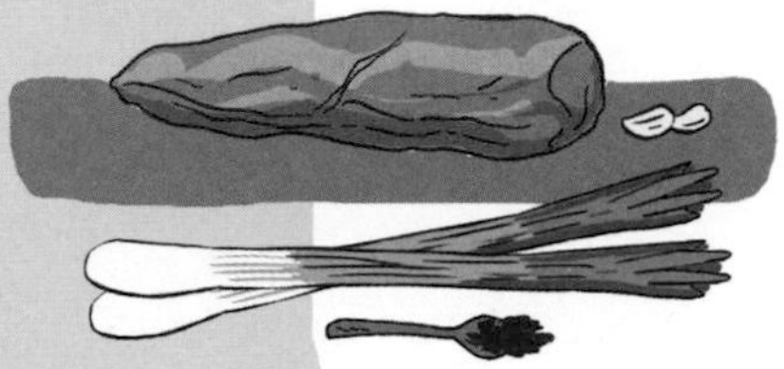

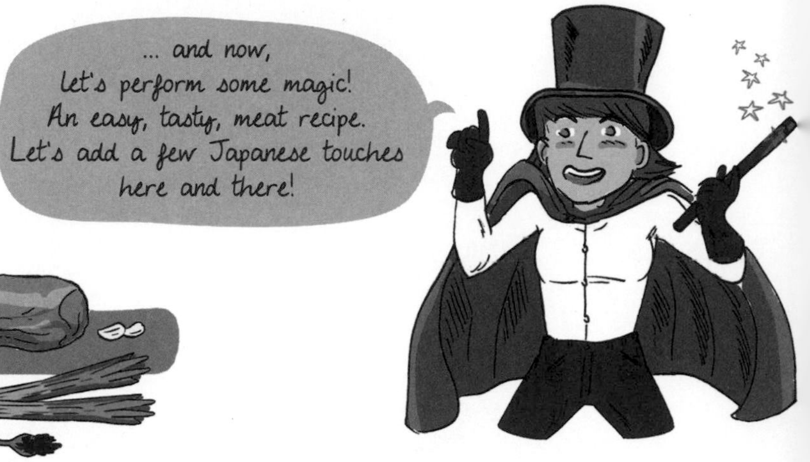
... and now, let's perform some magic! An easy, tasty, meat recipe. Let's add a few Japanese touches here and there!

1. Season the meat with a little salt and pepper then cut it into 2 big pieces.

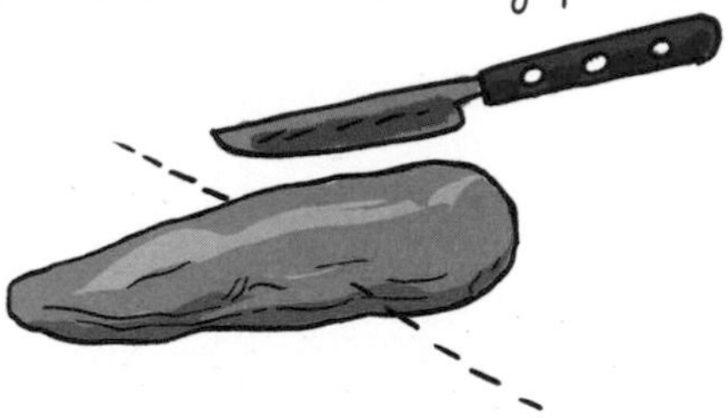

2. Add a little oil to a frying pan and brown the pork for a few seconds on each side over high heat to seal in the flavor.

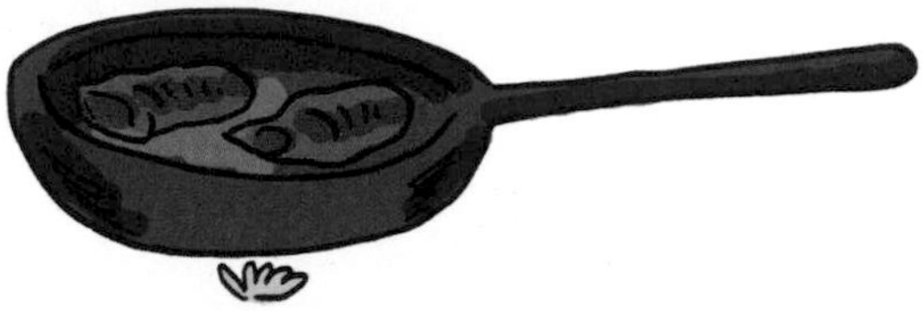

3. Place the meat, sliced leeks and garlic cloves in a pot.

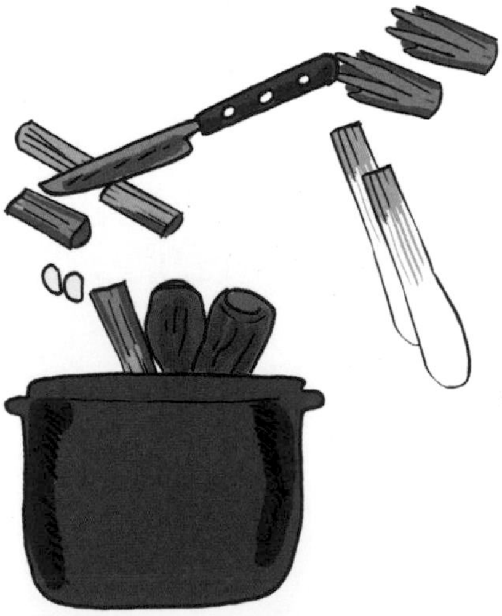

4. Pour the water over the ingredients to barely cover them and bring to a boil over high heat.

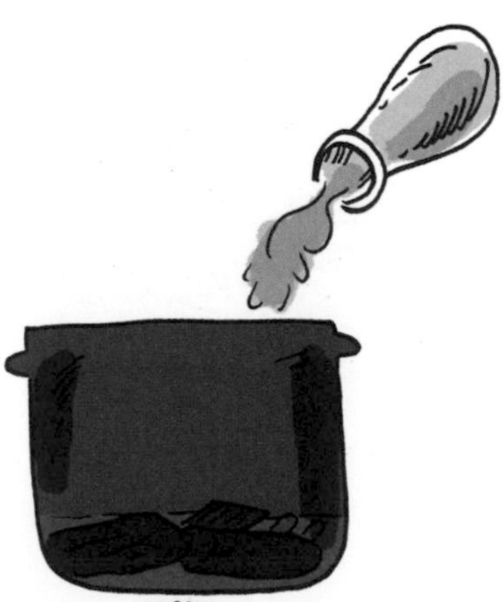

5. Reduce the heat to low and add a teaspoon of black tea leaves (jasmine or oolong).

6. Let the pork simmer for about 20–25 minutes until done (this depends on the thickness of the pork). Turn off the heat and let it sit for 15 minutes.

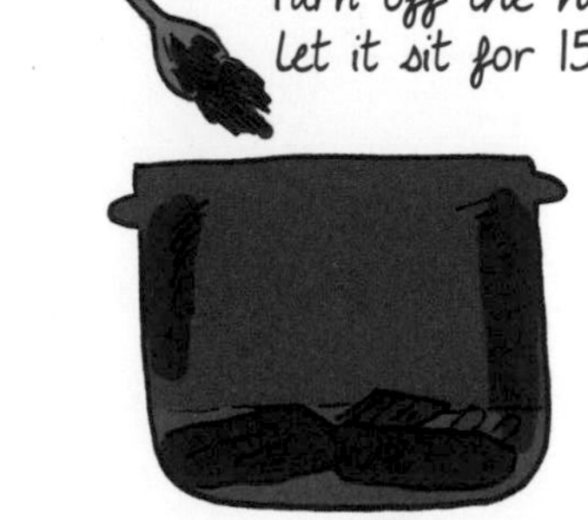

7. Take the pork out, let it cool and slice it into serving pieces. Reserve the cooking liquid and other ingredients.

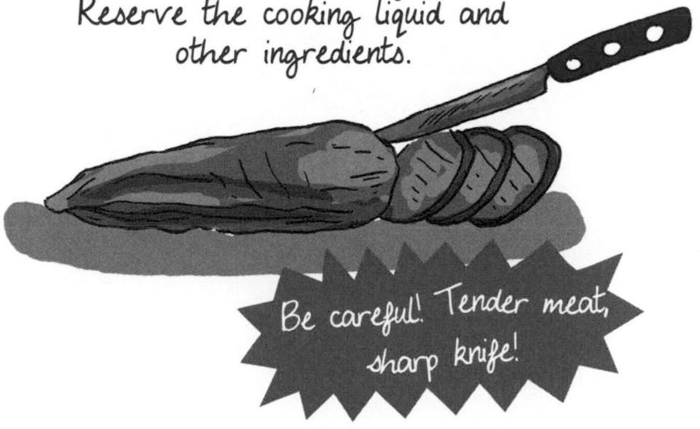
Be careful! Tender meat, sharp knife!

The meat is ready; now let's prepare a sauce that will truly add a Japanese touch to the dish. Pay attention!

8. To make the Sauce, combine the miso, mirin and sake or white wine in a small saucepan. Mix well over medium heat. Turn off the heat immediately once the Sauce begins to boil.

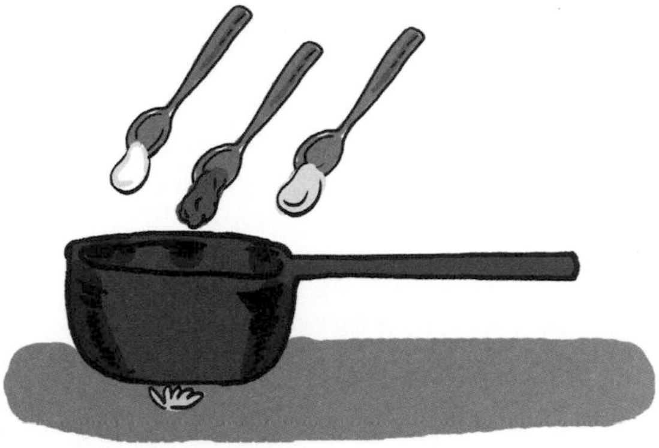

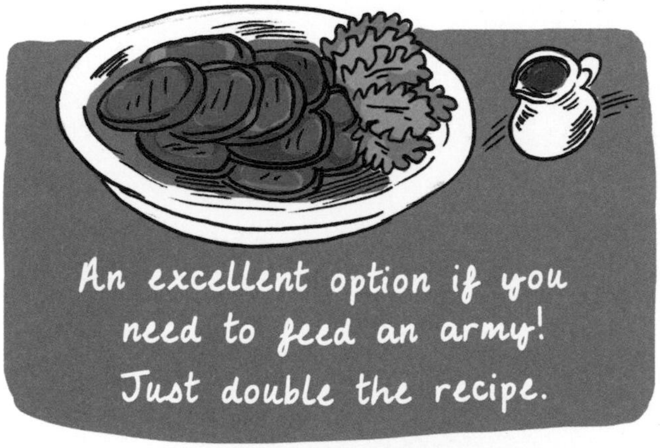
An excellent option if you need to feed an army! Just double the recipe.

Ta-daaah! Serve in a large platter with a salad. Put the Sauce in a small jug to serve on the side. This dish is a great excuse for inviting some friends over!

And now, ladies and gentlemen, the final trick! The magic of reusing leftovers.

The cooking liquid in the pot preserves the essence of the tea, the meat and the leek. Save that in an airtight container in the refrigerator to use for your soups (see page 39 Hearty Vegetable Soup).

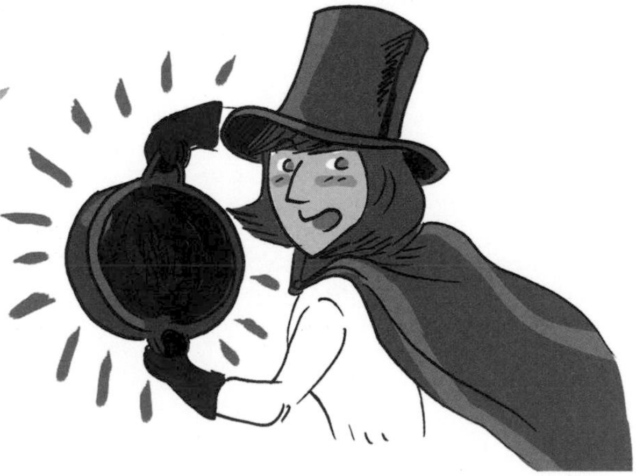

Nikujyaga Meat Stew with Vegetables

Look who's back! Granny, Gourmand Gohan's star chef! This meat and potato stew, very popular in Japanese homes, has a story...

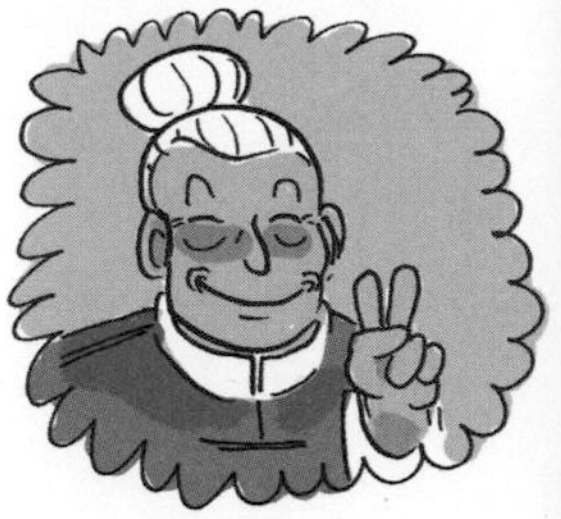

Serves 4
Time: 45 minutes.

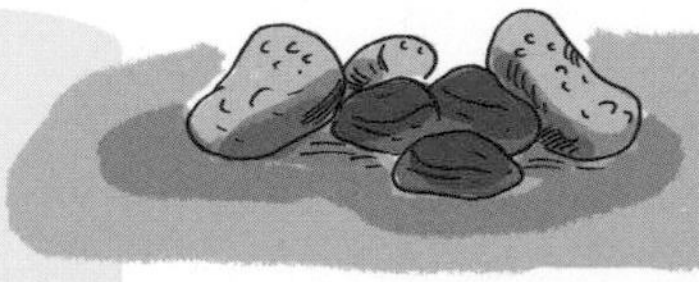

1½ lbs (650 g) beef or pork cubes
Cooking oil, to fry the meat
4 potatoes
1 carrot
8 green beans
1 onion
2 tablespoons sugar
1 tablespoon dashi powder
3 tablespoons soy sauce
1¾ cups (400 ml) water
3 tablespoons sake or white wine
2 tablespoons mirin

According to legend, this dish was introduced to Japan by Marshal Togo Heihachiro in the late 19th century.

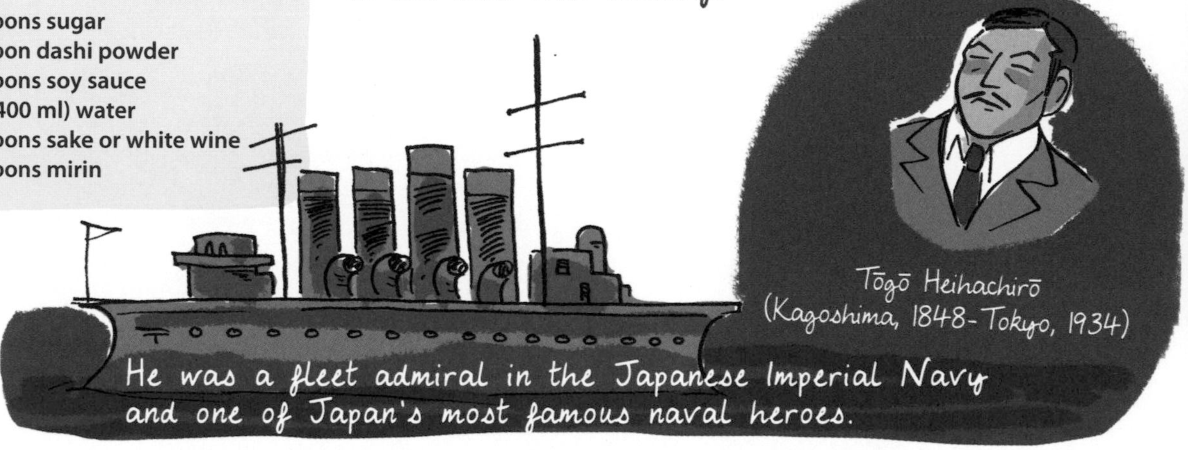
Tōgō Heihachirō
(Kagoshima, 1848-Tokyo, 1934)
He was a fleet admiral in the Japanese Imperial Navy and one of Japan's most famous naval heroes.

Heihachiro trained with the British Royal Navy where he enjoyed the ship's stews so much, the minute he got back to Japan, he asked his own chefs to replicate the dish.

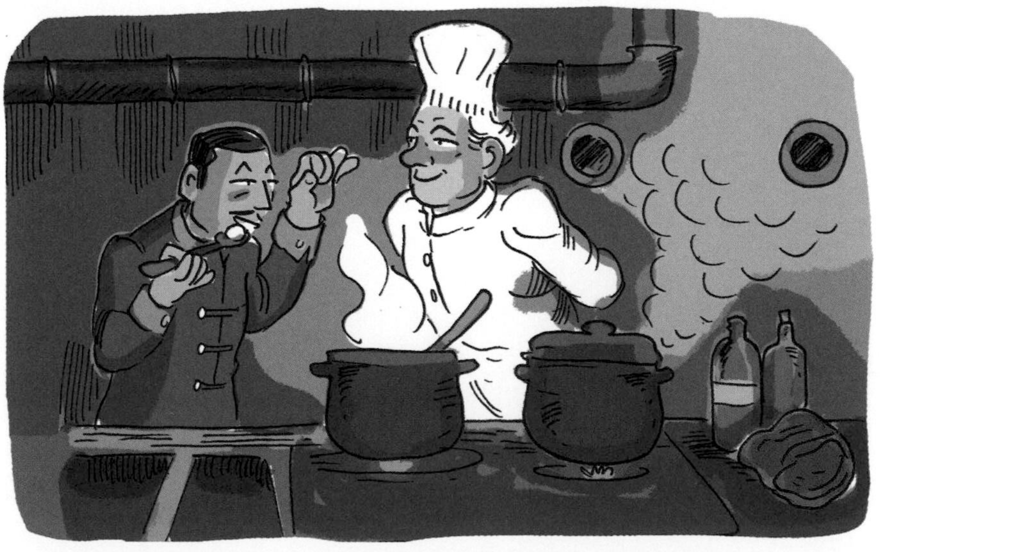

The Nikujyaga is a Japanese version of that dish. Now let's take a look at the recipe.

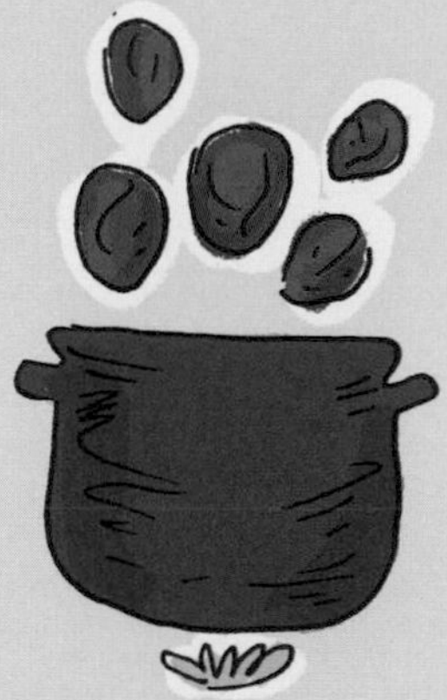

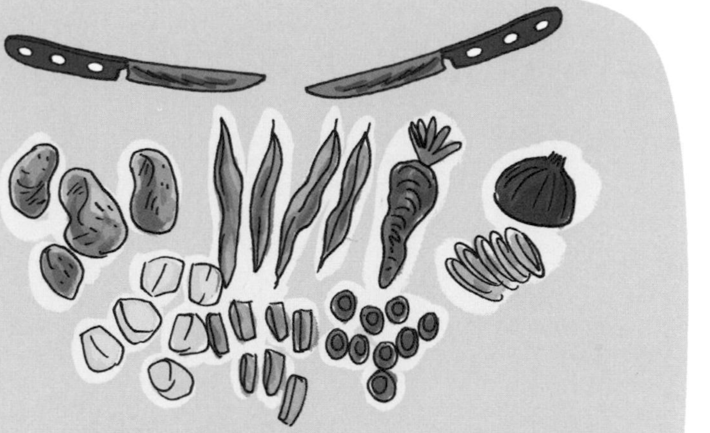

1. Slice the meat into chunks and brown it in a large pot over medium heat with a little cooking oil.

2. Cut the potatoes, carrot, green beans and onion into chunks and as soon as the meat is brown, add them to the pot.

3. Cook the vegetables, stirring with a wooden spoon, until the onion begins to brown. Then add the other ingredients.

4. Bring to a boil, reduce the heat to medium and simmer for about 30 minutes until the stock thickens and all the ingredients are cooked.

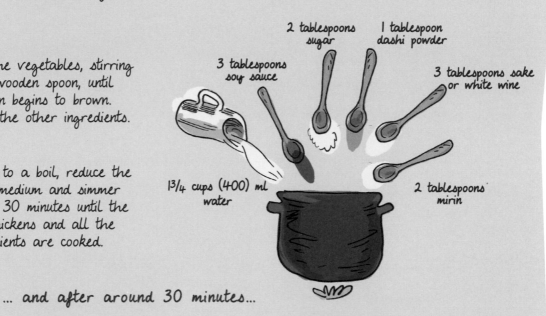

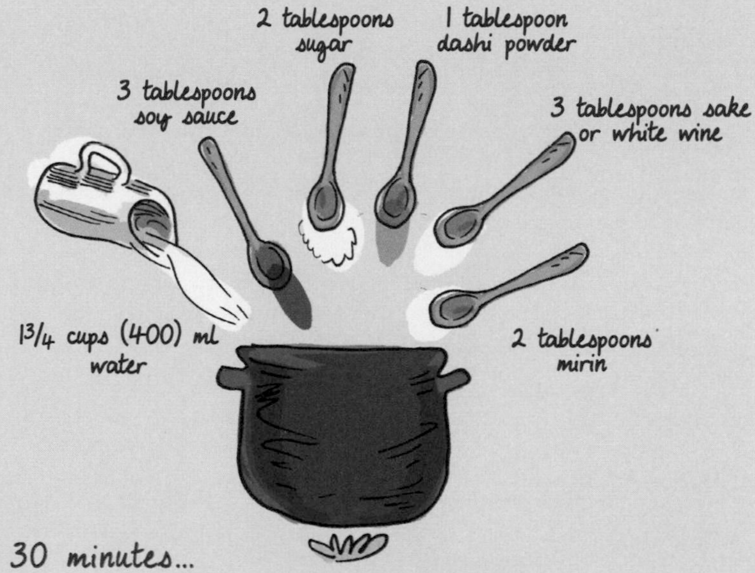
2 tablespoons sugar
1 tablespoon dashi powder
3 tablespoons soy sauce
3 tablespoons sake or white wine
1¾ cups (400) ml water
2 tablespoons mirin

... and after around 30 minutes...

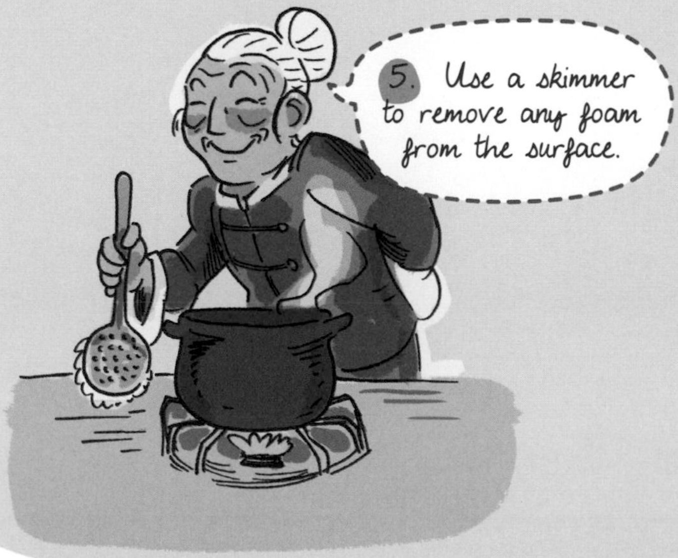
5. Use a skimmer to remove any foam from the surface.

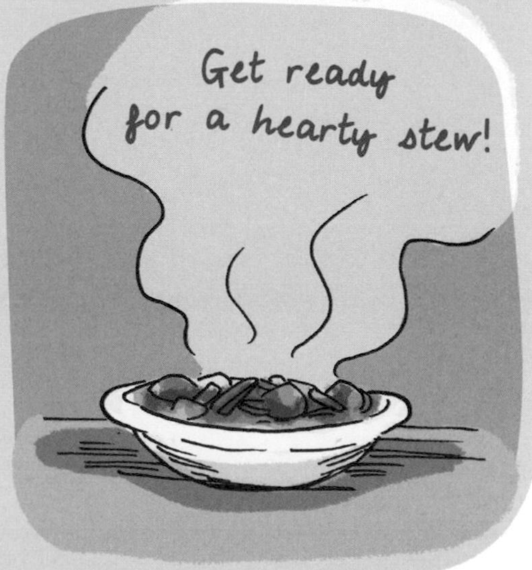
Get ready for a hearty stew!

Japanese Ginger Pork   Buta No Shogayaki

Here's another traditional Japanese dish. The secret is in the marinade ... a combination of ginger, honey, soy and mirin. This is a very savory dish which will win your friends' hearts.

Serves 2
Time: 30 minutes

1 lb (450 g) thin pork steaks
1 onion, peeled
2 tablespoons freshly grated ginger
2 tablespoons honey
2 tablespoons soy sauce
2 tablespoons mirin
Salt and pepper, to taste
Oil, for frying

1. Flatten the pork steaks with a large cleaver to make them thinner and broader. If you have a mallet, you can beat them to flatten.

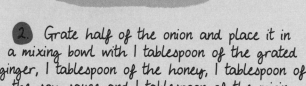

2. Grate half of the onion and place it in a mixing bowl with 1 tablespoon of the grated ginger, 1 tablespoon of the honey, 1 tablespoon of the soy sauce and 1 tablespoon of the mirin.

3. Mix all the ingredients well to form a smooth marinade.

4. Marinate the pork in the marinade we just prepared for at least one hour, then add a little salt and pepper to taste.

5. Finely slice the other half onion you've set aside...

... and sauté it in a skillet with a little oil.

6. When the onion turns golden brown, drain the pork fillets, reserving the marinade, and add the pork to the pan. Cook them for around 3 minutes on each side until done.

7. Pour the reserved marinade over the pork and let it simmer over medium heat until the sauce thickens, about 10-15 minutes.

Ready to serve ...
Yummy yummy!

A perfect match with rice and a fresh salad!

Tarutaru (Tartar) Sauce

This is the Japanese version of French tartar sauce. The main ingredient in French tartar sauce is mayonnaise. However we use Tofu Mayonnaise (see page 76) instead—a healthier option!

Makes 1 cup (225 g)
Time: 20 minutes

1 scallion (spring onion)
A few black olives
1 hard boiled egg
A pinch of parsley
Juice of ½ lemon
Pinch of salt
½ portion (¾ cup/175 g) Tofu
   Mayonnaise (page 76)

Maiko, there're some jars of Tofu Mayonnaise left and I don't want to waste it...

Don't worry. I will use it to make ... Tarutaru Sauce

1. First we just need to mince the scallion, the black olives, the boiled egg and the parsley.

2. Then mix everything in a bowl, stirring with a wooden spoon.

3. Add the lemon juice, a pinch of salt and keep stirring ...

4. Finally pour in the Tofu Mayonnaise and mix it until it's perfectly blended.

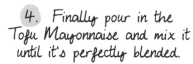

Ta daaaaaaa! A smooth, delicious sauce that goes fantastically well with any meat dish!!

Chicken with Tarutaru Sauce Tori Nanban

So, do you want to know how to serve the Tarutaru Sauce? Here is a basic meat preparation—another easy recipe that makes use of what you have on hand.

Serves 2-3
Time: 20 minutes

- 1⅓ cups (150 g) cornstarch
- 2 chicken breasts
- 1 tablespoon soy sauce
- 2 tablespoons mirin
- 3 tablespoons rice vinegar
- 2 tablespoons oil, for frying
- 1 cup (120 g) Tarutaru Sauce (page 92), to serve

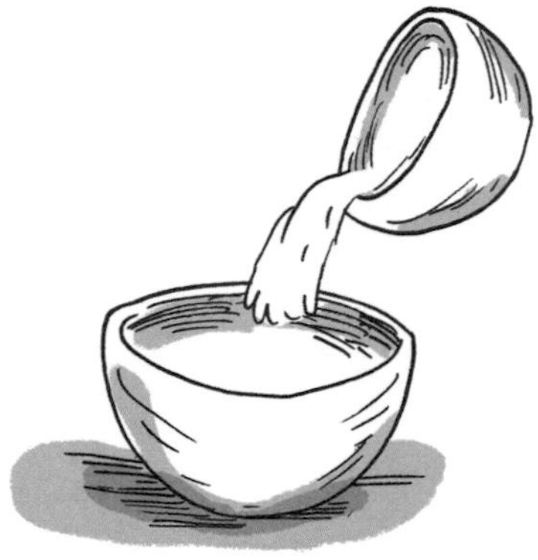

1. Pour the cornstarch into a mixing bowl.

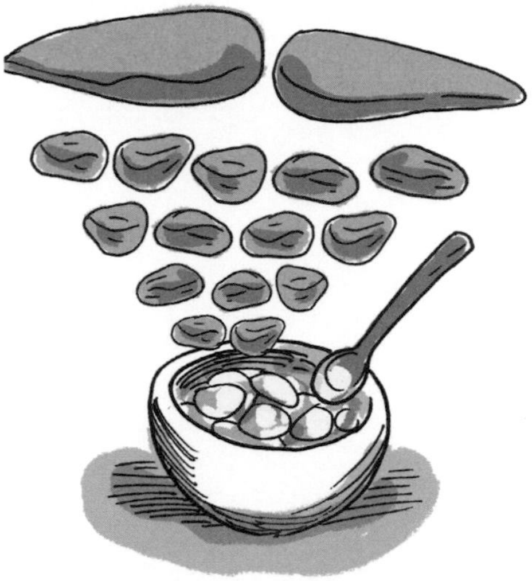

2. Slice the chicken breasts into bite-sized pieces... and dredge them in the cornstarch.

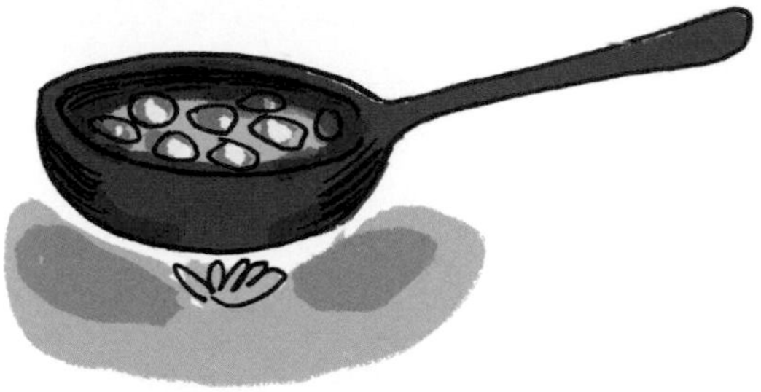

3. Heat some oil in a skillet and fry the chicken pieces over medium heat.

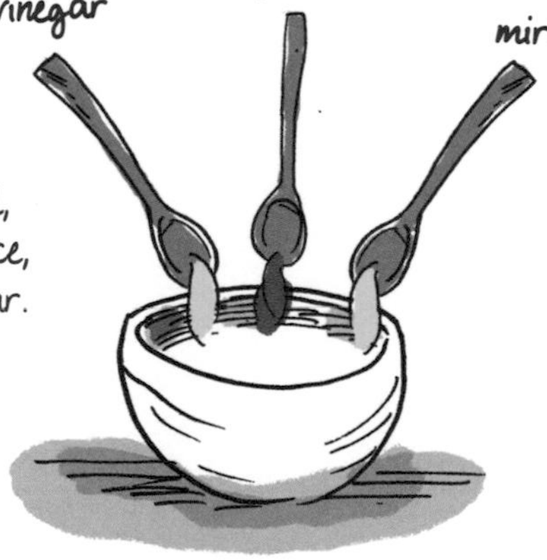
rice vinegar
soy sauce
mirin

4. In another bowl, combine the soy sauce, mirin and rice vinegar.

5. As soon as the chicken begins to get crispy, add the sauce mixture we just prepared. Let it simmer until the sauce becomes thick and caramelized, so the sauce sticks to the chicken pieces.

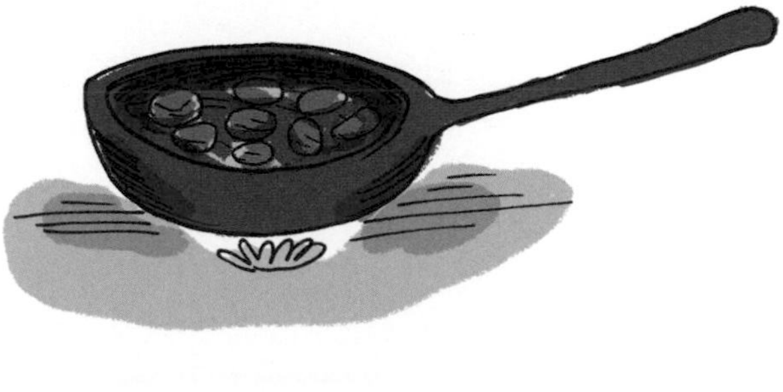

6. Serve the fried chicken on a plate with a garden salad and the Tarutaru Sauce.

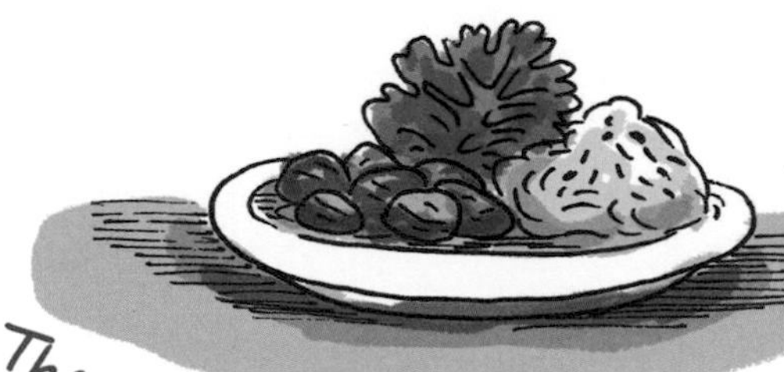

The meat's flavor goes so well with the Tarutaru's smooth texture!

Chapter 6

FISH & SEAFOOD

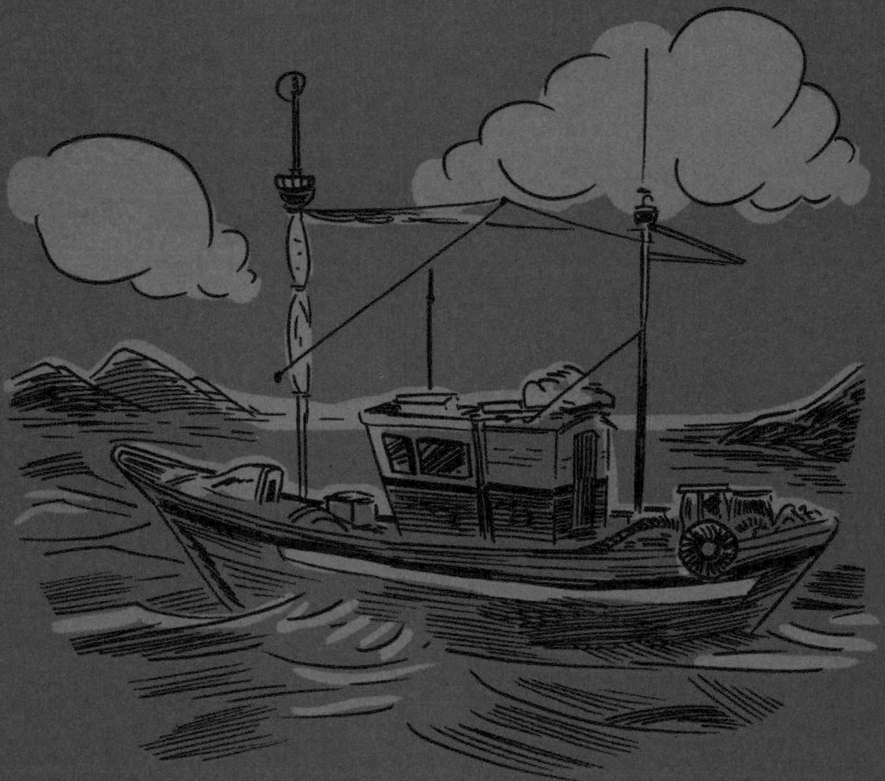

Not all seafood in Japan is eaten as sushi! We are happy to show you some other delicious Japanese seafood recipes that may surprise you! Grilled, fried and steamed fish dishes are a great way to balance your menus. Always buy fresh fish, if possible locally caught, and try these recipes using different kinds of fish and seafood available at your local fish market. Enjoy!

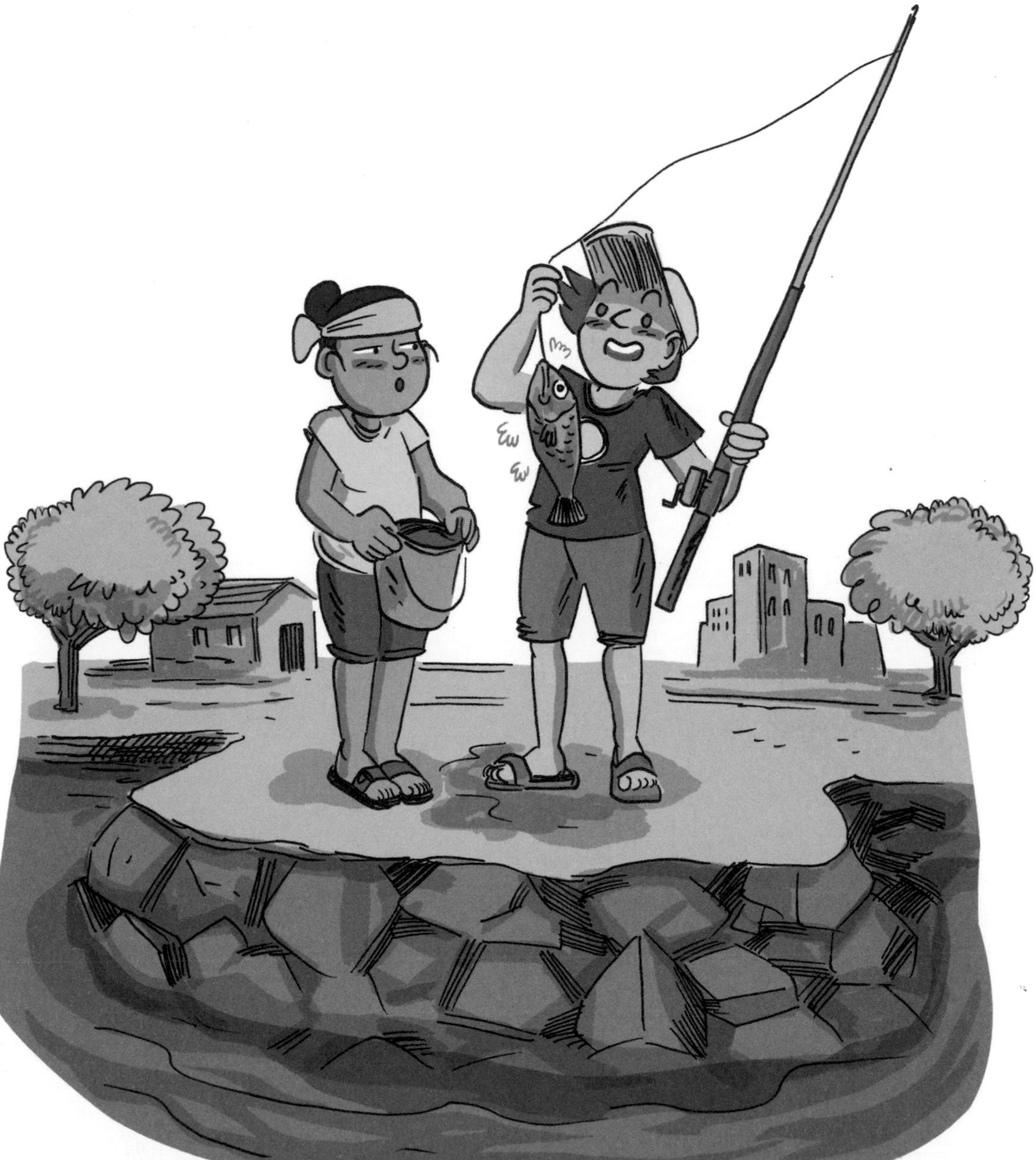
Ew
Ew

Marinated Mackerel Fillets Nanbanzuke

This "Southern Barbarian Preserved" fish recipe (no kidding, that's the literal translation!) refers to the ancient origins of this dish that arrived in Japan around the 17th century and quickly became popular as a way of preserving fish. Fresh mackerel (or any other fish) is marinated in a vinegar sauce with some vegetables. Prepare it early to allow the fish to marinate for an hour or more before serving.

Serves 4-6
Time: 40 minutes (plus at least 1 hour to marinate it)

- 2¼ lbs (1 kg) fresh mackerel or other fish fillets
- Flour, to dredge the fish
- Oil, for frying
- 1 small carrot, peeled
- 1 red bell pepper, deseeded
- 1 yellow bell pepper, deseeded
- 1 green bell pepper, deseeded
- 1 onion
- 1 lemon, thinly sliced

Sauce

- 3 tablespoons soy sauce
- 3 tablespoons sake
- 3 tablespoons water
- 2 tablespoons sugar
- 2 tablespoons mirin
- 3 tablespoons rice vinegar

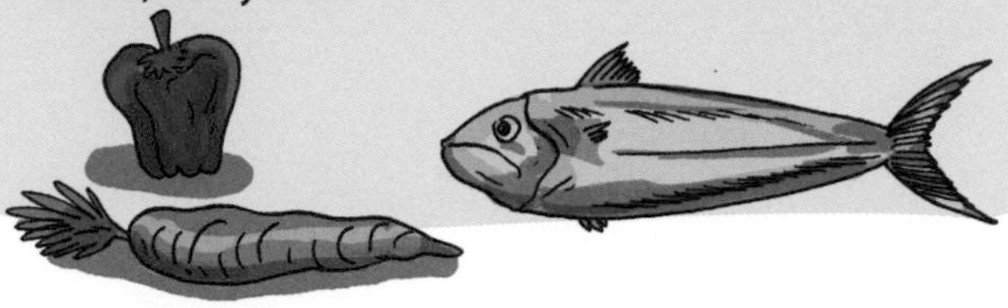

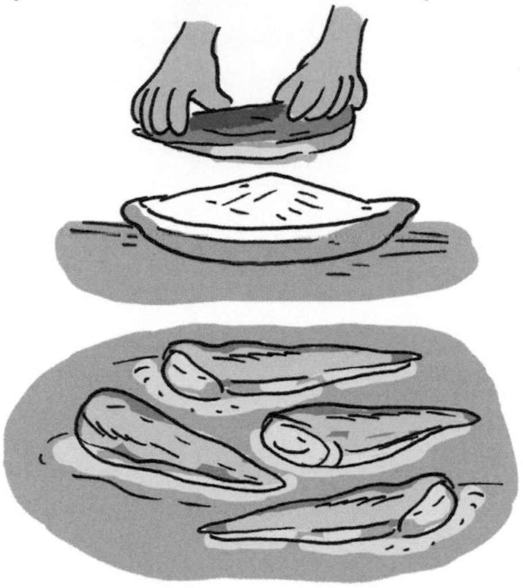

1. Clean and dry the fish fillets with paper towels. Put some flour in a plate and dredge the fish fillets in the flour to lightly coat them.

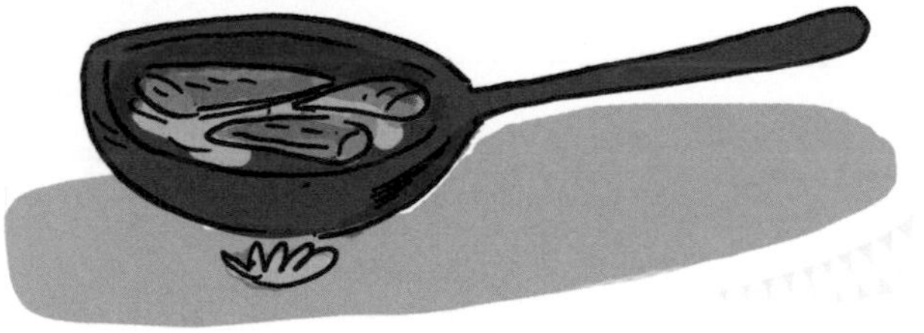

2. Cover the bottom of a skillet with oil and fry the fish until browned on both sides, about 5 minutes.

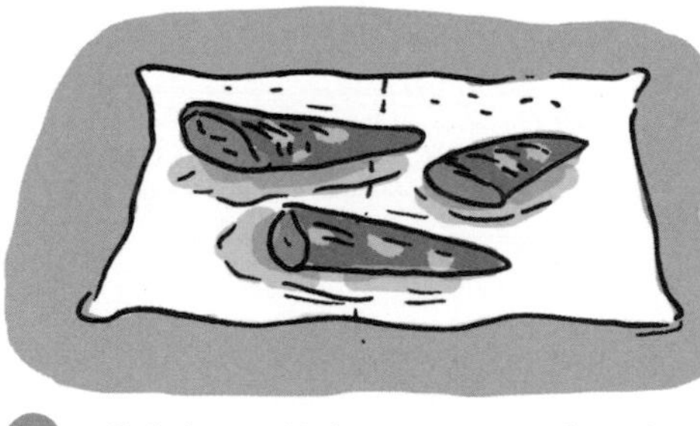

3. Put the fillets on paper towels to drain off the oil.

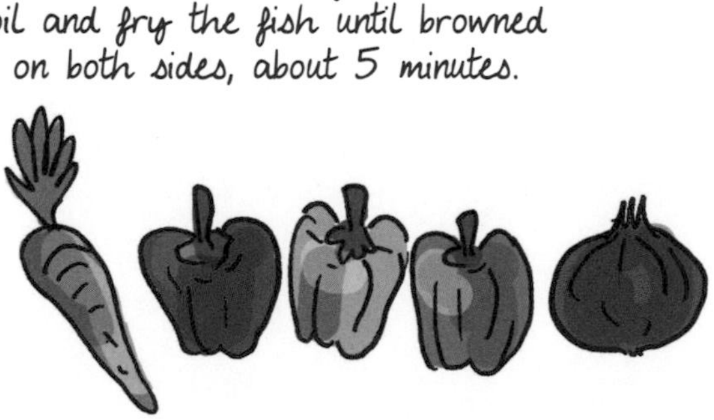

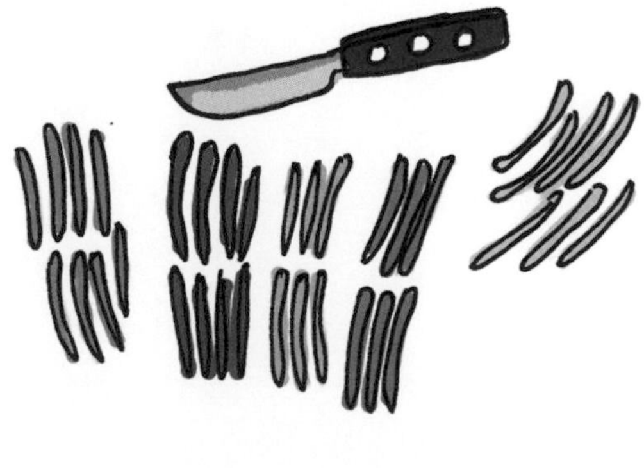

4. Slice the carrot and bell peppers into thin, even strips. Do the same with the onion.

5. Ok, now focus your attention on this magical Sauce we're going to prepare in a pot. Heat the following ingredients in a saucepan over medium heat.

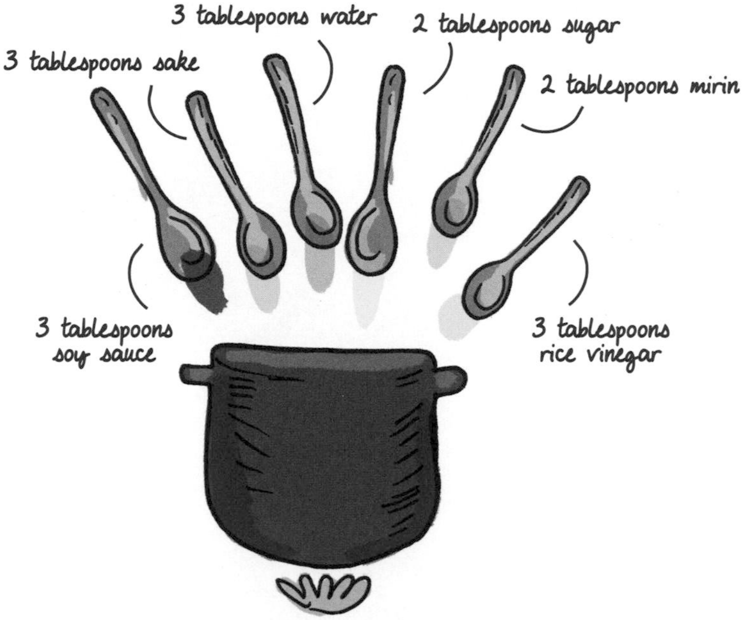
3 tablespoons water
2 tablespoons sugar
3 tablespoons sake
2 tablespoons mirin
3 tablespoons soy sauce
3 tablespoons rice vinegar

6. As the sauce starts to blend, add the veggie sticks and simmer them for around 15 minutes, stirring with a wooden spoon until they soften.

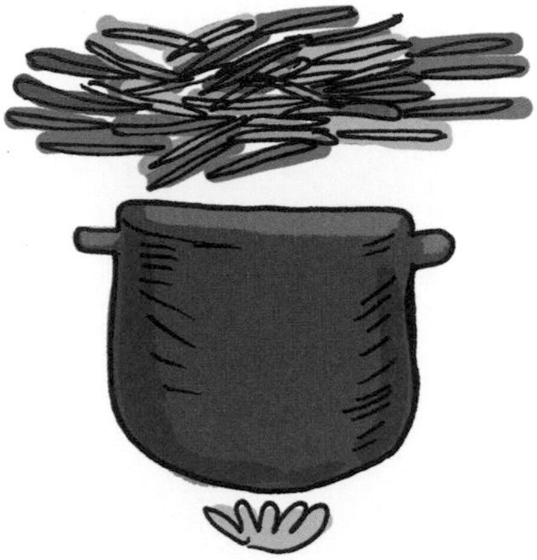

7. Place the drained mackerel fillets in a shallow serving platter.

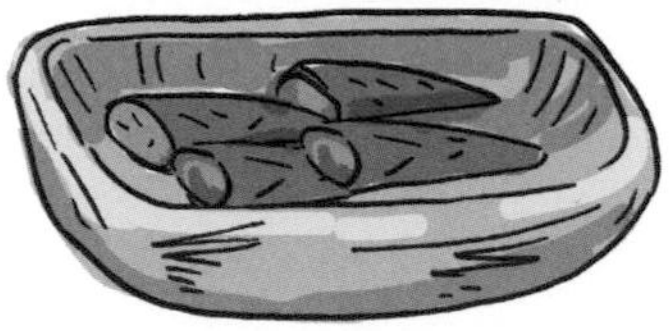

8. Then you just cover them with the cooked veggies and sauce and add some fresh lemon slices on top!

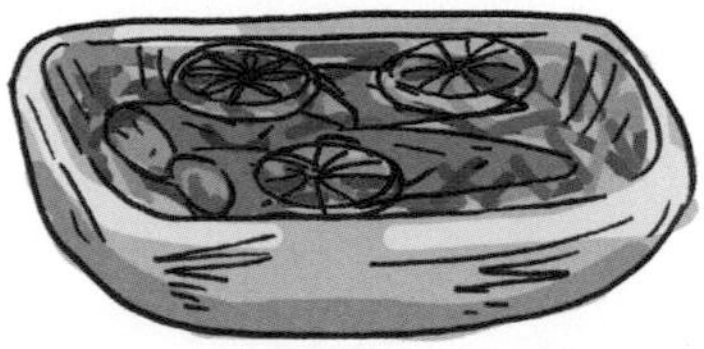

9. And now test your patience, because you need to allow the fish to marinate for at least one hour in the fridge.

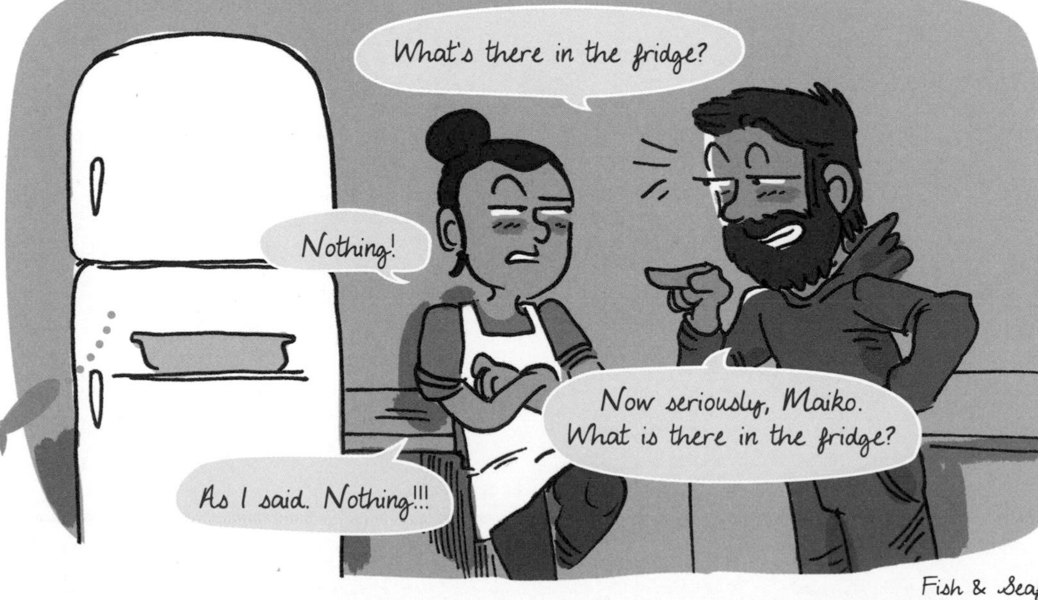
What's there in the fridge?
Nothing!
Now seriously, Maiko. What is there in the fridge?
As I said. Nothing!!!

Crispy Fried Prawns Ebifurai

Ebifurai literally means "fried prawns". Shellfish are always excellent as an appetizer or in combination with other simple dishes because of their distinctive flavor. This is a very simple preparation that allows you to eat each prawn in just one bite.

Serves 4
Time: 20 minutes

1 lb (450 g) large fresh prawns
Salt and pepper, to taste
1 egg, beaten
Flour, to dredge
Panko breadcrumbs

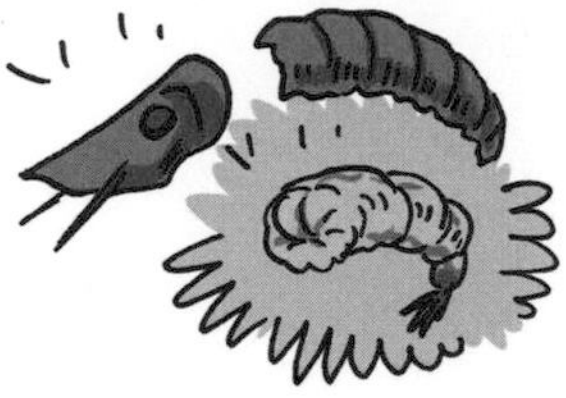

1. Remove the shells and heads from the prawns.

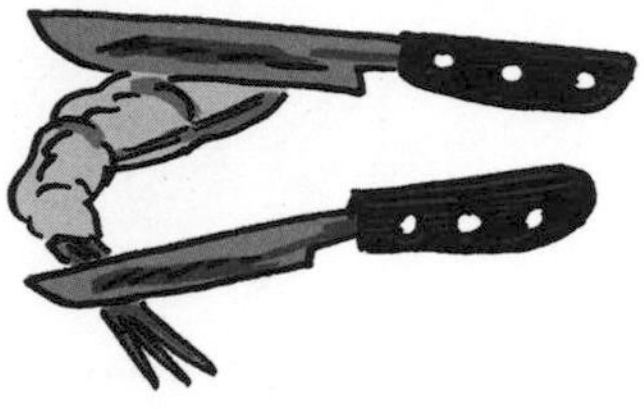

2. Cut off the tails and cut each prawn in half (or into 3 bite-sized chunks depending on the size).

3. Sprinkle some salt and pepper on them.

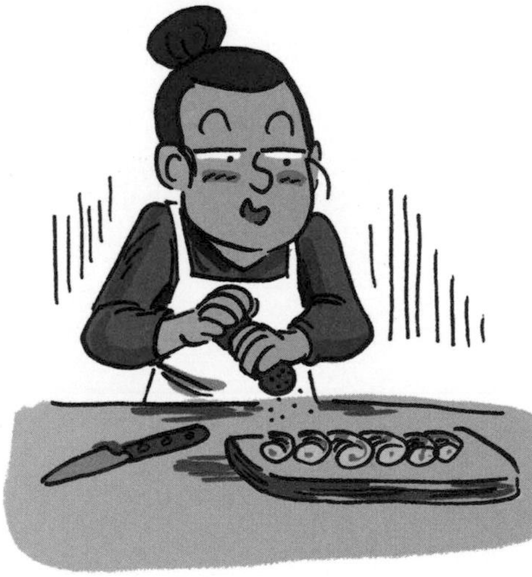

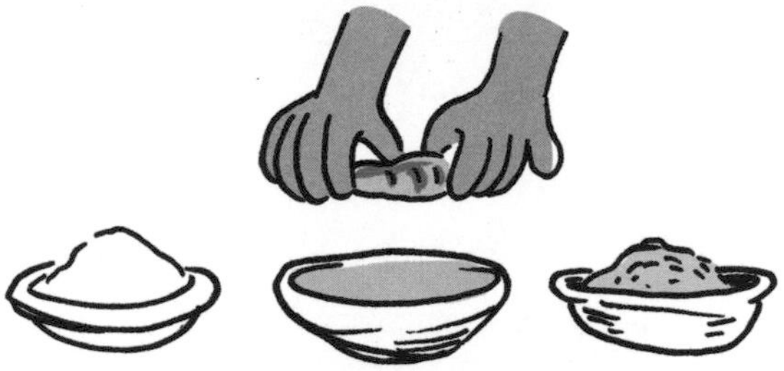

4. Dip the prawn pieces in the beaten egg then in the flour and finally in the breadcrumbs.

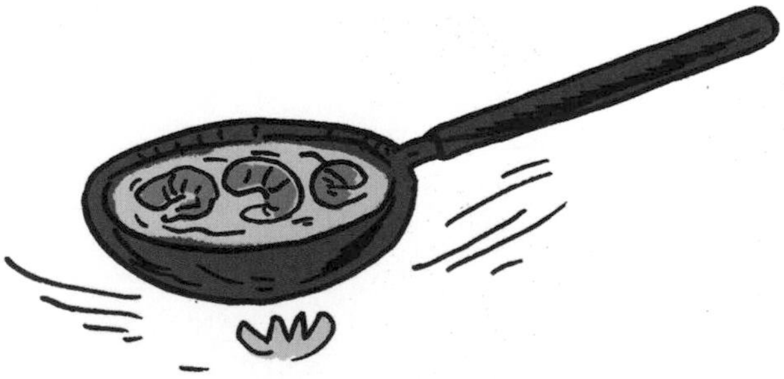

5. Heat about 2 in (5 cm) of oil in a skillet or wok over high heat until almost smoking and deep-fry the breaded prawn pieces for about 2 minutes until golden brown.

Crispy fried prawns are so simple and good!

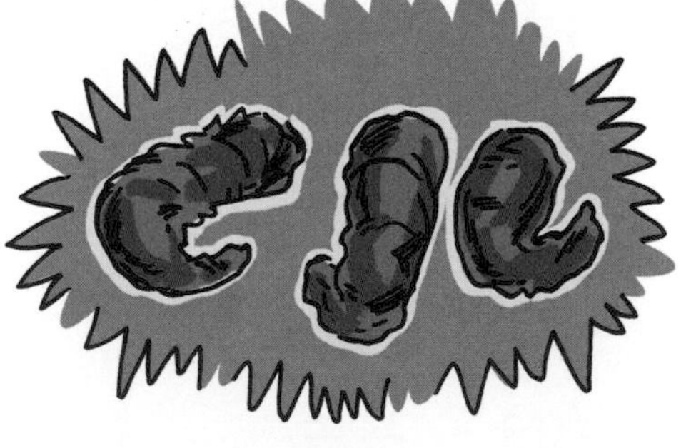

The Tarutaru Sauce that is on page 92 also goes great with this recipe!

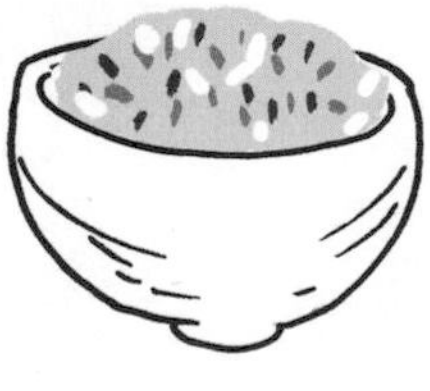

Sardine Meatballs Iwashi no Tsumire

Iwashi-no-tsumire or "sardine meatballs" are very popular in Japan. They are eaten in different ways depending on the season and are especially popular in winter because of their nutrients. They go very well with a rich miso-based soup in cold weather. They are also great served with soy sauce and rice.

Serves 4
Time: 30 minutes

3 cans of sardines (total around 15 oz/450 g)
Salt, to taste
1 carrot, peeled and grated
1 tablespoon freshly grated ginger
1 tablespoon cornstarch
½ cup (125 ml) sake or white wine
1 tablespoon miso paste
2 tablespoons oil, for frying

1. Drain the sardines and remove any bones. Place them into a bowl, then mash them with a fork. Add a pinch of salt.

2. Now add the grated carrot and grated ginger.

3. Add the cornstarch, sake or white wine, and miso. Mix everything together until it forms a smooth dough.

4. Take a handful of the mixture and form a large meatball.

... The size is up to you!

5. Put some oil in a pan over medium heat and fry the balls on all sides for 5 to 10 minutes until they turn golden brown ... yummy!!!

These balls can also be served in a pot of vegetable and miso soup.

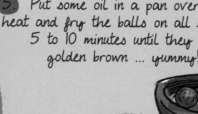

Kabayaki

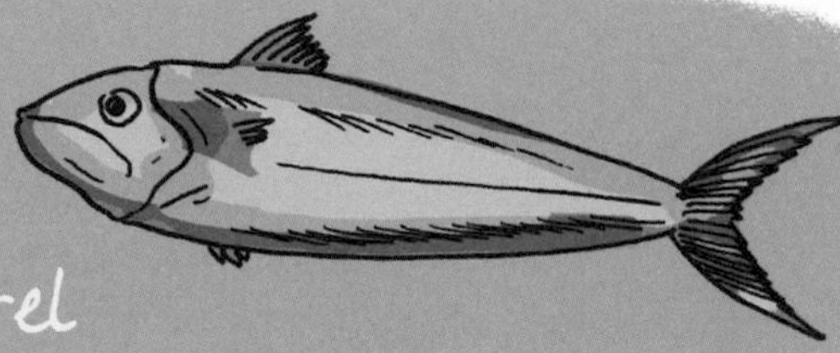

The return of the Mackerel

Pan-fried Fish with Kabayaki Sauce

Mackerel is probably the most beloved fish in Japan because of its dark, rich taste. There are infinite ways of preparing it including some very old traditional recipes. Here we fry it and serve it with kabayaki, a sweet sauce similar to teriyaki.

Serves 4
Time: 20 minutes

- 2 lbs (900 g) fresh mackerel or other fish fillets
- 3 tablespoons mirin
- 3 tablespoons sake or white wine
- 3 tablespoons soy sauce
- 3 tablespoons sugar
- 2 tomatoes, for serving
- Oil, for frying

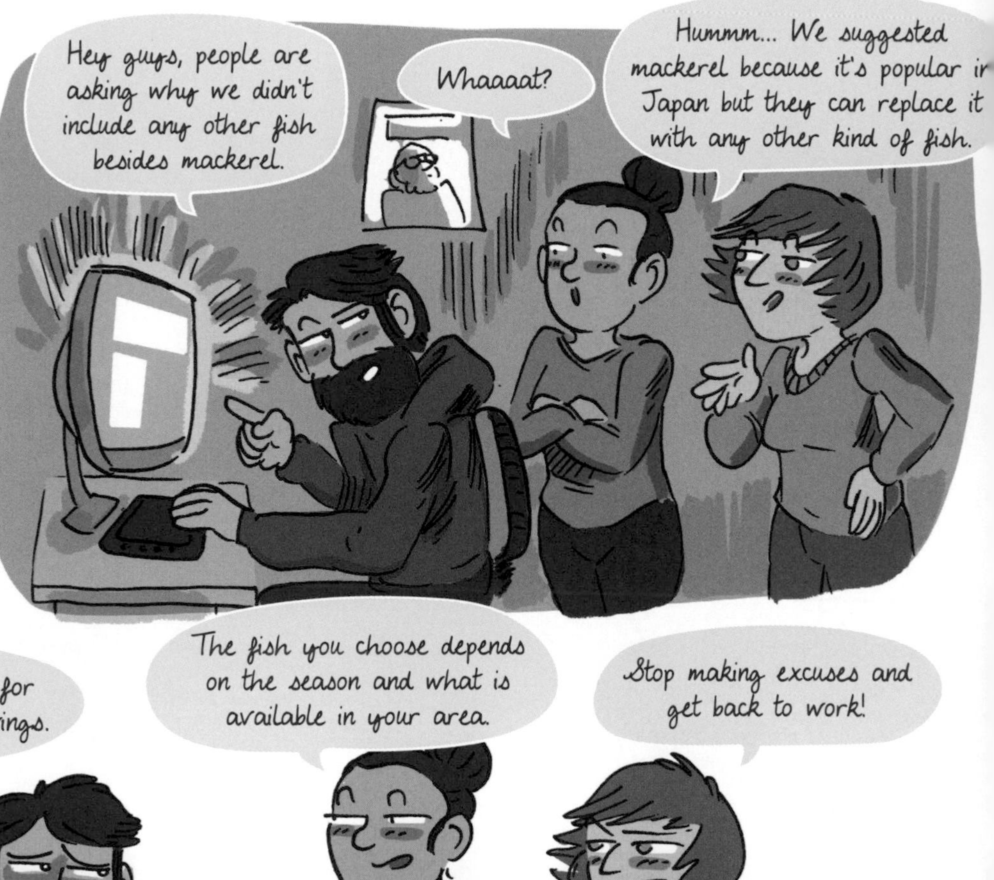

Hey guys, people are asking why we didn't include any other fish besides mackerel.
Whaaaat?
Hummm... We suggested mackerel because it's popular in Japan but they can replace it with any other kind of fish.

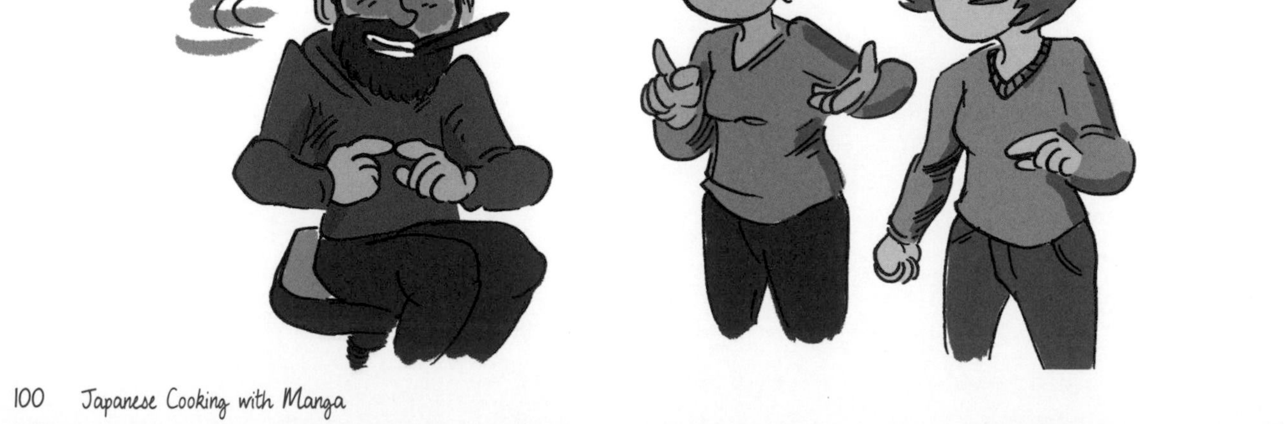

Well, and it's also easier for me to reuse the same drawings.
The fish you choose depends on the season and what is available in your area.
Stop making excuses and get back to work!

1. Clean and dry the fish fillets using paper towels. Then add the mirin and sake or white wine to a small saucepan and bring it to a boil over medium heat. Allow the alcohol to evaporate.

2. When it boils, add the soy sauce and sugar.

3. Let the sauce simmer for a few more minutes over medium heat until it thickens, then remove from the heat.

4. Add a little oil to a skillet and pan-fry the fish fillets till they are cooked. (Use any fish of your choice, you've got the power!)

Easy and tasty like no other dish!

5. Slice some delicious fresh tomatoes and lay them on a platter, then cover them with the mackerel fillets and spoon the sauce over the top.

Why is there a bone in my mouth? Who likes unwanted bones in their mouth? Bones scare readers off and stop them from learning to cook.
Does he complain about absolutely everything? I swear I'll hit him if he brings something else up.
I was hoping he'd choke on the bone and finally shut up.

Braised Fish with Ginger & Miso

Mackerel with miso sauce is a traditional recipe and a classic home cooked dish. The rich flavor of the miso is complemented by the sliced ginger and if you cook it slowly you get a delicious sauce. Serve it with some vegetables and enjoy!

Serves 4-6
Time: 40 minutes

2 lbs (900 g) fresh mackerel or other fish fillets
Salt and pepper, to taste
8 thin slices ginger
1¼ cups (300 ml) sake or dry sherry
2 tablespoons brown sugar
2 tablespoons mirin
3 tablespoons miso paste

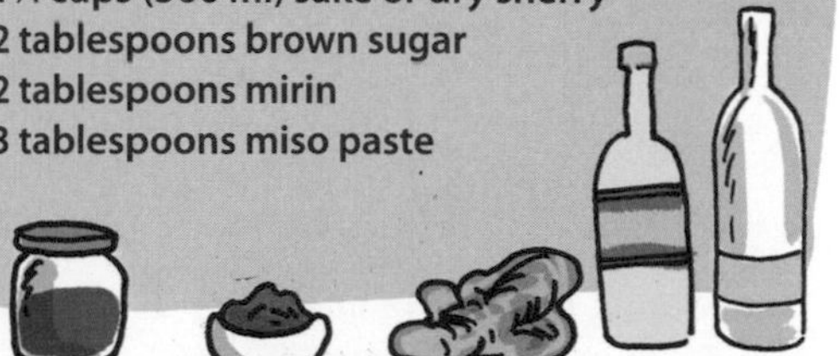

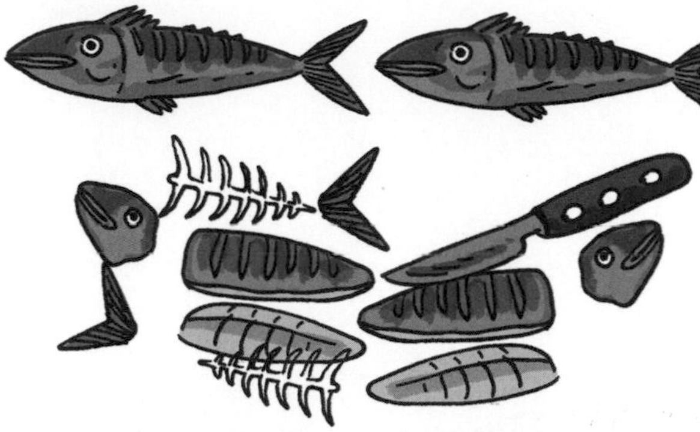

1. If your fishmonger hasn't already done it for you, fillet the fish and discard the heads, spines, tails and guts.

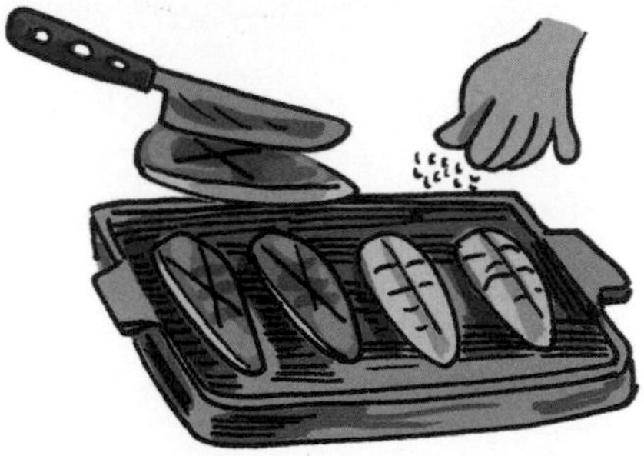

2. Make a few X cuts on the skin sides of the fillets and add salt and pepper on the other side.

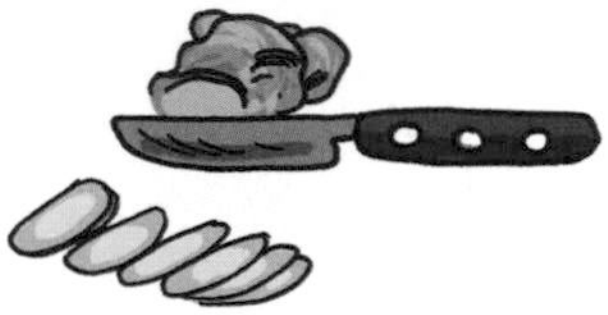

3. Cut aprox 8 thin slices of ginger.

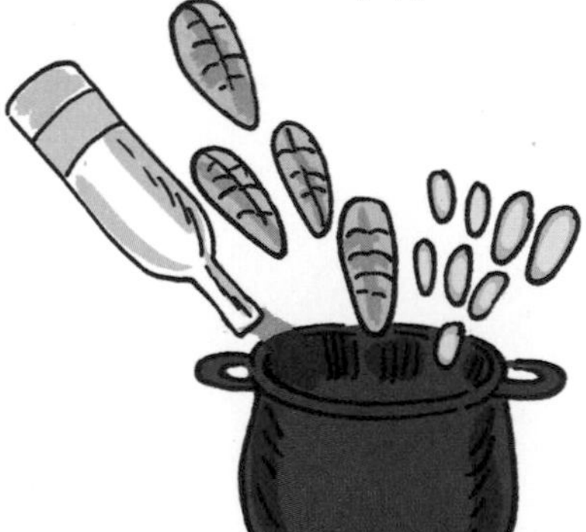

4. Add the sake or dry sherry to a pot and add the fish fillets and the slices of ginger.

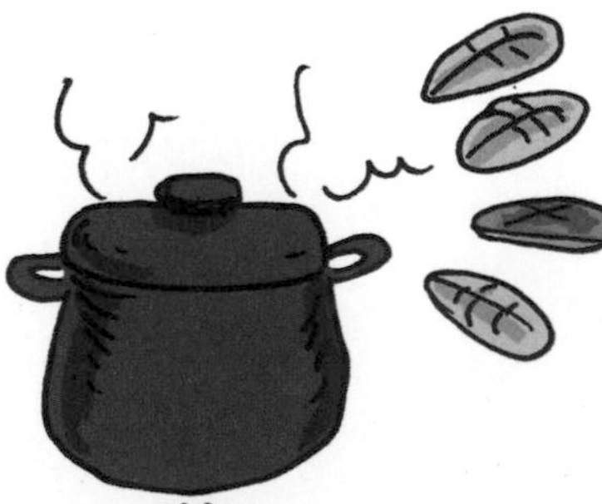

5. Cover the pot and bring to a boil over medium heat!

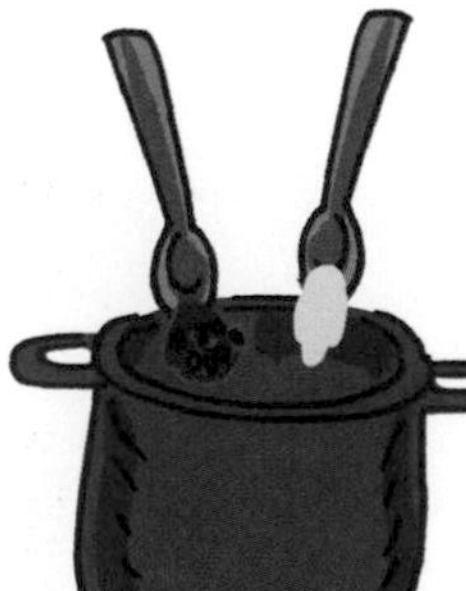

6. When it comes to a boil, remove the fish and set aside. Then add the sugar and the mirin.

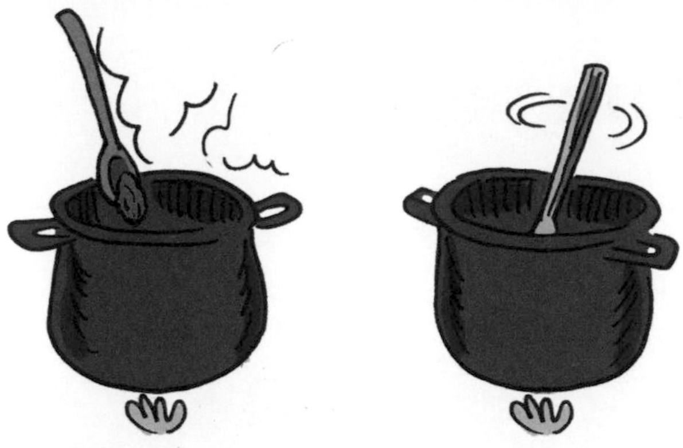

7. When the mixture comes to a boil again, add the miso and stir well to combine everything.

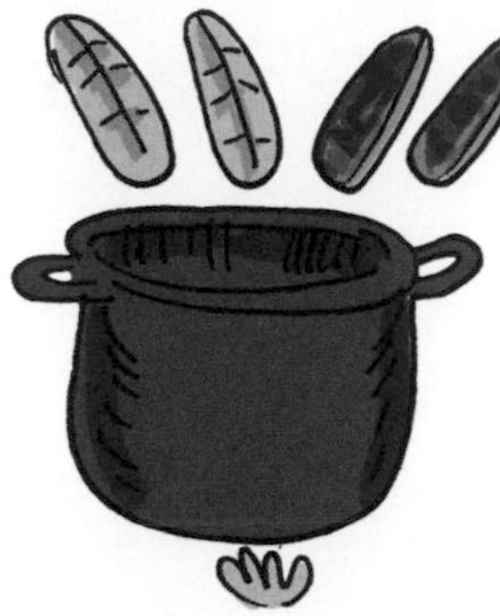

8. Put the mackerel fillets back into the pot and let them simmer a few more minutes to complete the cooking process.

Serve the mackerel fillets and sauce with poached asparagus and rice and you'll have a perfect meal!

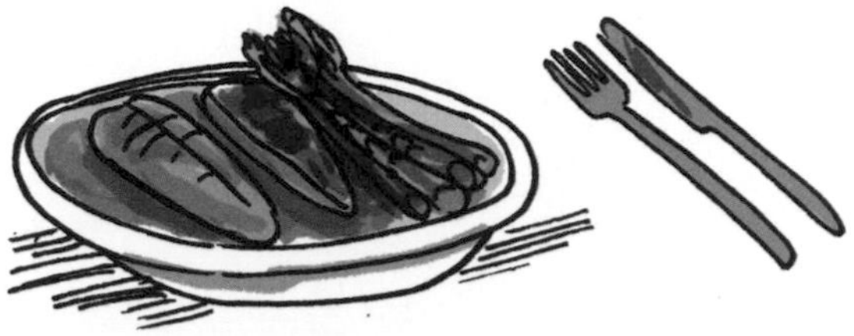

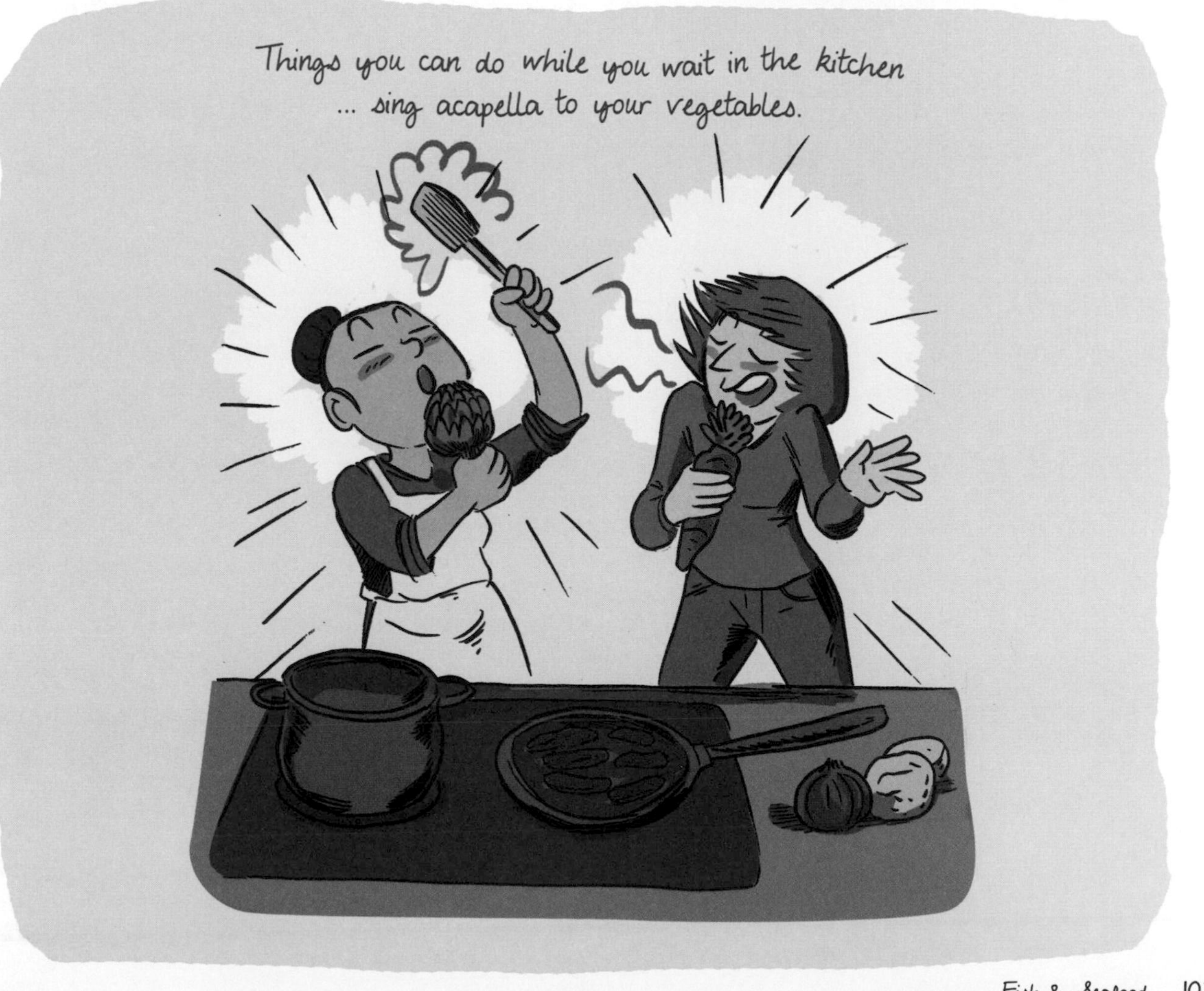
Things you can do while you wait in the kitchen
... sing acapella to your vegetables.

Fish and Vegetable Tempura

Tempura is a popular method of deep-frying seafood and vegetables until crispy and golden brown. The key is in the batter. You can use this technique to fry any kinds of vegetables, fish or shellfish and here we'll use a combination of codfish, mushrooms and asparagus. Fry them quickly and enjoy them while hot!

Serves 3-4

Time: 20 minutes

1½ lbs (650 g) fresh codfish or other fish fillets
12 stalks asparagus, trimmed
10 shiitake mushrooms, stems removed
Flour, to dredge the fish and veggies
Sunflower oil, for deep-frying

Tempura Batter

½ cup (75 g) flour
2 tablespoons cornstarch
½ teaspoon yeast
1 teaspoon rice vinegar
¾ cup (200 ml) water

Tempura Dipping Sauce

4 tablespoons soy sauce
4 tablespoons mirin
¾ cup (200 ml) water
1 teaspoon dashi powder

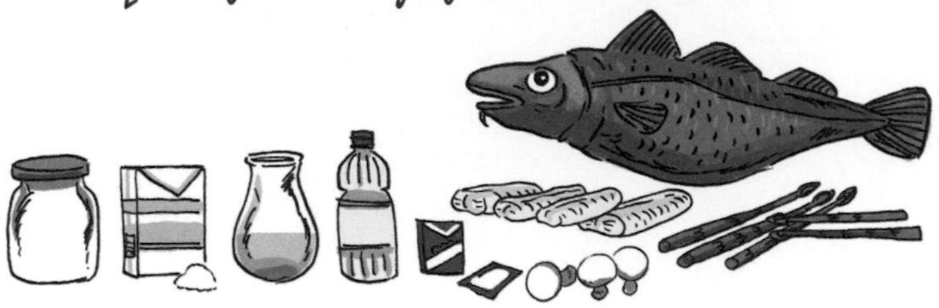

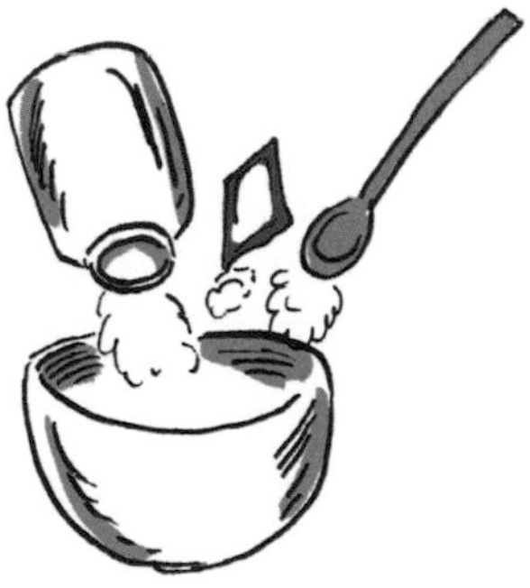

1. Clean and dry the fish fillets using paper towels. Make the Tempura Batter by mixing the flour, cornstarch and yeast together in a bowl.

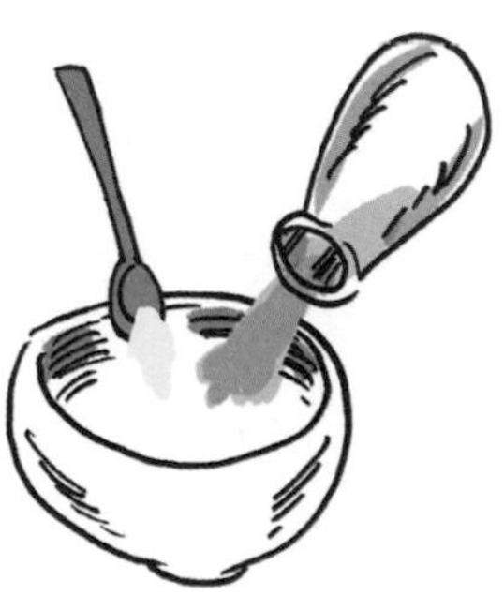

2. Add the rice vinegar and then slowly add the water.

3. Mix everything with a wooden spoon. No need to break up the lumps; in tempura they add variety to the texture.

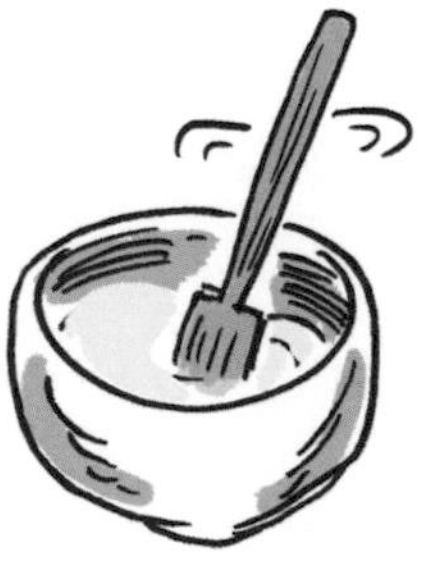

4. Cut the asparagus stalks in half (removing and discarding the tough ends), slice the mushrooms ... ... and also cut the codfish fillets into long strips. Use the size of your finger to guide you.

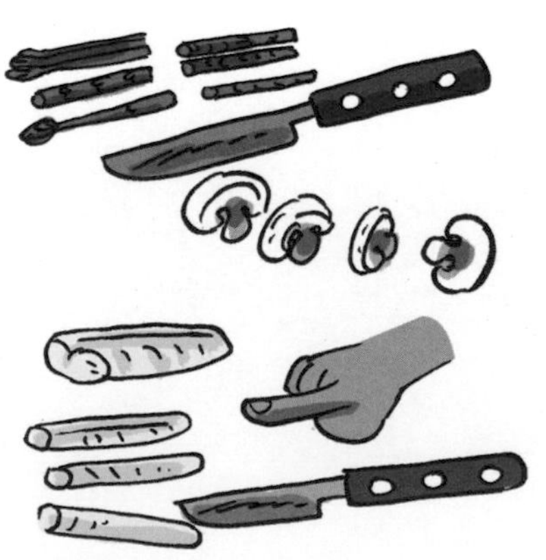

5. Pour 3 cups (700 ml) of sunflower oil into a saucepan or wok and heat it until very hot.

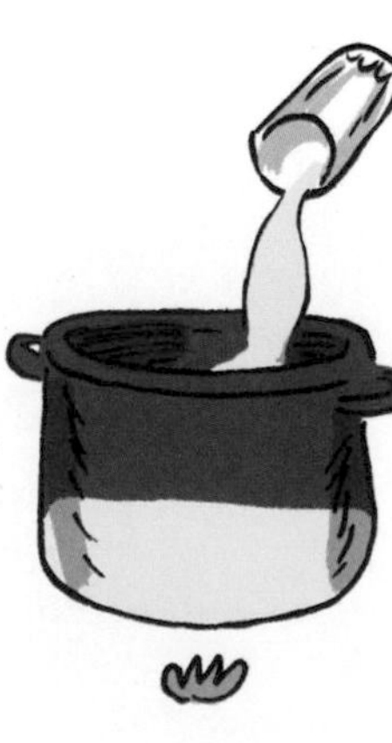

6. Dredge each ingredient in flour first and then dip them in the Tempura Batter that you have just prepared.

7. Fry each piece for 2 or 3 minutes and remove them with tongs, placing them on a plate with absorbent paper towels to drain off the oil.

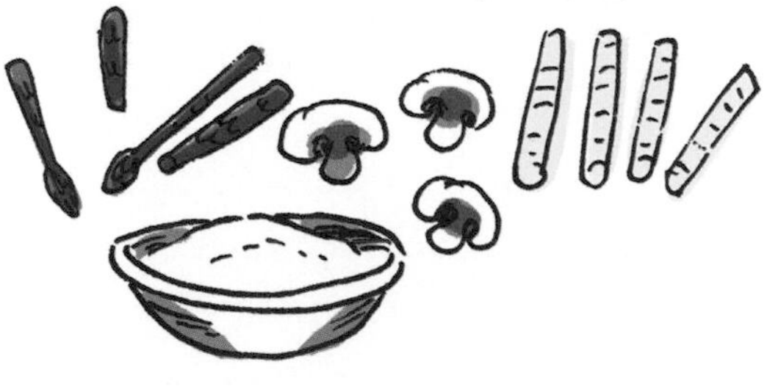

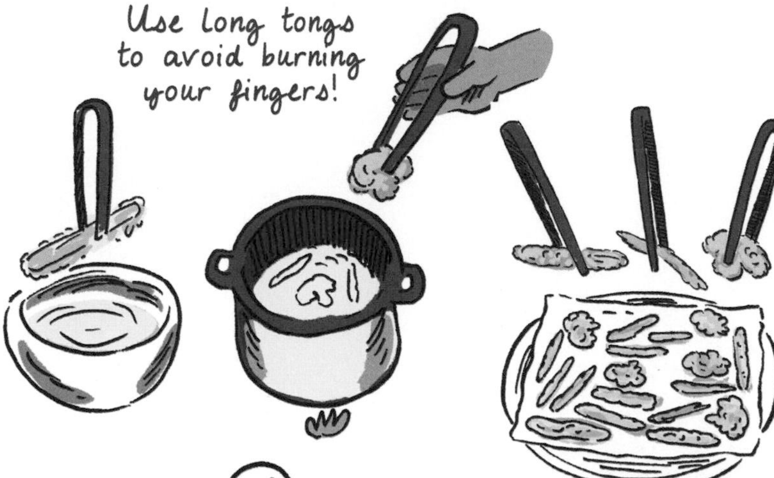
Use long tongs to avoid burning your fingers!

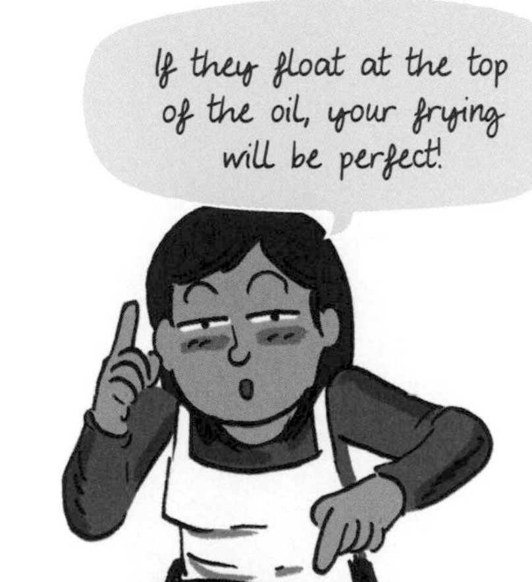
If they float at the top of the oil, your frying will be perfect!

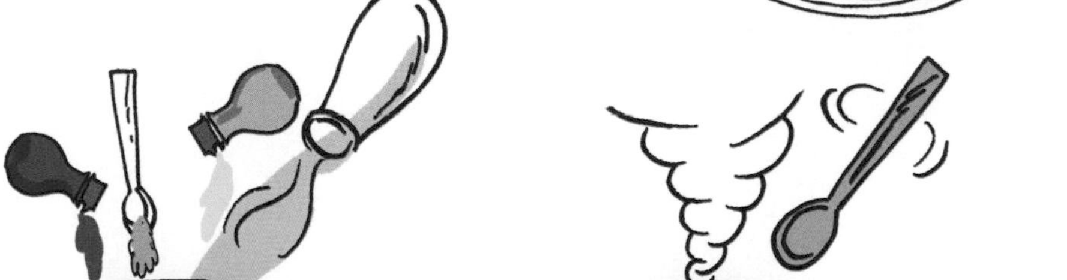

8. Notice that the oil should always be "roiling" hot to prevent the tempura pieces from sinking to the bottom.

9. To top it all off, prepare the Tempura Dipping Sauce by combining the soy sauce, mirin, water and dashi powder in a saucepan. Mix well and heat until just boiling. Remove from the heat and serve in small individual serving bowls.

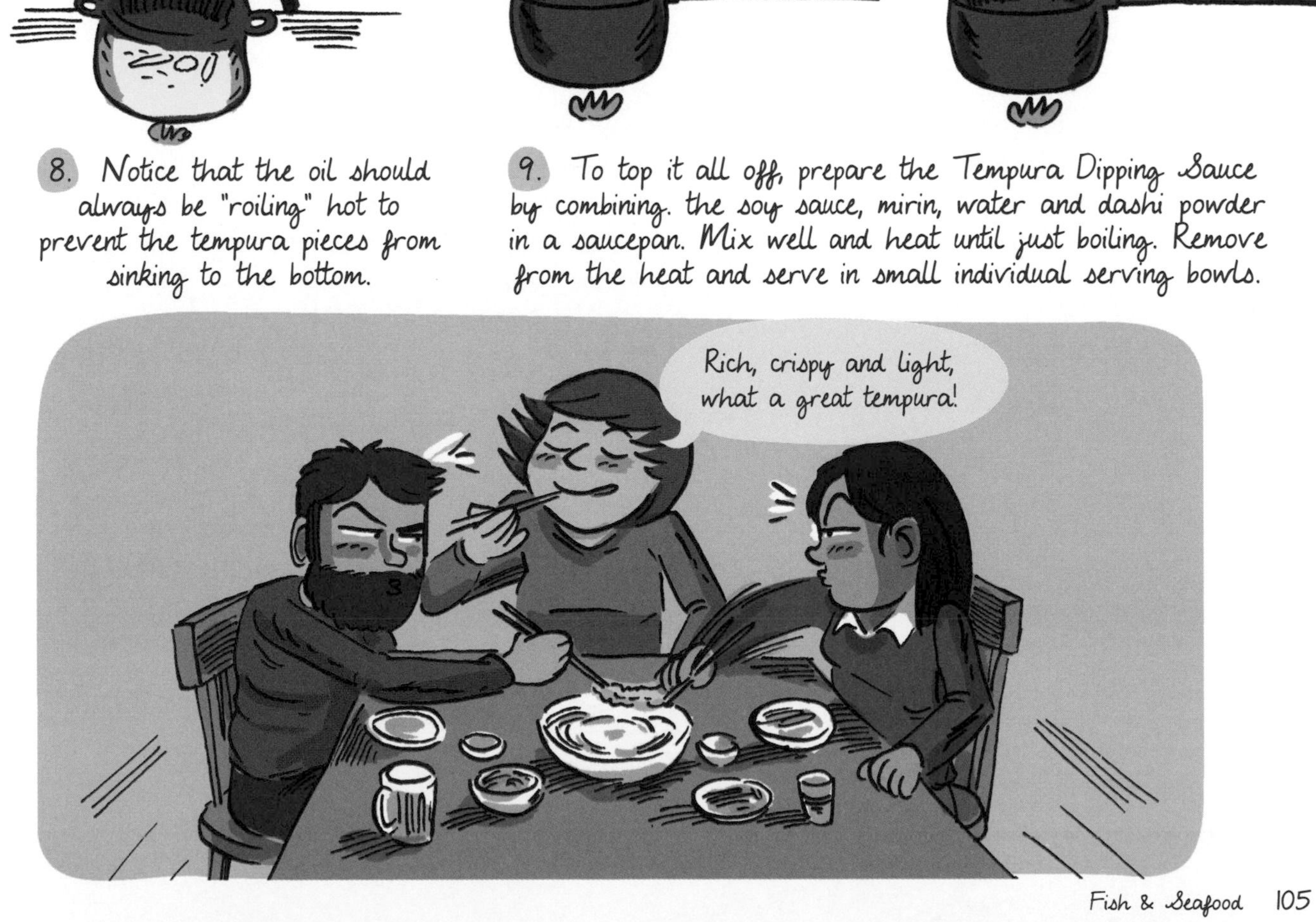
Rich, crispy and light, what a great tempura!

Chapter 7

NOODLES & RICE

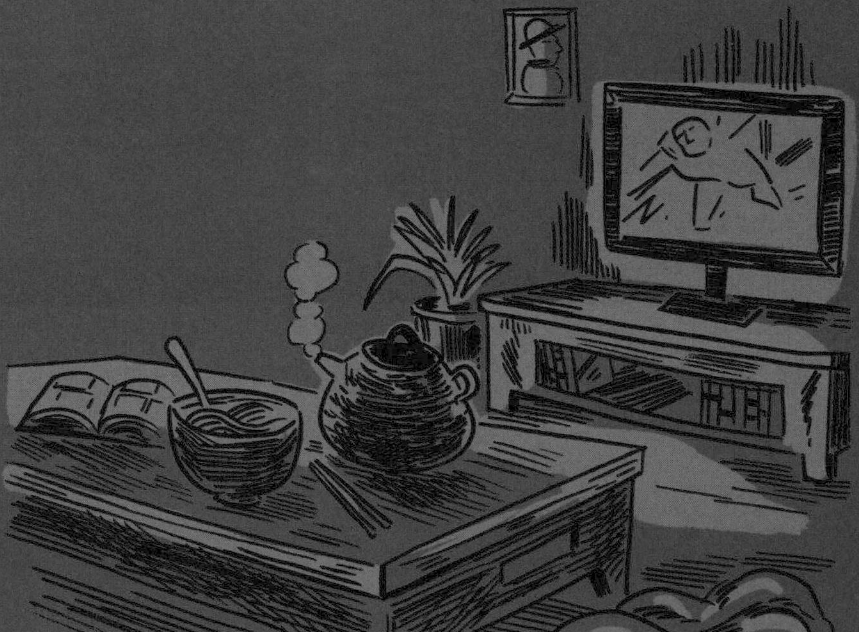

Noodle and rice dishes are easy to prepare and everybody loves them! These recipes are perfect when you don't have much time or you need something quick for your lunch at work. Or when there is an important game on TV and you don't want to miss it! Sometimes the best recipes are the simplest ones ... so be creative and have fun!

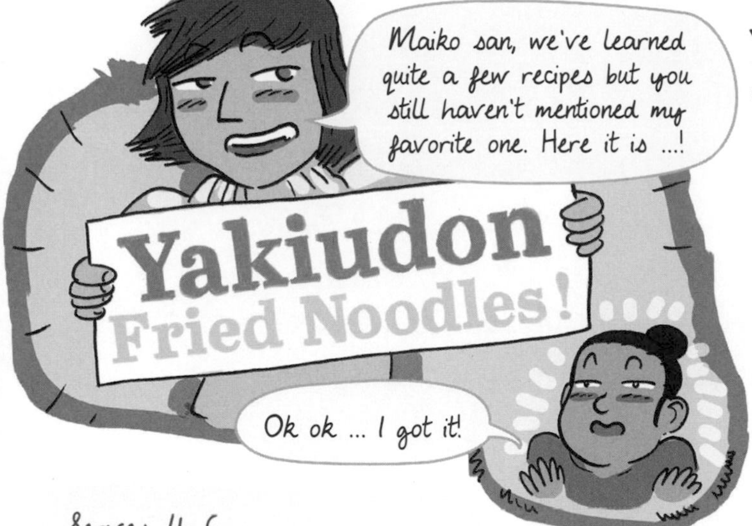
Maiko san, we've learned quite a few recipes but you still haven't mentioned my favorite one. Here it is ...!
Yakiudon Fried Noodles!
Ok ok ... I got it!

Yakiudon is a variation on a popular dish called yakisoba. The main difference is it uses udon noodles instead of soba noodles. This is a classic *izakaya* or Japanese pub dish and is a good example of healthy "fast food". It can be prepared with either vegetables, meat or fish, and the secret lies in the sauce! Here we use canned anchovies and fresh prawns but you can also use chicken or pork or cabbage and carrots.

Serves 4-6
Time: 30 minutes

1 scallion (spring onion)
Oil, for frying
1 small can (2 oz/60 g) anchovies in oil
2 cloves garlic, thinly sliced
1 small onion, peeled and diced
A handful of spinach leaves, washed
1 lb (450 g) dried udon noodles
½ cup (125 ml) dashi stock (mix 1½ tablespoons dashi powder with ½ cup hot water)
7 tablespoons sake or white wine
4 tablespoons soy sauce
16 fresh prawns (about 1 lb/450 g), shelled but with heads and tails left on
1 tablespoon freshly grated ginger

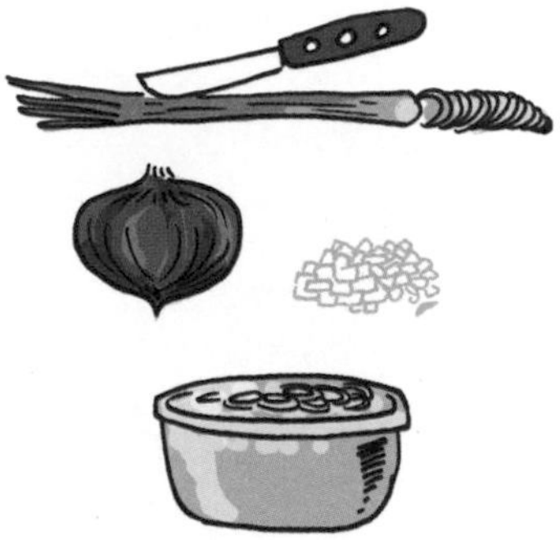

1. Thinly slice the scallion (green leaves also) and soak in water to soften. Drain and set aside. Chop the onion.

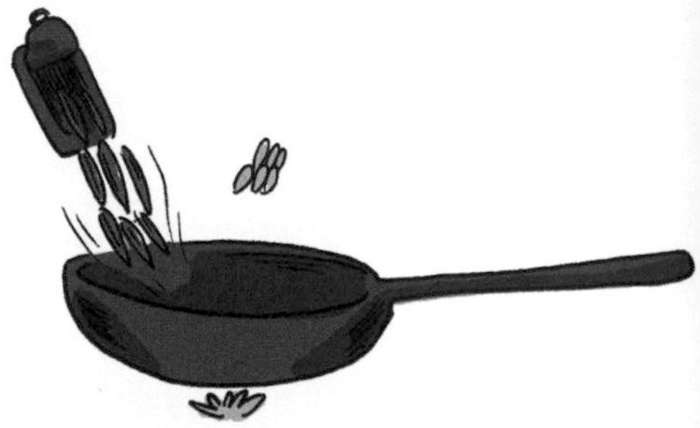

2. Add a little oil to a large skillet, add the anchovies and sliced garlic and stir.

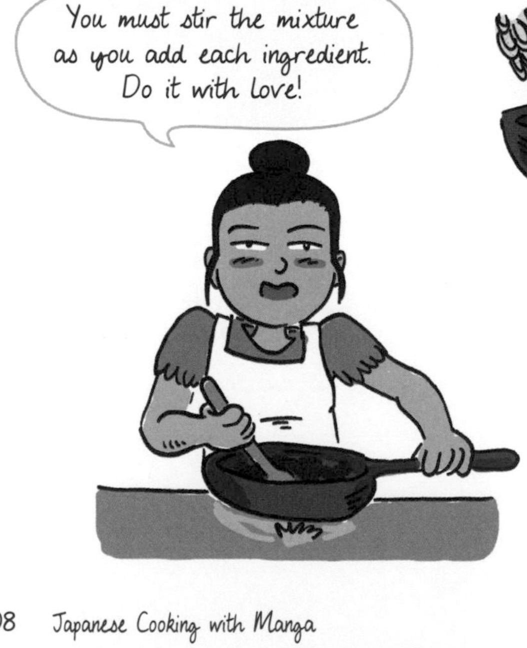
You must stir the mixture as you add each ingredient. Do it with love!

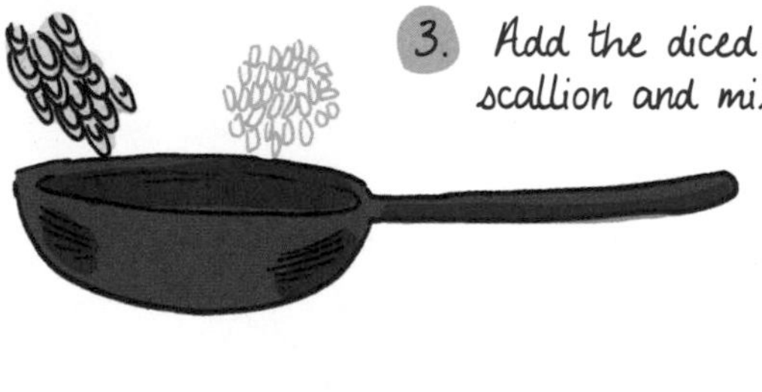

3. Add the diced onion and scallion and mix well.

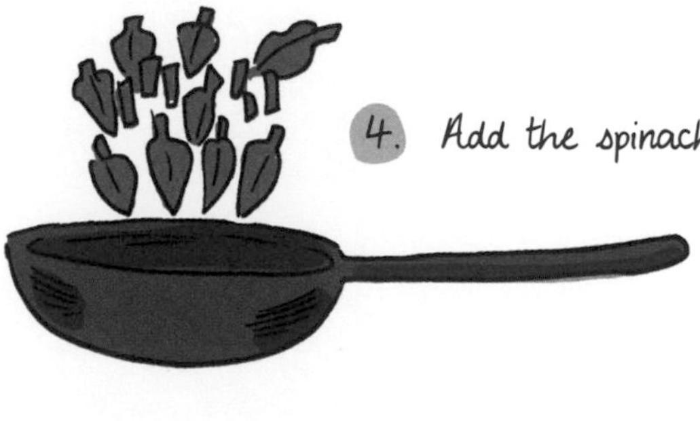

4. Add the spinach leaves.

5. Now, add the...

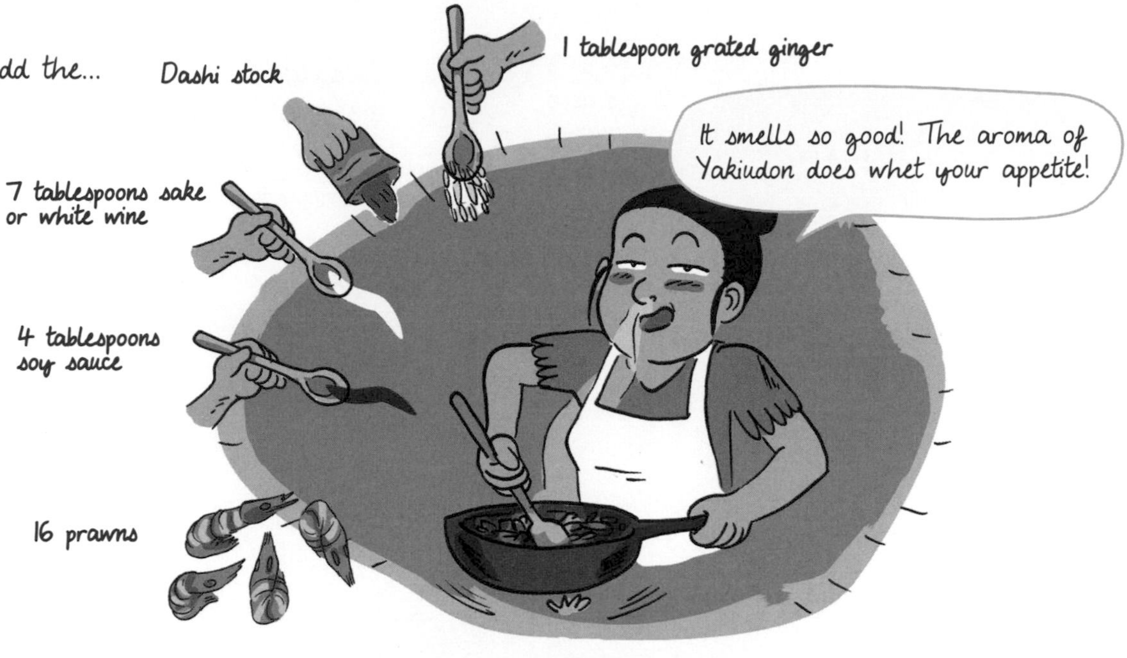
Dashi stock
1 tablespoon grated ginger
7 tablespoons sake or white wine
4 tablespoons soy sauce
16 prawns
It smells so good! The aroma of Yakiudon does whet your appetite!

... Continue mixing and cooking for about 5 minutes, then turn off the heat and prepare the noodles.

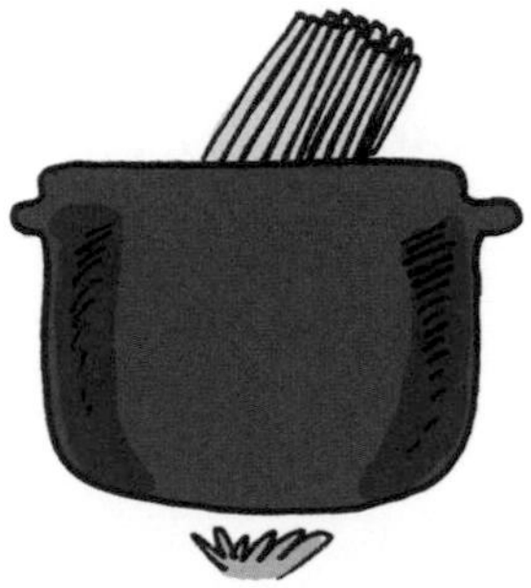

6. Bring a pot of water to a boil and add the noodles. Cook them for around 8 minutes until done.

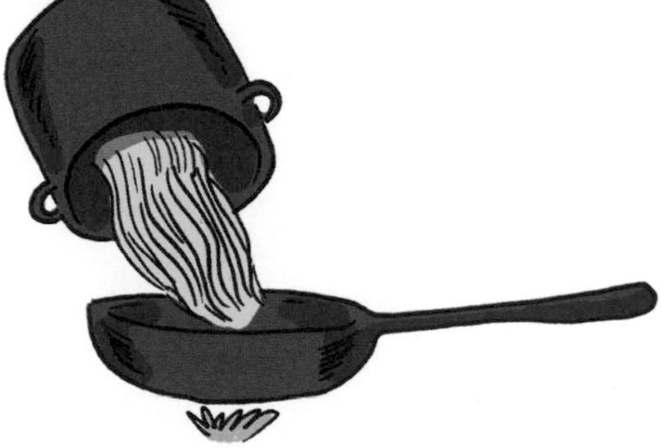

7. When cooked, drain them well and pour into the pan with the other ingredients. Stir well to combine well.

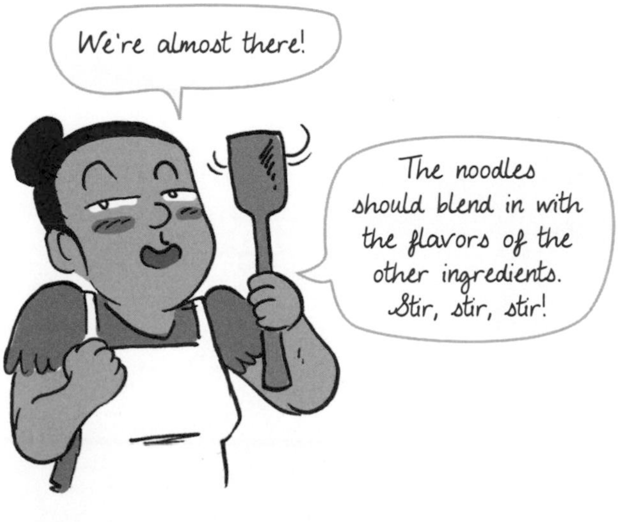
We're almost there!
The noodles should blend in with the flavors of the other ingredients. Stir, stir, stir!

A delicious Yakiudon, ready to win over any dinner guest with its colors and aroma!

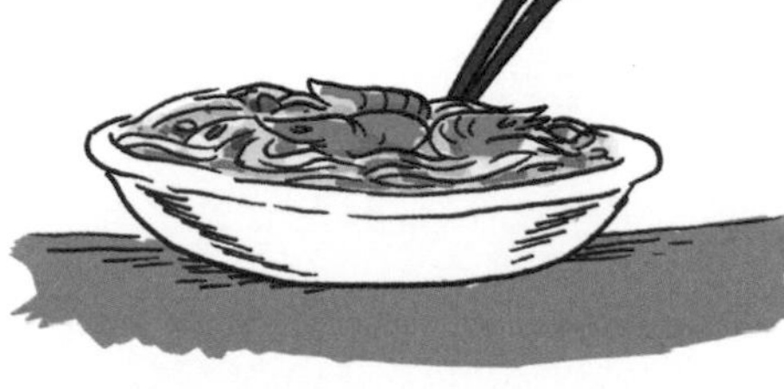

Quick & Easy Salmon Rice Shake Gohan

Here is a very simple rice recipe that is ideal for summer and perfect when you need something for your lunchbox at work. You can try different variations, but we recommend this basic option.

Serves 2
Time: 30 minutes

1 scallion (spring onion)
1 cup (200 g) uncooked Japanese rice
2 cups (480 ml) water
3 tablespoons mayonnaise
3 tablespoons soy sauce
1 tablespoon black sesame seeds
1 packet smoked salmon (around 7 oz/200 g), thinly sliced

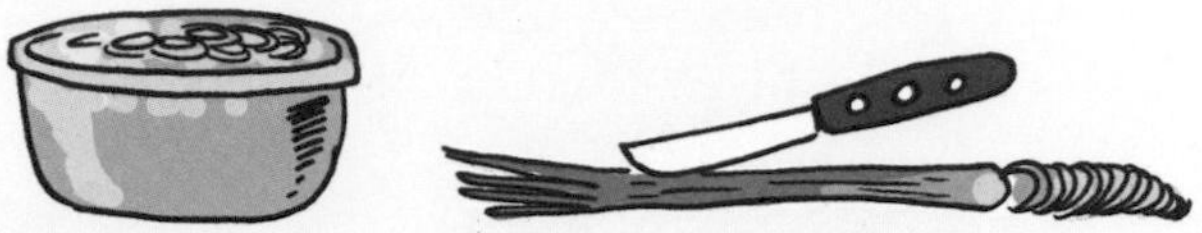

1. Thinly slice the scallion and soak in water to soften. Drain and set aside.

2. Put the uncooked rice and water in a pot, cover and bring to a boil.

3. Turn down the heat and let it simmer for 15 minutes, then turn off the heat.

4. Let it stand for 10 minutes. (so the rice will absorb all the water).

5. Add all the other ingredients to the pot of cooked rice.

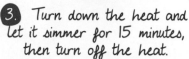

Soy sauce

Black sesame seeds

Scallion

Sliced smoked salmon

Mayonnaise

6. Stir until well mixed.

Tadaaaaaa!!!!!!
Superrrrrr easyyyyyyy
and very tastyyyyy!!!!!

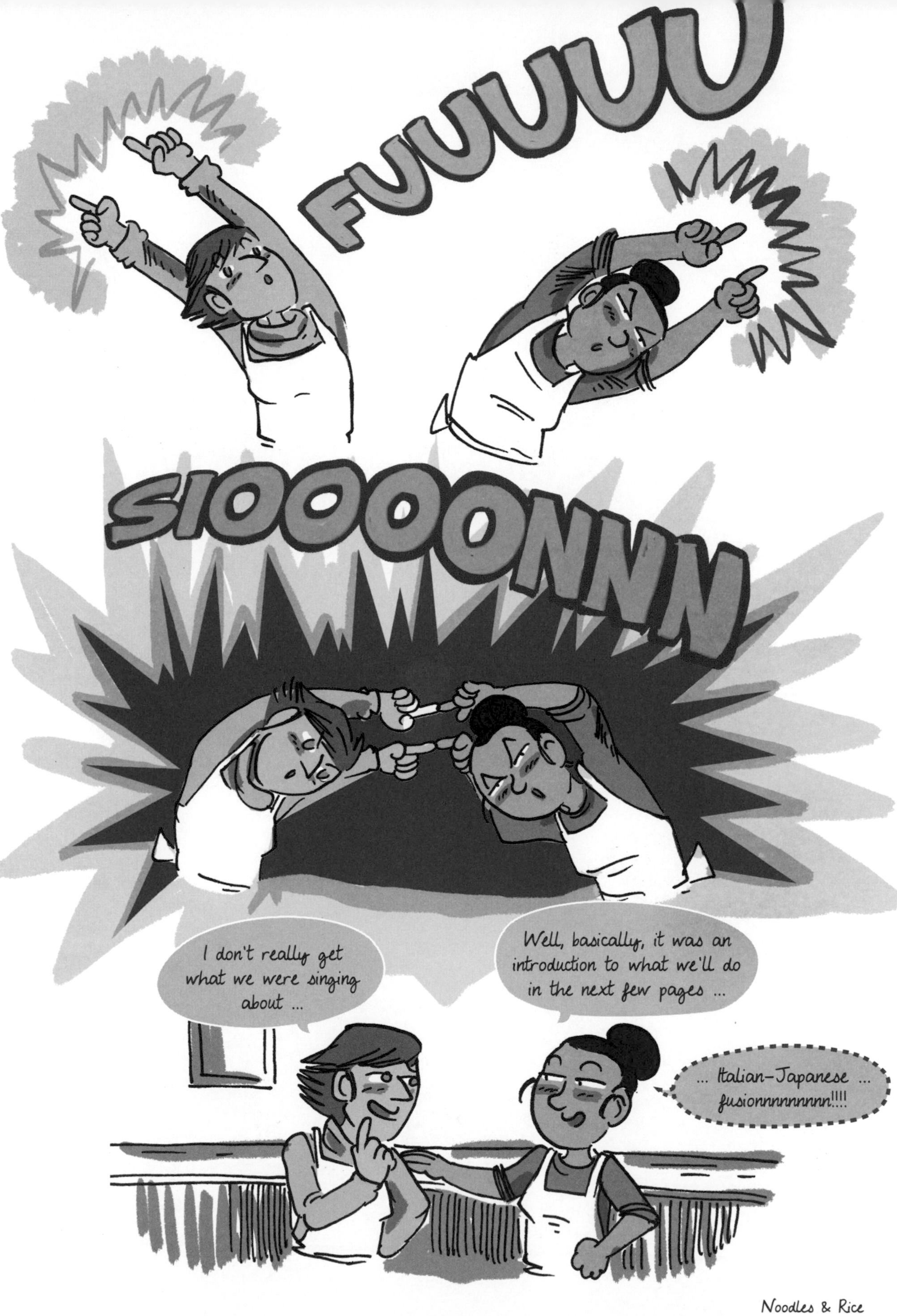
FUUUUU
SIOOOONNNN
I don't really get what we were singing about ...
Well, basically, it was an introduction to what we'll do in the next few pages ...
... Italian-Japanese ... fusionnnnnnnnnn!!!!

Japanese-style Car(u)bonara Pasta

Carbonara is one of the most popular Italian pasta sauces and here we offer a variation that changes the main ingredient in the sauce from cream to Tofu Mayonnaise. You will love this version ... try it!

Serves 2
Time: 20 minutes

1 onion, peeled and minced
3–4 shiitake mushrooms
1 clove garlic
3 thick bacon strips
   (4 oz/125 g)
4 tablespoons Tofu
   Mayonnaise (page 76)
⅓ cup (35 g) grated Parmesan
   cheese
Salt and pepper, to taste
½ lb (250 g) dried penne or
   any other pasta you want

1. Mince the onion, slice the mushrooms and garlic. Cut the bacon into small bits.

2. Sauté the bacon along with the garlic in a skillet, then add the onion and finally the mushrooms.

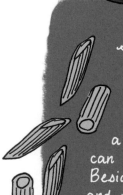

3. Keep your eyes peeled, here comes the trick: instead of cream, we'll now add our Tofu Mayonnaise!

4. Season with the grated Parmesan, salt and pepper. Turn off the heat and set aside.

5. Bring a pot of water to a boil and add your favorite pasta. Cook for 7-10 minutes or until al dente.

Select a type of pasta suitable to the sauce you're making. Spaghetti is great for tomato sauces, but heavier or richer sauces such as this one need a kind of pasta that can "contain" them. Besides penne, fusilli and rigatoni also work well.

6. Pay attention to the time and taste the pasta to check if is cooked or not.

"Al dente" really makes a difference!

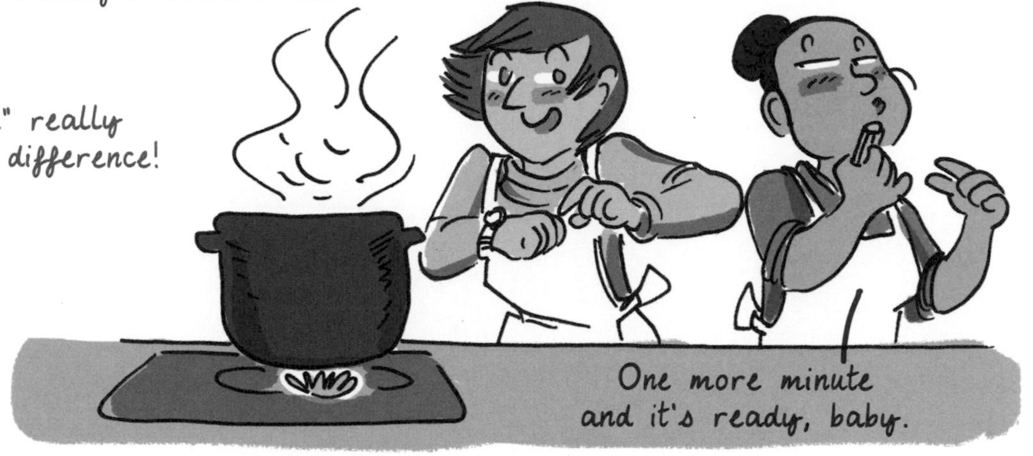
One more minute and it's ready, baby.

7. When the pasta is done, drain it well.

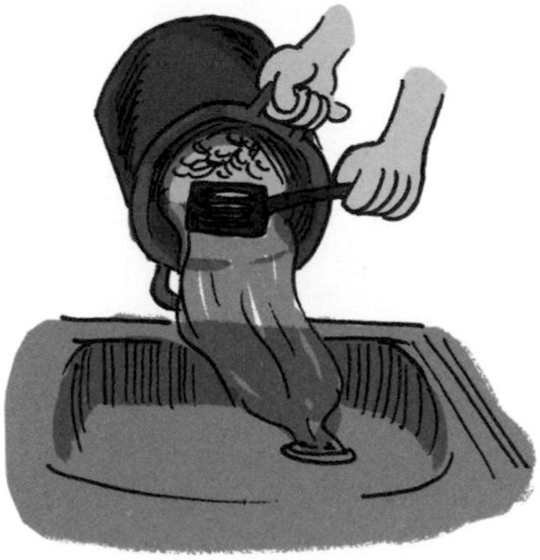

8. The pour the sauce over the pasta and heat it over very low heat.

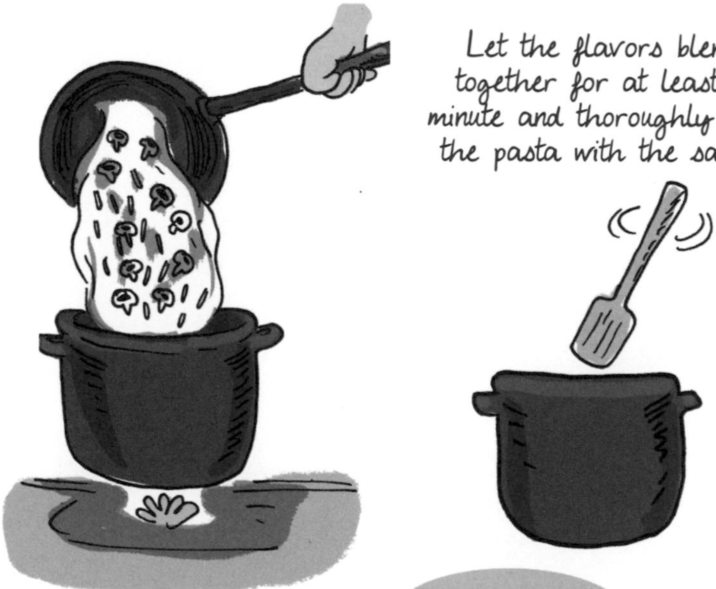

Let the flavors blend together for at least a minute and thoroughly coat the pasta with the sauce.

PRO TIP:
Save some cooking water from the pasta to make the sauce thinner in case it becomes too thick.

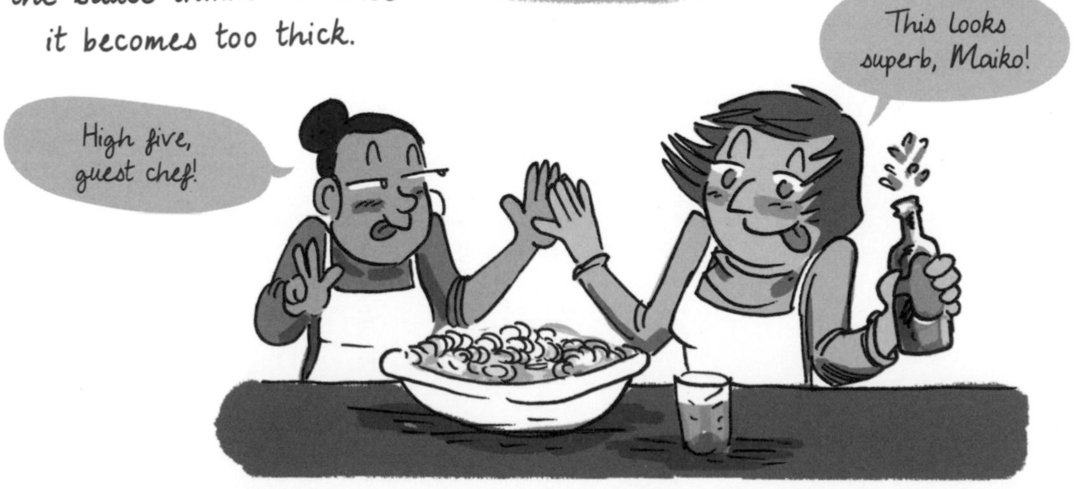
High five, guest chef!
This looks superb, Maiko!

"Sea and Mountain" Fried Rice Yakimeshi

Yakimeshi literally means "fried rice" and is a typical homestyle dish. It's very easy to prepare and another excellent option when you need something fast for your lunchbox. "Sea and mountain" refers to the combination of tuna and bacon, but other ingredients like cooked chicken, ham, sausage or vegetables can also be used.

Serves 3
Time: 35 minutes (not including time needed to cook the rice)

1½ cups (300 g) uncooked Japanese rice
2½ cups (600 ml) water
Oil, for frying
4 thick strips bacon (5 oz/150 g), sliced into small bits
3 eggs
2 cans (4 oz/115 g per can) tuna, drained well
2 garlic chives, thinly sliced
1 stock cube, dissolved in 2–3 tablespoons hot water
Salt and pepper, to taste
4–5 lettuce leaves, thinly sliced, to garnish
Soy sauce, to taste

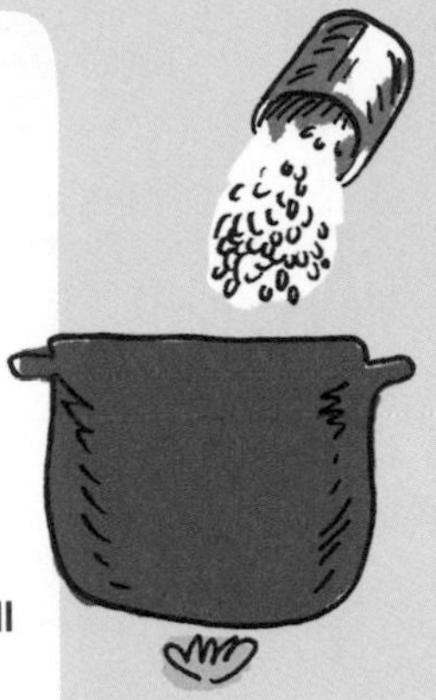

1. Cook the rice (see page 110). When it is cooked, allow it to cool for an hour or two.

2. Sauté the bacon bits in a pan until crispy. Let the fat melt!

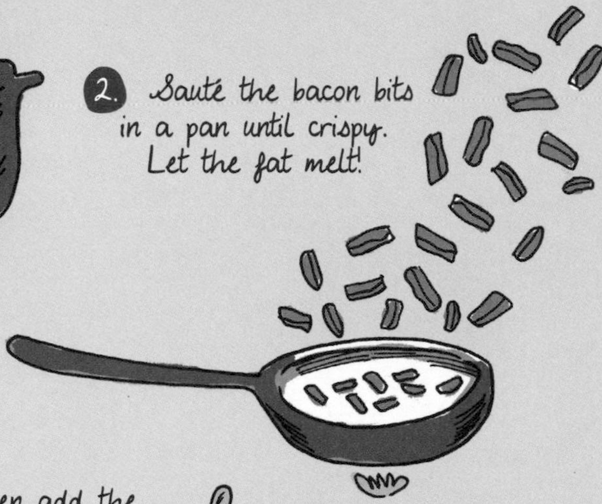

3. Transfer the rice to a large bowl and add the tuna, omelette strips, garlic chives and soup stock.

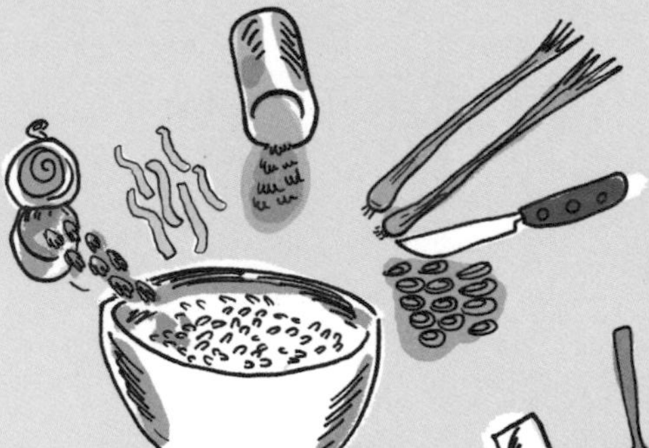

4. Then add the bacon bits ... and toss!

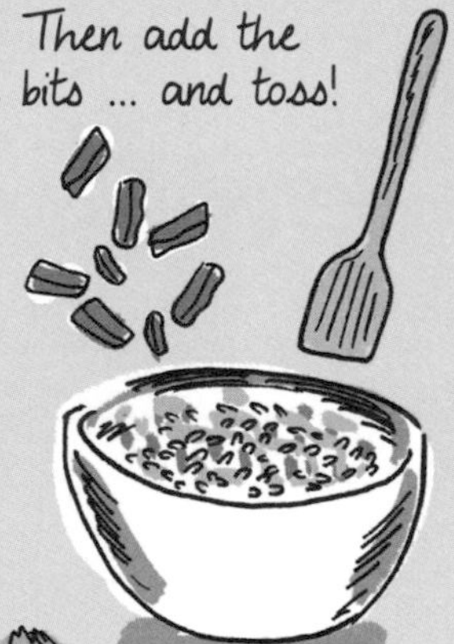

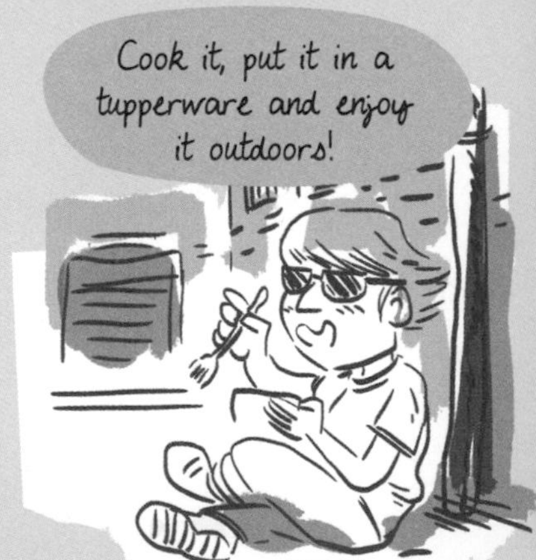
Cook it, put it in a tupperware and enjoy it outdoors!

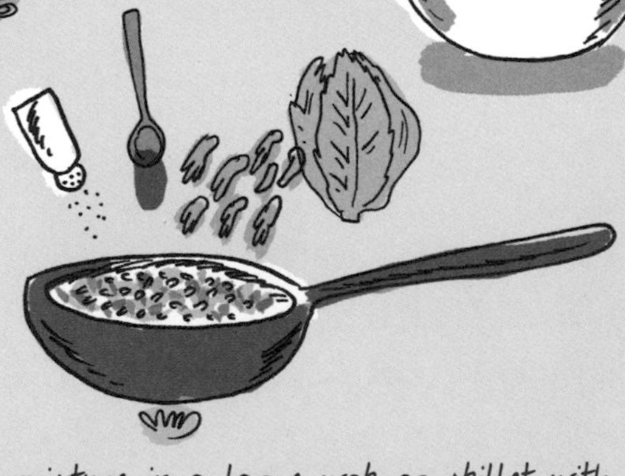

5. Stir-fry the rice mixture in a large wok or skillet with a little oil for about 8-10 minutes. Once it's ready, sprinkle the sliced lettuce leaves on top. Season with salt and pepper. Then add a little soy sauce, salt and pepper, to taste.

Delicious and light!

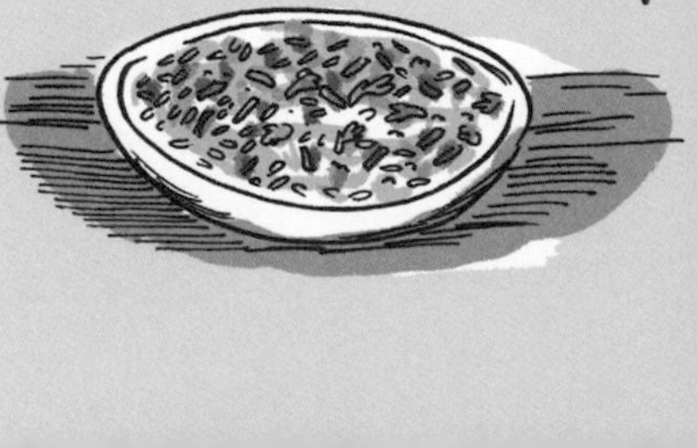

Rice Stuffed Omelettes Omu-rice

Omu-rice is an English–Japanese term which means "omelette and rice". It is a very popular dish in Japanese homes that you also find in restaurants. We show you the most typical way of cooking it, but you'll find many variations using beef instead of chicken, bechamel sauce instead of tomato sauce, or even replacing the rice with noodles (omu-soba).

Serves 2
Time: 30 minutes (not including time needed to cook the rice)

1 cup (200 g) uncooked Japanese rice
2 cups (480 ml) water
1 small onion, peeled and diced
1 small carrot, peeled and diced
2 skinless chicken breasts
Oil, for frying
½ cup (75 g) fresh or frozen peas
1 cup (250 ml) chicken stock
1 tablespoon soy sauce
3 tablespoons ketchup
⅓ cup (35 g) grated cheese
4 eggs

1. Cook the rice following the instructions on page 110.

2. Dice the onion, carrot and chicken breasts ...

3. ... and fry them slowly in a pan with a little oil over medium heat.

Don't forget to add the cup of chicken stock!

Let it simmer until it thickens.

4. Add the peas and the chicken stock. Simmer until it thickens.

5. Add the soy sauce and ketchup and mix well. Continue cooking for 6-8 minutes until the chicken is cooked, then turn off the heat.

6. When the rice is ready, you just need to pour it into the skillet with the other ingredients and season it with the grated cheese! Be generous!

7. Let it simmer over very low heat for a couple of minutes, occasionally stirring. It must get smooth! Turn off the heat.

8. Now make the omelettes.

2 eggs
whisk
... pour into a large skillet and swirl the egg all around the pan so it is large and thin.
Fry 2 minutes over low heat.

(Repeat this process to make two large omelettes, one for each person.)

9. Place one omelette in a bowl so the edges stick out over the rim ... and the omelette sits inside the bowl ...

Yep!
It's a flying saucer!

... then pour half of the rice mixture into the bowl on top of the omelette ...... and put a large plate on top of the bowl.

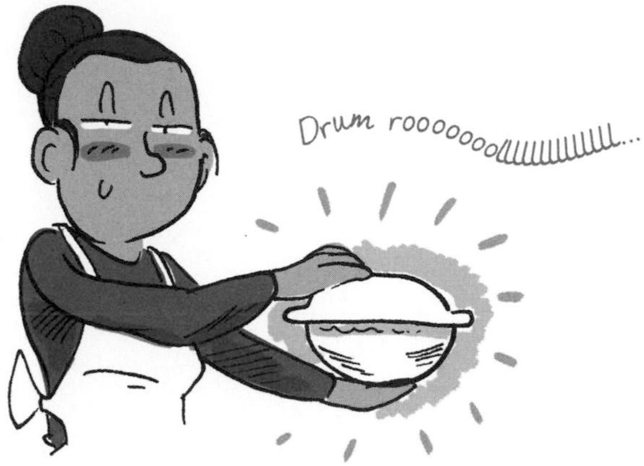
Drum roooooooollllllllll...

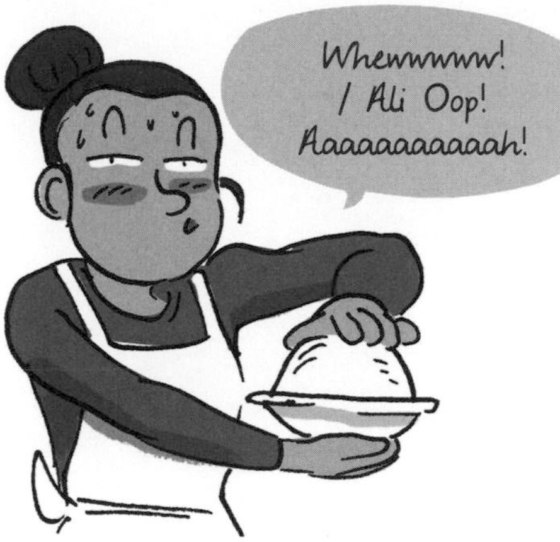
Whewwwww! / Ali Oop! Aaaaaaaaaaah!

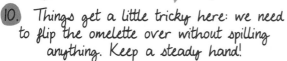

10. Things get a little tricky here: we need to flip the omelette over without spilling anything. Keep a steady hand!

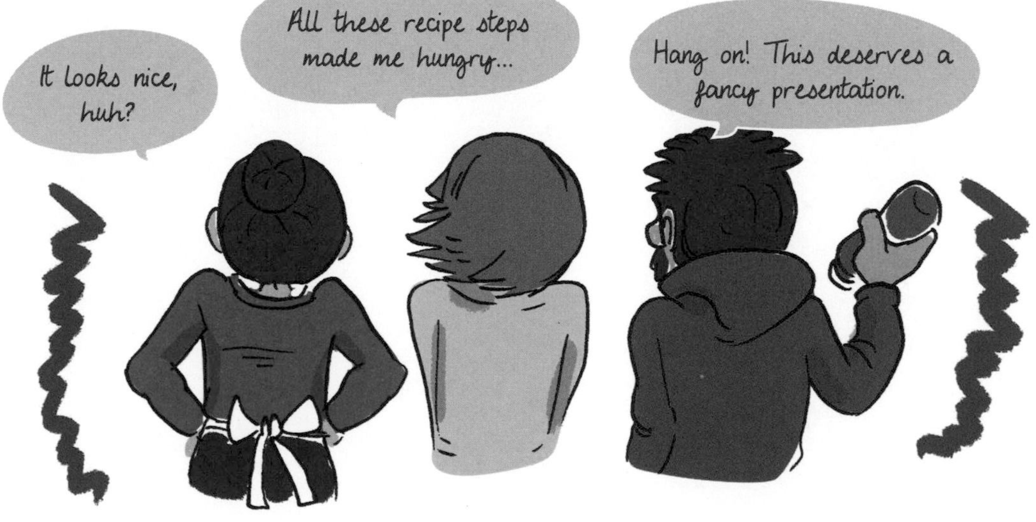
It looks nice, huh?
All these recipe steps made me hungry...
Hang on! This deserves a fancy presentation.

Use your creativity, with a bit of ketchup or mayonnaise, to create some fun decorations to surprise your friends and make the dish entertaining!!!

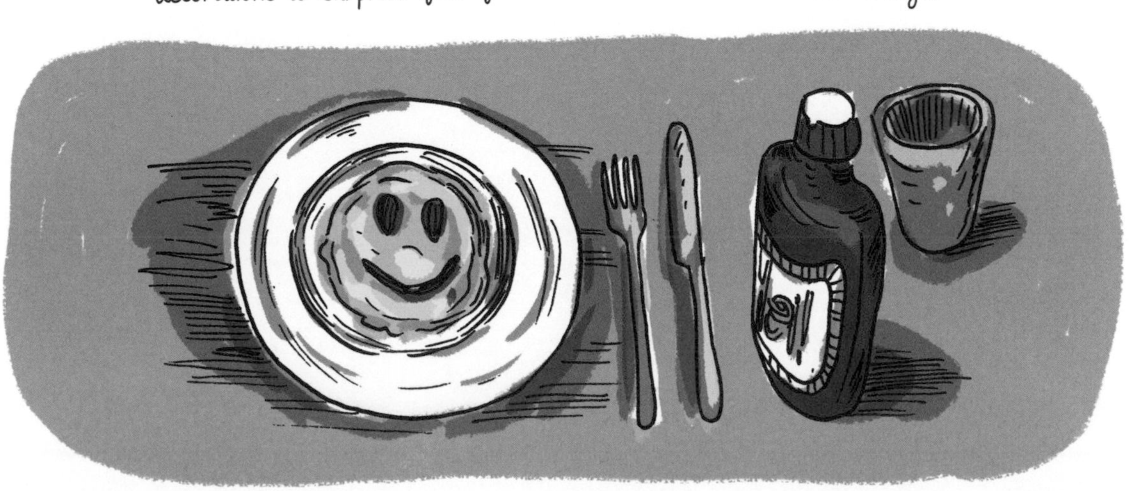

Chapter 8

DESSERTS & DRINKS

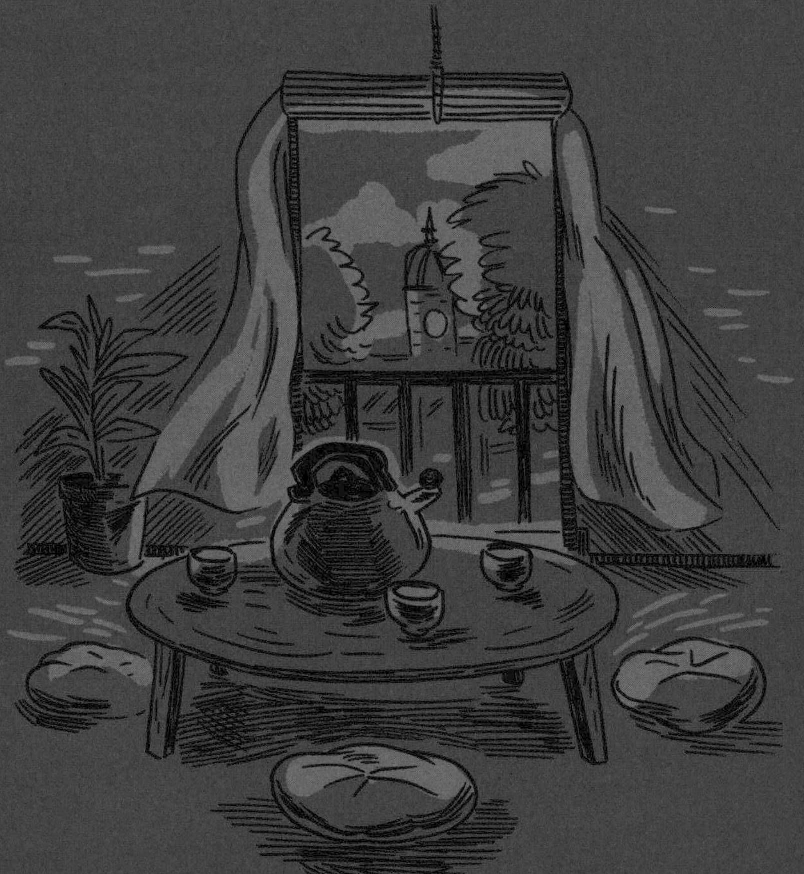

We couldn't end this book without letting you try some delicious Japanese desserts. You will discover some new and amazing textuuuures here!!! These desserts are delightful after a meal or as a sweet snack in the afternoon. Remember that to create good desserts you need to be a bit disciplined to measure all the ingredients accurately and cook them for the right amount of time.
Love and dedication will do the rest! Surprise your family and friends with these recipes and share some healthy food with them!

Black Sesame Flan

This is a very easy recipe to make. And it's a great way to finish any meal. The individual flans have a very soft texture and a creamy, delicate flavor!

Serves 4
Time: 20 minutes + 4 hours cooling

1¼ cups (300 ml) milk
¾ cup (200 ml) cream
⅓ cup (70 g) sugar
1 tablespoon honey
4 tablespoons black sesame seeds
1 tablespoon gelatin powder
½ cup (125 ml) water

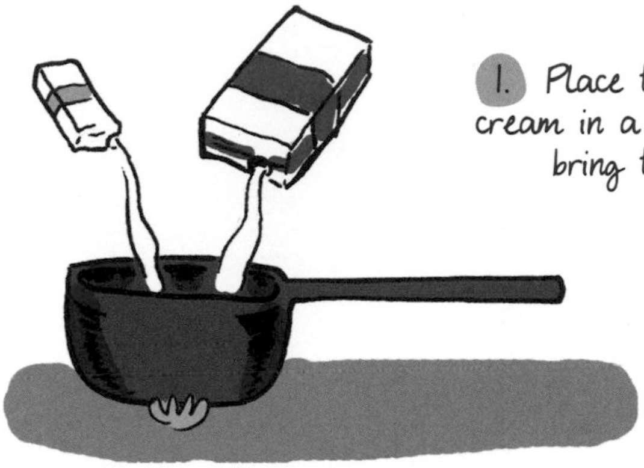

1. Place the milk and cream in a saucepan and bring to a boil.

2. When the mixture boils, lower the heat and add the

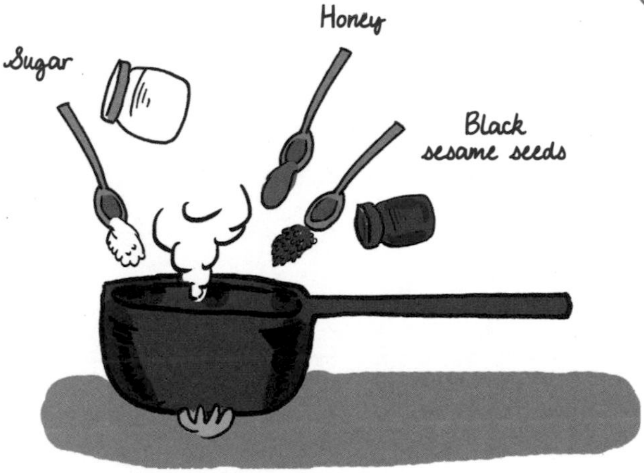

Sugar
Honey
Black sesame seeds

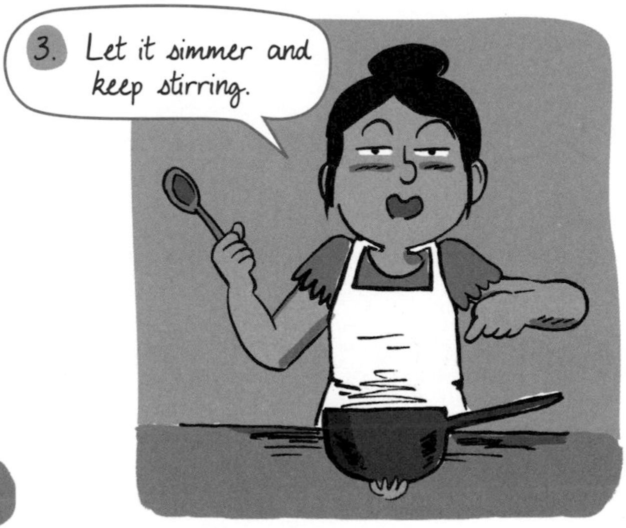

3. Let it simmer and keep stirring.

4. Pour the gelatin powder into a glass with the water.

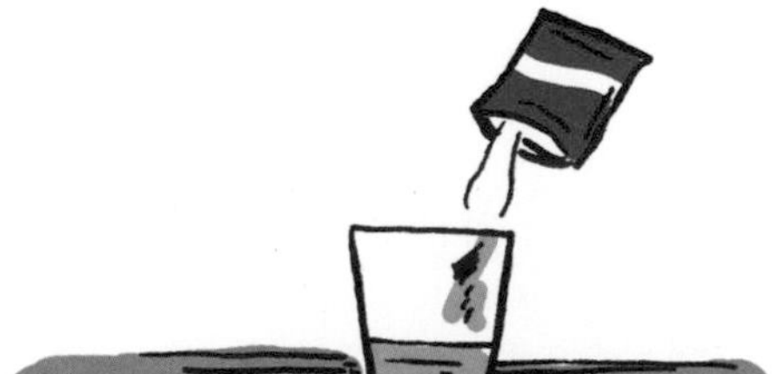

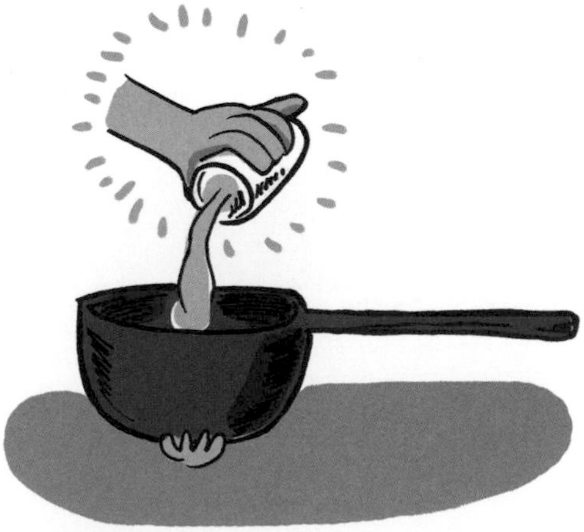

5. Add this to the pan and continue to stir over low heat.

6. Turn off the heat and let it cool for a few minutes. Then pour the mixture into 4 different cups or small bowls or flan molds (any glass or ceramic containers will do).

7. Put the flans in the fridge to cool.

Several hours are needed for the flans to set, around 3 to 4 hours. Make them the night before if you have guests coming!

It is sooooooo smooth!!!

It tastes really good! Although due to its stonelike color it might seem a bit weird at first ...

Green Tea Cake with Apricots

This is perfect for breakfast, dessert or tea time. Matcha (green tea) powder adds softness and a bright green color that contrasts well with the apricot bits. Spongy and tasty!

Serves 4
Time: 75 minutes

- 5 tablespoons (100 g) unsalted butter
- ¾ cup (80 g) icing sugar
- 2 eggs
- 1 teaspoon matcha (green tea) powder
- 1 packet (3 g) yeast
- 1 cup (150 g) flour
- ½ cup (80 g) chopped apricots

1. Preheat the oven to 360°F (180°C).

2. Place the butter on a plate in a warm place to soften, without letting it melt (for example over a pot of warm water).

3. Beat the butter with a spatula in a bowl and slowly add the icing sugar.

4. Add the eggs and continue beating to form a smooth mixture.

5. Now add the Matcha powder

Flour   Yeast

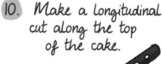

6. Keep beating until all the ingredients are well combined.

7. Pour the mixture into a greased baking pan.

8. Bake in the oven at 360°F (180°C) for 10 minutes.

9. Remove the cake from the oven and sprinkle the dried apricots on top.

10. Make a longitudinal cut along the top of the cake.

11. Put it back in the oven for 30-40 minutes. The exact time will depend on the strength of your oven, so keep watching!

Once cooked, take it out of the mold and let it cool. Now yes, it's ready to taste!

Matcha Frappuccino

A surprising way to get creative with a simple frappuccino. You might even decide to give up coffee!

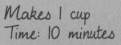

Makes 1 cup
Time: 10 minutes

1 teaspoon matcha (green tea) powder
¼ cup (50 ml) water
⅔ cup (150 ml) milk
Sugar, to taste (optional)
Mini marshmallows, to top

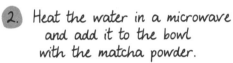

1. Sift the matcha powder into a bowl.

2. Heat the water in a microwave and add it to the bowl with the matcha powder.

3. Whisk the tea with a miniblender to foam it.

4. Pour the milk into the cup you will be using to serve the tea, adding the sugar (if using) and heat it in a microwave.

5. Whisk the milk with a miniblender to foam it.

6. Now add the matcha tea foam ...

7. ... top it off with mini marshmallows. Spongy, soft and sweet all in one!

Green Tea & Chestnut Chocolates

This easy dessert recipe will win over family and friends whenever you have a special occasion. You just need a handful of chestnuts, chocolate and some matcha tea powder to create a truly spectacular flavor and color combination!

Makes 20 chocolates
Time: 45 minutes

20 raw chestnuts in their shells (about ½ lb/250 g)
6 oz (150 g) cooking chocolate (milk chocolate or dark chocolate, as you prefer)
4 tablespoons honey
2 tablespoons matcha (green tea) powder

1. Boil the chestnuts for 20-25 minutes or until cooked (taste one to check if they are cooked). Drain and let them cool.

2. Once cooled, peel and cut the chestnuts into small pieces.

3. Melt your favorite kind of chocolate in a double boiler.

4. Add the chestnut bits to the chocolate.

5. Add the honey.

6. Mix until well combined.

7. Grease your hands with a little butter and shape the chocolate into small balls!

8. Sprinkle each chocolate with matcha powder to coat them.

Success guaranteed!

... put the chocolates in the fridge for a while so they become firm.

Mother-in-law proof... ;-)

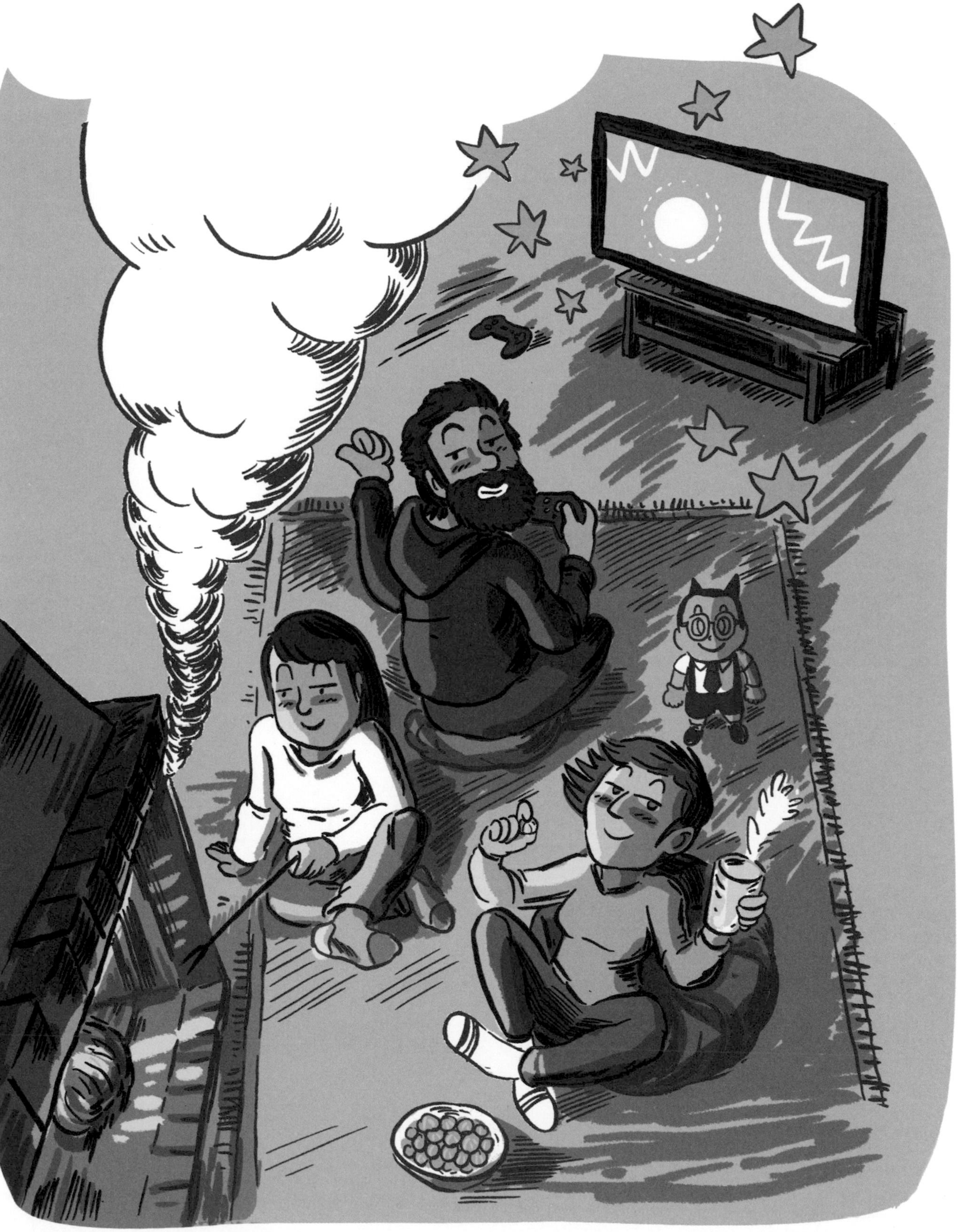

Mushi-pan Banana Muffins

Now we're going to make another very typical homestyle Japanese dessert. In Japan, you'll find countless kinds of mushi-pan! The name means "steamed bread" and when cooked it is like a spongy muffin with a fruity flavor. Pay attention! Here we use banana but you can get creative and use any other kind of fruit that is in season!!!

Serves 4
Time: 20 minutes

1 large ripe banana
1 tablespoon coconut oil
1 teaspoon baking powder
1 tablespoon sugar
½ cup (75 g) flour
1 teaspoon cocoa powder
½ cup (120 ml) milk

1. Peel and slice the banana. Save 4 slices for later to top the muffins.

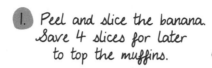

2. Mash the banana in a bowl together with the coconut oil and the other ingredients.

1 teaspoon baking powder

1 tablespoon sugar

½ cup flour

1 teaspoon cocoa powder

½ cup (120 ml) milk

3. Now you just need to mix it well until you get a very smooth dough.

4. Pour the mixture into 4 greased muffin molds or paper muffin cups ...

5. ... and top each one with a banana slice.

Add water to a steamer and steam the muffins for 15 minutes over high heat.

6. Place a kitchen towel under the steamer's lid to prevent water condensation dripping onto the muffins.

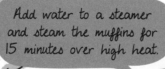

There's only one left, we're gonna have to share it...

Are you kidding me?

Japanese Twig Tea Kuki-cha

Kuki-cha is a kind of tea that has twigs and stems as well as leaves. It has a slightly sweet and nutty flavor. You can buy it in Asian stores or order it online. It is rich in minerals and great for your tummy. We couldn't finish our book without dedicating one page to the Japanese tea ceremony, a central element of Japanese culture.

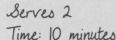

Serves 2
Time: 10 minutes

2 cups (500 ml) mineral water
4 teaspoon *kuki-cha* (2 per person)
2 tea strainers (one per person)

1. Pour the water into a kettle ... put it on the stove and wait for it to boil.

2. Put 2 teaspoons of kuki-cha into each tea strainer.

3. Place a tea strainer into each cup and add the boiling water. Let it steep for about 2 minutes to infuse the water with its unique aroma and color, then remove it.

The most important thing is to sit in a quiet and comfortable place, away from any noise, accompanied by friends and some delicious cakes or cookies. Take a minute to meditate on all the good things in your life!

A simple ritual like this is a great way to take care of ourselves and our friends.

Published by Tuttle Publishing, an imprint of Periplus Editions (HK) Ltd.

www.tuttlepublishing.com

Library of Congress Control Number: 2018941049

ISBN: 978-4-8053-1433-3

Distributed by

North America, Latin America & Europe
Tuttle Publishing
364 Innovation Drive
North Clarendon, VT 05759-9436 U.S.A.
Tel: 1 (802) 773-8930; Fax: 1 (802) 773-6993
info@tuttlepublishing.com | www.tuttlepublishing.com

Japan
Tuttle Publishing
Yaekari Building 3rd Floor
5-4-12 Osaki Shinagawa-ku
Tokyo 141-0032
Tel: (81) 3 5437-0171 | Fax: (81) 3 5437-0755
sales@tuttle.co.jp | www.tuttle.co.jp

Asia Pacific
Berkeley Books Pte. Ltd.
61 Tai Seng Avenue, #02-12
Singapore 534167
Tel: (65) 6280-1330 | Fax: (65) 6280-6290
inquiries@periplus.com.sg | www.periplus.com

21 20 19 18 5 4 3 2 1
Printed in China 1805RR

Acknowledgments

First of all we want to thank the Tuttle staff for their effort in doing this book and placing their trust in us. We are happy to publish it after its start as a small self-publication. It was born as a project made with a lot of love and passion and we are proud to see it develop and grow.

Thanks also to the new friends and readers we have made since we started this project at all the little markets. Your beautiful words have encouraged us to keep going.

And of course a big thank you to all our families and friends for their encouragement and their support. Without them this couldn't be possible.

Best wishes and delicious meals for everybody.

Alexis, Ilaria & Maiko

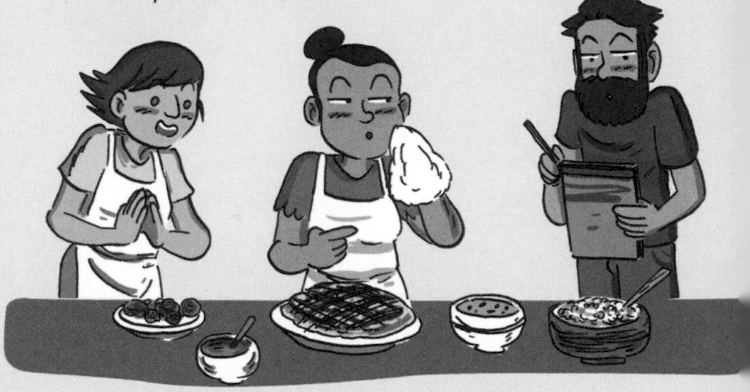

ABOUT TUTTLE:
"Books to Span the East and West"

Our core mission at Tuttle Publishing is to create books which bring people together one page at a time. Tuttle was founded in 1832 in the small New England town of Rutland, Vermont (USA). Our fundamental values remain as strong today as they were then—to publish best-in-class books informing the English-speaking world about the countries and peoples of Asia. The world has become a smaller place today and Asia's economic, cultural and political influence has expanded, yet the need for meaningful dialogue and information about this diverse region has never been greater. Since 1948, Tuttle has been a leader in publishing books on the cultures, arts, cuisines, languages and literatures of Asia. Our authors and photographers have won numerous awards and Tuttle has published thousands of books on subjects ranging from martial arts to paper crafts. We welcome you to explore the wealth of information available on Asia at **www.tuttlepublishing.com**.